Praise for *The Narcissism Epidemic*

"A must-read for anyone who is a parent, a relationship partner, in the workforce, in school, or on the job market. Twenge and Campbell not only define narcissism but detail its antecedents, consequences, and underlying processes in a way that brings together so much of what one sees in modern western culture. Grounded in research and peppered with media and anecdotal stories, *The Narcissism Epidemic* offers practical, much-needed solutions to coping in the age of entitlement."

—Kathleen Vohs, Ph.D., University of Minnesota McKnight Land-Grant Professor and coeditor of *Self and Relationships: Connecting Intrapersonal and Interpersonal Processes*

"This insightful book shows us how the epidemic of narcissism touches almost all aspects of our lives. Twenge and Campbell's astute analysis and salient anecdotes powerfully map the problem and the high price we all pay. They expertly show us the kinds of actions we can take to free ourselves of the epidemic's ruthless grip and how the future well-being of humane society depends on our doing so."

—Diane E. Levin, Ph.D., Professor of Education at Wheelock College and coauthor of *So Sexy So Soon: The New Sexualized Childhood and What Parents Can Do to Protect Their Kids*

The Narcissism Epidemic

Living in the Age of Entitlement

Jean M. Twenge, Ph.D.,

and W. Keith Campbell, Ph.D.

FREE PRESS

New York London Toronto Sydney

Free Press
A Division of Simon & Schuster, Inc.
1230 Avenue of the Americas
New York, NY 10020

First Free Press hardcover edition April 2009

For information about special discounts for bulk purchases,
please contact Simon & Schuster Special Sales at 1-866-506-1949 or
business@simonandschuster.com

Manufactured in the United States of America

7 9 10 8

Library of Congress Control No.: 2008044705

ISBN-13: 978-1-4165-7598-6
ISBN-10: 1-4165-7598-7

To our daughters:

Kate (J.M.T.)

and

McKinley and Charlotte (W.K.C.)

CONTENTS

The Narcissism Epidemic

Introduction

The Growing Narcissism in American Culture

We didn't have to look very hard to find it. It was everywhere.

On a reality TV show, a girl planning her sixteenth birthday party wants a major road blocked off so a marching band can precede her grand entrance on a red carpet. A book called *My Beautiful Mommy* explains plastic surgery to young children whose mothers are going under the knife for the trendy "Mommy Makeover." It is now possible to hire fake paparazzi to follow you around snapping your photograph when you go out at night—you can even take home a faux celebrity magazine cover featuring the pictures. A popular song declares, with no apparent sarcasm, "I believe that the world should revolve around me!" People buy expensive homes with loans far beyond their ability to pay—or at least they did until the mortgage market collapsed as a result. Babies wear bibs embroidered with "Supermodel" or "Chick Magnet" and suck on "Bling" pacifiers while their parents read modernized nursery rhymes from *This Little Piggy Went to Prada*. People strive to create a "personal brand" (also called "self-branding"), packaging themselves like a product to be sold. Ads for financial services proclaim that retirement helps you return to childhood and pursue your dreams. High school students pummel classmates and then seek attention for their violence by posting YouTube videos of the beatings.

Although these seem like a random collection of current trends, all are rooted in a single underlying shift in the American psychology: the relentless rise of narcissism in our culture. Not only are there more narcissists than ever, but non-narcissistic people are seduced by the increasing emphasis on material wealth, physical appearance, celebrity worship, and attention seeking. Standards have shifted, sucking otherwise humble people into the vortex of granite countertops, tricked-out MySpace pages, and plastic surgery. A popular dance track repeats the words "money, success, fame, glamour" over and over, declaring that all other values have "either been discredited or destroyed."

The United States is currently suffering from an epidemic of narcissism. Merriam-Webster's dictionary defines an epidemic as an affliction "affecting . . . a disproportionately large number of individuals within a population," and narcissism more than fits the bill. In data from 37,000 college students, narcissistic personality traits rose just as fast as obesity from the 1980s to the present, with the shift especially pronounced for women. The rise in narcissism is accelerating, with scores rising faster in the 2000s than in previous decades. By 2006, 1 out of 4 college students agreed with the majority of the items on a standard measure of narcisstic traits. Narcissistic Personality Disorder (NPD), the more severe, clinically diagnosed version of the trait, is also far more common than once thought. Nearly 1 out of 10 of Americans in their twenties, and 1 out of 16 of those of all ages, has experienced the symptoms of NPD. Even these shocking numbers are just the tip of the iceberg; lurking underneath is the narcissistic culture that has drawn in many more. The narcissism epidemic has spread to the culture as a whole, affecting both narcissistic and less self-centered people.

Like a disease, narcissism is caused by certain factors, spreads through particular channels, appears as various symptoms, and might be halted by preventive measures and cures. Narcissism is a psychocultural affliction rather than a physical disease, but the model fits remarkably well. We have structured the book according to this model, explaining the epidemic's diagnosis, root causes, symptoms, and prognosis.

Like the obesity epidemic, the narcissism epidemic has not affected everyone in the same way. More people are obese, just as more people are narcissistic, but there are still those who exercise and eat right, and still those who are humble and caring. Even the less self-absorbed have witnessed narcissistic behavior on TV, online, or in real-life interactions with friends, family, or coworkers. The mortgage meltdown that led to the financial crisis of 2008 was caused, in part, by the narcissistic overconfidence of homebuyers who claimed they could afford houses too expensive for them and greedy lenders who were willing to take big risks with other people's money. In one way or another, the narcissism epidemic has touched every American.

In the last few years, *narcissism* has become a popular buzzword, used to explain the behavior of everyone from hooker-obsessed former New York governor Eliot Spitzer to famous-for-being-famous Paris Hilton. Others have diagnosed themselves: former presidential candidate John Edwards explained his extramarital affair by stating, "In the course of several campaigns, I started to believe that I was special and became increasingly egocentric and narcissistic." As the *New York Times* noted, narcissism "has become the go-to diagnosis by columnists, bloggers, and television psychologists. We love to label the offensive behavior of others to separate them from us. 'Narcissist' is among our current favorites."

Despite the popularity of narcissism as a label, it is difficult to find scientifically verified information on it outside academic journal articles. Many websites on narcissism are based on some combination of conjecture, personal experience, and poorly understood psychoanalytic theories. Christopher Lasch's 1979 bestselling book, *The Culture of Narcissism*, though fascinating, was written before any serious research explored the personality and behavior of narcissists. Books such as *Why Is It Always About You?* and *Freeing Yourself from the Narcissist in Your Life* were written by established psychotherapists and use case studies of individuals with NPD. This approach is important, but largely ignores the scientific data on the topic.

We take a different approach in this book, describing the now-extensive scientific research on the truth about narcissists and why they behave the way they do. We believe that with a topic as complex as narcissism, the empirical research is the place to begin.

Narcissism is an attention-getting term, and we do not use it lightly. We discuss some research on NPD, but primarily concentrate on narcissistic personality traits among the normal population—behavior and attitudes that don't go far enough to merit a clinical diagnosis but that can nevertheless be destructive to the individual and other people. This "normal" narcissism is potentially even more harmful because it is so much more common. Of course, much of what we discuss applies to individuals with NPD as well.

Narcissism is not simply a confident attitude or a healthy feeling of self-worth. As we explore in chapters 2 and 3, narcissists are overconfident, not just confident, and—unlike most people high in self-esteem—place little value on emotionally close relationships. We will also address other myths, such as "narcissists are insecure" (they're typically not), and "it's necessary to be narcissistic to succeed today" (in most contexts, and long term, narcissism is actually a deterrent to success).

Understanding the narcissism epidemic is important because its long-term consequences are destructive to society. American culture's focus on self-admiration has caused a flight from reality to the land of grandiose fantasy. We have phony rich people (with interest-only mortgages and piles of debt), phony beauty (with plastic surgery and cosmetic procedures), phony athletes (with performance-enhancing drugs), phony celebrities (via reality TV and YouTube), phony genius students (with grade inflation), a phony national economy (with $11 trillion of government debt), phony feelings of being special among children (with parenting and education focused on self-esteem), and phony friends (with the social networking explosion). All this fantasy might feel good, but, unfortunately, reality always wins. The mortgage meltdown and the resulting financial crisis are just one demonstration of how inflated desires eventually crash to earth.

The cultural focus on self-admiration began with the shift toward focusing on the individual in the 1970s, documented in Tom Wolfe's article on "The Me Decade" in 1976 and Lasch's *The Culture of Narcissism*. In the three decades since, narcissism has grown in ways these authors never could have imagined. The fight for the greater good of the 1960s became looking out for number one by the 1980s. Parenting became more indulgent, celebrity worship grew, and reality TV became a showcase of narcissistic people. The Internet brought useful technology but also the possibility of instant fame and a "Look at me!" mentality. Using botulinum toxin to smooth facial wrinkles to perpetuate a youthful face birthed a huge industry. The easy accessibility of credit allowed people to look better off financially than they actually were.

Jean's first book, *Generation Me: Why Today's Young Americans Are More Confident, Assertive, Entitled—and More Miserable Than Ever Before*, explored the cultural shifts in self-focus that affected people born after 1970 and—because the trends continued to accelerate—especially those born in the 1980s and '90s. In *The Narcissism Epidemic*, we widen our focus to Americans of all ages, and to the entire culture. Younger people bear the brunt of the changes because this is the only world they have ever known, but retirement ads promising extravagant fantasies (own your own vineyard!) suggest that the epidemic has reached far up the age scale. And although we present data on the growing number of narcissistic individuals, we concentrate on the rise in cultural narcissism—changes in behavior and attitudes that reflect narcissistic cultural values, whether the individuals themselves are narcissistic or simply caught up in a societal trend.

When observing cultural change—especially changes in the negative direction—one runs the risk of mistaking one's aging for a true shift in culture. Change is difficult to take when you're older, and it's easy to conclude that the world is going to hell in a handbasket. We have tried to avoid this bias by finding as much hard data and considering as many perspectives as we could. Many cultural changes were eminently quantifiable: the fivefold increase in plastic surgery and cosmetic procedures in just ten years, the growth of celebrity gossip magazines, Americans spending more than they earn and racking up huge amounts of debt, the growing size of houses, the increasing popularity of giving children unique names, polling data on the importance of being rich and famous, and the growing number of people who cheat. We also journeyed outside the research data by gathering stories and opinions through our online survey at www.narcissismepidemic.com (we have changed respondents' names and, in some cases, identifying information). Since this is a book about culture, we explore media events, pop culture happenings, and Internet phenomena. We also talked to our students to get perspectives from the younger generation. We were somewhat shocked to find that many graduate students—most in their mid-twenties—think things have gotten worse in their lifetimes. Undergraduates are more accepting of the current culture but often report feeling tremendous pressure to self-promote and keep up in a materialistic world.

The kernel of the idea for this book was planted in 1999 in a basement office at Case Western Reserve University in Cleveland. We were both working as postdocs—a kind of research limbo between graduate school and hoped-for professorships—in the lab of Roy Baumeister, a well-known social psychologist. There's not much to do in Cleveland, especially in the winter, so we ended up talking a lot in our shared office.

Sometimes we were actively procrastinating—Jean recalls one conversation about weight loss in which our fellow postdoc Julie Exline described a diet pill that supposedly contained a tapeworm. Before she could even finish the story, Keith began yelling "Urban legend!" and looked it up on the nascent Internet (he was right). Most of the time, though, we talked about ideas. Keith would describe his latest study on the behavior of narcissistic people, and Jean would talk about trends in American culture and how they were showing up in personality traits. Almost immediately we thought about looking at trends in narcissism, but in 1999 the standard measure of narcissism had only been around for 10 years, which wasn't long enough to do a solid study of change over time.

That study would have to wait for the summer of 2006, when Jean was seven months pregnant and couldn't do much but sit at her computer. By then, we had both married and settled into jobs across the country from each other (Keith at the University of Georgia, far from where he grew up in Southern California, and Jean at San Diego State University, far from where she grew up in Minnesota and Texas). Our coauthors on this project were renowned narcissism and aggression researcher Brad Bushman and two former students (now faculty), Joshua Foster and Sara Konrath. The rise in college students' narcissism over the generations was clear, and when we released the study in February 2007, it was covered by the Associated Press and many other news outlets. It was an interesting first day back on the job for Jean after a four-month maternity leave. One TV crew setting up a standard "walking" shot asked Jean to carry her briefcase so she would "look more professional." "Guys," Jean said, "That's not my briefcase. It's my breast pump."

When Jean got home that night, the full impact hit her: the story had been covered by the NBC *Nightly News*, Fox News Channel, and National Public Radio, and both Jay Leno and Conan O'Brien made jokes about it. The AP story appeared in more than one hundred newspapers around the country, prompting a slew of editorials, newspaper columns, and e-mails. Much of the feedback was positive, but we also received intense questioning and harsh criticism, some of it based on misunderstandings about what narcissism is and how it is measured.

That was when we realized we'd hit a nerve. We also realized that the narcissism epidemic went far beyond the changing personalities of college students. The American culture was shifting in a fundamental way, and we wanted to document it—and figure out how to stop it. Every time we turned on the TV, it seemed that another symptom of narcissism was rearing its ugly head—Botox ads, the mortgage meltdown, fake paparazzi. We found so many examples of narcissism in American culture that we had to stop collecting them. This book could have been twice as long.

The rise in cultural narcissism is a complex story, often with nuanced arguments. We urge you not to jump to conclusions too quickly, and to refrain from overgeneralizing. When we show that narcissism doesn't usually lead to success, that doesn't mean it never does. When we link materialism to narcissism, that doesn't mean that wanting a big house necessarily makes you a narcissist (and the same goes for wanting plastic surgery). When we say parents shouldn't tell kids they are special, that doesn't mean we think they should say, instead, "You're *not* special." When we note that narcissism is linked to aggression, that doesn't mean all crime will rise along with narcissism. Some religions now promote self-admiration, but that doesn't mean those religions are bad. And although the culture is now more narcissistic, of course there are exceptions like people volunteering to help others or serving in the military. Although we certainly use sound bites sometimes, we also try to explain the complexities as much as we can. In some cases, we go into the necessary detail in the notes and appendices, available at www.narcissism epidemic.com.

We focus most of our discussion on narcissism in the United States, because we are both American citizens and most of the data are from the U.S. However, many global trends originate in the United States, and outbreaks of the narcissism epidemic have popped up in Europe, Asia, and Australia. These range from made-for-video school shootings in Finland to "Little Emperor Syndrome" in China. We discuss the global reach of the narcissism epidemic in Chapter 16.

We spend a good amount of the book on solutions—our prescriptions to salve (if not entirely cure) the narcissism epidemic. Some are personal, such as practicing gratitude, changing the way you parent, or avoiding narcissistic relationship partners. Others are more structural, such as teaching children friendship skills and rewarding the practice of saving money instead of spending. Most chapters end with some solutions, and we expand on these ideas in the final chapter.

Our hope is that this book becomes the starting point for a discussion about the current state of American culture. We have a personal interest as well: between us, we have three young daughters, and we are concerned about how the culture will affect them as they grow up. While they are young, it's relatively easy to steer clear of the "Little Princess" onesie and the "Bling" pacifier, but then the culture creeps in the door—especially since exposure to adolescent values now begins at about four, with young girls (including Keith's older daughter) watching tween shows like *Hannah Montana* and eight-year-olds having makeover parties for their birthdays. The narcissism epidemic seems to have hit girls especially hard. Who knows—by the time our daughters graduate from high school, one of the most common graduation presents might be a breast augmentation. (We're not kidding; the number of teens getting breast augmentations jumped 55% in just one year from 2006 to 2007, and some parents do indeed pay for them as graduation gifts).

We want this book to be a wake-up call. In contrast to the obesity epidemic, which has been widely publicized, Americans have become inured to the incivility, exhibitionism, and celebrity obsession caused by the narcissism epidemic. It's taken for granted that a baby bib saying "Supermodel" is "cute." "Having changed ourselves, we no longer perceive our transformation," wrote Roger Kimball in the *New Criterion*. We've gotten so turned around that some people now argue that narcissism is good (as we discuss in Chapter 3, narcissism has some short-term benefits to the self, but is not good for other people, society, or even the narcissist himself in the long run). Even when trends are recognized for their negative effects—such as the fistfights on YouTube or teens posting inappropriate pictures of themselves online—people rarely connect the dots to see that these trends are all related to the rise in narcissism.

Recognizing the narcissism epidemic is the first step to stopping it. The analogy to the obesity epidemic is useful here. Definite steps are being taken to combat obesity: soda machines are being removed from schools, exercise programs suggested, and nutrition education plans implemented. Not so with narcissism. In many cases, the suggested cure for narcissistic behavior is "feeling good about yourself." After all, the thinking goes, fourteen-year-old Megan wouldn't post revealing pictures of herself on MySpace if she had higher self-esteem. So parents redouble their efforts, telling Megan she's special, beautiful, and great. This is like suggesting that an obese person would feel much better if she just ate more doughnuts. Megan wants everyone to see just how beautiful and special she is, and it's not because she thinks she is ugly—it's because she thinks she's hot and, perhaps more importantly, because she lives in a narcissistic society where she might garner praise, status, and "friends" by displaying blatant sexuality.

In fact, narcissism causes almost all of the things that Americans hoped high self-esteem would prevent, including aggression, materialism, lack of caring for others, and shallow values. In trying to build a society that celebrates high self-esteem, self-expression, and "loving yourself," Americans have inadvertently created more narcissists—and a culture that brings out the narcissistic behavior in all of us. This book chronicles American culture's journey from self-admiration, which seemed so good, to the corrosive narcissism that threatens to infect us all.

SECTION 1

THE DIAGNOSIS

CHAPTER 1

The Many Wonders of Admiring Yourself

It all began with such good intentions.

American culture encourages self-admiration with the belief that it will improve our lives. Admiring yourself feels good and makes you happy. If you believe in yourself, you are more likely to keep trying even when you don't succeed the first time. Self-respect is no longer restricted to the privileged few: you can feel good about yourself no matter what your race, sex, or sexual orientation is.

Our country's focus on self-admiration has certainly been successful in raising Americans' opinions of themselves. Self-esteem is at an all-time high in most groups, with more than 80% of recent college students scoring higher in general self-esteem than the average 1960s college student. Middle school students, often the focus of self-esteem-boosting efforts, have skyrocketed in self-esteem, with 93% of late 2000s tweens scoring higher than the average eleven- to thirteen-year-old did in 1980. Total self-esteem has not increased among high school seniors, but 3 out of 4 report they are satisfied with themselves, up from 2 out of 3 in 1975. One out of 3 now say they are "completely satisfied," versus 1 out of 4 in 1975. Younger generations are also markedly higher in other traits related to self-admiration, including individualism, assertiveness, and extraversion. The changes have affected older people as well; college-educated women born in the 1930s grew increasingly focused on their individual selves as they lived through the indulgent decades of the 1970s and 1980s. Especially these days, Americans love to love themselves. (In the next chapter, we will explain the important differences between self-esteem and narcissism; here we explore self-admiration as American culture promotes it, as a general feeling of self-love that does not distinguish between a healthy sense of self-worth and the unhealthy narcissism that can instead result).

American culture has embraced the value of self-admiration with a big, warm hug. As an NBC public service announcement puts it, "You may not realize it, but everyone is born with their one true love—themselves. If you like you, everyone else will, too." One young man expressed this view by covering his entire right side with a tattoo saying "Believe in Yourself" in graffiti-style writing (with "Rely on No One" written underneath). Every culture is shaped by its fundamental core beliefs, and in America today there are few values more fiercely held than the importance of self-admiration. Most of us don't tattoo it on our bodies, but it is tattooed onto the flesh of our body of cultural beliefs.

Not that long ago, messages of self-admiration were directed toward people who really needed them. The 1987 book *Learning to Love Yourself*, for example, was written for the adult children of alcoholics who endured the emotional abuse of their parents. Now, however, self-admiration is considered extremely important for everyone, at all times. "Loving yourself means knowing how great you are and not letting any person, any place, or any thing ever get in the way of that," writes Diane Mastromarino in her aptly titled 2003 book, *The Girl's Guide to Loving Yourself: A Book About Falling in Love with the One Person Who Matters Most . . . You*. Joel Osteen, pastor of the largest church in the United States, writes: "God wants us to have healthy, positive self-images. He wants us to feel good about ourselves." Self-esteem is considered, as one author put it, our "national wonder drug."

Unfortunately, the good intentions behind self-admiration sometimes seems to cross the line into narcissism. When Chidi Ogbuta of Allen, Texas, got married, her wedding cake was in the shape of herself. Her wedding pictures feature Ogbuta and her husband cutting into what looks like her twin. (One commentator on cnn.com asked, "What part of the cake did they save to eat on their one year anniversary? Her head?") A popular poster proclaims, "The most important thing is how you see yourself," above a picture of a small orange kitten looking in the mirror and seeing a large lion. Thus, this teaches, it is important to see yourself as much better—bigger, stronger, more capable—than you actually are. And maybe quite a bit better: "The best thing about Jesus was that he had a mom that believed he was the son of God," says self-help author Wayne Dyer at his seminars. "Imagine how much better the world would be if all of our moms thought that way." In other words, we should all be raised to believe that we are the second coming of Christ—God's greatest gift to mankind.

A substantial cottage industry has grown up around self-admiration. A quick search on Google reveals 191,000 hits for "how to love yourself" with such tips as "Make a note every time someone says something nice about you," "Stop all criticism," and "Look at yourself in the mirror and say, 'You look great!' " Some sites even recommend caressing your body. Others are eager for your self-admiration to lead to their self-money, selling "Love Yourself Affirmation Cards," a "Love Yourself, Heal Your Life" workbook, or a "Soaring Self-Esteem" subliminal audio recording. You can buy T-shirts that say "I ❤ ME" or "Love Yourself." Sports stars regularly credit "believing in yourself" for their success rather than the more likely reasons such as God-given talent and years of hard work.

Parents are told that even newborns can experience the benefits of self-admiration. *The Breastfeeding Book*, by Martha and William Sears, notes that one of the benefits of breastfeeding is milder-smelling stools. This is great for parents, but it's good for baby, too: "When the baby looks at the face of the diaper-changing caregiver and sees happiness rather than disgust, he picks up a good message about himself—perhaps a perk for budding self-esteem." Given the popularity of encouraging self-admiration in children, this will probably be just the first time the child will learn that his poop doesn't stink.

Many self-help books maintain that loving yourself is a cure-all. If we just believe in ourselves, this advice goes, anything is possible. The 2007 megabestseller *The Secret* promises that you can get anything you want (especially material things) simply by visualizing it. (Apparently neither of us authors really wanted to win the MegaMillions jackpot, because we didn't.) Interviewed on *Larry King Live* about Lindsay Lohan and other young stars' troubles with alcohol and drugs, *The View*'s Joy Behar said, "They have everything you'd ever want in life—they've finally achieved their faces on TV. Meanwhile that little voice inside is saying, 'You're not good enough. Not good enough.' And yet there are people who live in poverty who say I am good enough. It's all what you think of yourself." According to this view, young stars like Lindsay Lohan and Paris Hilton wouldn't have as many problems if they just loved themselves enough. (Lohan declared herself "a role model to younger generations as well as generations older than me," and Hilton has a large picture of herself over her living room couch, so we'll leave it to you to decide if either one of them is lacking in self-admiration.) Britney Spears, another young star not known for her humility, also just needs more self-admiration, according to a psychologist quoted in a celebrity magazine. Britney should look at herself in the mirror every day and say, "I love me," she advised. "Britney needs that capital 'I'."

One of the most popular current cultural messages is telling kids they are special. "I am special" appears on T-shirts, stickers, and even car seats. One day Keith opened up the weekly lesson plans for his daughter's preschool (in Athens, Georgia) to find that the three-year-olds were going to start every day by singing a song that went "I am special / I am special / Look at me." He suggested that the "I promise to listen to my Dad and stop kicking him in the face when he tries to dress me" song would be better. The teacher told Keith she got the "I am special" song from a national educational resource for preschools. In the end, she decided against the song when Keith told her that most young children already have high self-esteem, and that feeling "special" was linked to narcissism. Of course, one "I am special" song is not going to turn a child into a narcissistic nightmare, just as a single raindrop won't get a child wet. But just as a rainstorm will leave a child soaked, a deluge of these "special" messages could have a negative impact. Today's culture rains enough narcissism to get everyone wet.

The emphasis on self-admiration for children is relatively new. Parents may have always thought their children were special, but until recently they did not expect the rest of the world to treat them that way. In a recent study of the mothers and grandmothers of three-year-old children, American mothers universally agreed that their children needed to have high self-esteem. When asked, "Do you think a person's self-esteem could ever be too high?" the mothers all said "No." More than two-thirds of the grandmothers, however, said people could certainly have overly high self-esteem; such people were arrogant, self-centered, selfish, and spoiled. When they were raising their children, the grandmothers pointed out, parents did not actively promote their children's self-esteem.

Self-admiration is also not promoted so feverishly in other countries (although, as we discuss in Chapter 16, the rest of the world is starting to follow America's lead). Many other cultures emphasize self-criticism and working on one's weaknesses as the route to success in school and business. In the study on views of self-esteem, mothers and grandmothers in Taiwan both agreed that self-esteem was not very important. In fact, the concept of self-esteem is so unrecognized in their culture that neither Taiwanese nor Mandarin Chinese has a word for it.

And it isn't just Asia. Keith recently stayed with a family in northern British Columbia, Canada, on a fishing trip. At dinner one night, one of the young boys in the family mentioned that he had shot a rabbit at sixty-two yards with a .22. His mother immediately looked at him and said, "It isn't polite to brag." Keith was surprised by this—most American parents would have said, "Yes, it's true, my son is a budding Wild Bill Hickok." Keith told the family that in the United States we actually encourage kids to brag, and that if you put the rifle shot in slow motion on a YouTube video with some good background music, your child could be famous for a few minutes. The mother responded that where they live, they judge people by their character and what they have accomplished. She didn't think that system needed to be improved upon. Keith agreed.

But here in the United States, we have taken the desire for self-admiration too far—so far that our culture has blurred the distinction between self-esteem and narcissism in an extreme, self-destructive way. Most people understand that narcissism has a negative connotation, but don't recognize that the language of self-admiration skates dangerously close to the hole in the ice called narcissism—and often falls in. Treating your child as if he's Christ, singing "I am special," and wearing a shirt that says "Too Cool 4 You" instills narcissism, not basic self-worth. America has overdosed on self-admiration, and our "wonder drug" comes with serious side effects such as arrogance and self-centeredness. In the rush to create self-worth, our culture may have opened the door to something darker and more sinister.

CHAPTER 2

The Disease of Excessive Self-Admiration and the Top Five Myths About Narcissism

Self-admiration sounds great and is a central tenet of modern American culture. But self-admiration taken too far has a distinct downside: narcissism and all of the negative behaviors that flow from it.

Narcissism is a psychological term, but even people who have never taken a psychology class know it when they see it. Other common names for narcissism include arrogance, conceit, vanity, grandiosity, and self-centeredness. A narcissist is full of herself, has a big head, is a blowhard, loves the sound of his own voice, or is a legend in her own mind. A lot of self-absorbed jerks are narcissists, but so are a lot of smooth, superficially charming, and charismatic people (who, unfortunately, are later revealed to be self-centered and dishonest). A narcissist has an overinflated view of his own abilities, similar to the kitten that sees himself as a lion on the popular poster. Narcissists are not just confident, they're overconfident. In short, narcissists admire themselves too much.

The word *narcissism* comes from the Greek myth of Narcissus, an attractive young man who set out looking for someone to love. The beautiful nymph Echo falls in love with him and repeats everything Narcissus says, but he rejects her and she fades away. Narcissus keeps looking for the perfect mate until one day he sees his own reflection in the water. Narcissus falls in love with his own image and gazes at it until he dies. At that spot on the riverbank grew the flower now known as the narcissus (a subspecies of daffodil). The myth of Narcissus captures the tragedy of self-admiration, because Narcissus becomes frozen by his self-admiration and unable to connect with anyone outside himself—and his narcissism harms other people (in this case, Echo). The legend reflects real life, with the most serious consequences of narcissism falling upon others and society.

Today, thanks to the writings of Freud and others, we use the name of the mythical Narcissus to capture the personality trait of narcissism. The central feature of narcissism is a very positive and inflated view of the self. People with high levels of narcissism—whom we refer to as "narcissists"—think they are better than others in social status, good looks, intelligence, and creativity. However, they are not. Measured objectively, narcissists are just like everyone else. Nevertheless, narcissists see themselves as fundamentally superior—they are special, entitled, and unique. Narcissists also lack emotionally warm, caring, and loving relationships with other people. This is a main difference between a narcissist and someone merely high in self-esteem: the high self-esteem person who's not narcissistic values relationships, but the narcissist does not. The result is a fundamentally imbalanced self—a grandiose, inflated self-image and a lack of deep connections to others.

Narcissists also face an interesting psychological challenge: How do you keep feeling like a special and important person—especially if you aren't? One approach is simply to use other people as pawns in a grand game of deception. If you do this well—convincing yourself and everyone else that you are as terrific as you think you are—you can be a winner in the game of self-admiration.

Narcissists might brag about their achievements (while blaming others for their shortcomings), focus on their physical appearance, value material goods that display status ("Has anyone seen my BMW keys?"), use big gestures, constantly turn the conversation back to themselves, manipulate and cheat to get ahead, surround themselves with people who look up to them (such as a "posse" or entourage), seek out "trophy partners" who make them look good, and jump at opportunities to garner attention and fame. Because narcissists don't value warm or caring relationships, they can do all this with little concern for others, often manipulating and exploiting people and viewing others as tools to make themselves look and feel good.

Researchers have labeled these efforts to gain self-admiration "self-regulation strategies." The narcissist spends his or her life regulating his or her social relationships in order to maximize self-admiration. When it works, the narcissist feels a rush of esteem and pride; when it fails, the narcissist reacts with anger, blame, and sometimes rage. Think, for example, of the two faces of O. J. Simpson: the charming, likable sports star who ran through airports in Hertz ads, and the allegedly homicidal ex-husband who, as he relates in his book *If I Did It*, may have killed two people when he believed his ex-wife didn't show him enough respect. Both of O.J.'s faces are facets of narcissism. The violent side of narcissism inspired researcher Del Paulhus to label narcissism one of the "Dark Triad" (the other two are Machiavellianism, or manipulativeness, and sociopathy, which taps antisocial behavior). As Dr. Drew Pinsky noted, "Narcissists are a pleasure to be around. They are wonderful and entertaining. They are the life of the party and can really make you feel good. But God help you if you cross them."

MEASURING NARCISSISM IN INDIVIDUALS

When psychologists assess narcissistic personality traits in individuals, they usually use the Narcissistic Personality Inventory (NPI), developed in the 1980s by Robert Raskin and Howard Terry at the Institute of Personality Assessment and Research at the University of California at Berkeley. The most common form of the scale pairs 40 narcissistic statements with non-narcissistic ones, asking the respondent to choose which describes him or her best. Respondents are not told that the test measures narcissism. Try it yourself with this shortened version below (you'll have to remind yourself to be honest, since unlike most respondents you know what it measures):

In each of the following pairs, choose the one that you MOST AGREE with. Mark your answer by writing EITHER A or B in the space provided. Only mark ONE ANSWER for each attitude pair.

1. _____
   - A. The thought of ruling the world frightens the hell out of me.
   - B. If I ruled the world it would be a much better place.

2. _____
   - A. I prefer to blend in with the crowd.
   - B. I like to be the center of attention.

3. _____
A. I can live my life any way I want to.
B. People can't always live their lives in terms of what they want.

4. _____
A. I don't particularly like to show off my body.
B. I like to show off my body.

5. _____
A. I will never be satisfied until I get all that I deserve.
B. I will take my satisfactions as they come.

6. _____
A. I am no better or no worse than most people.
B. I think I am a special person.

7. _____
A. I find it easy to manipulate people.
B. I don't like it when I find myself manipulating people.

8. _____
A. I try not to be a show-off.
B. I will usually show off if I get the chance.

9. _____
A. I am much like everybody else.
B. I am an extraordinary person.

10. _____
A. I like having authority over other people.
B. I don't mind following orders.

SCORING:

Questions 3, 5, 7, and 10: Give yourself 1 point if you answered A.
Questions 1, 2, 4, 6, 8, and 9: Give yourself 1 point if you answered B.

0–3 points: You have scored low in narcissism.
4–5 points: You have scored about the same in narcissism as the average college student. This is a slightly above-average score for someone older than 40.
6–7 points: You have scored above average in narcissism.
8–10 points: You have scored significantly above average in narcissism.

The design of paired statements is a major strength of the NPI. People filling out the questionnaire don't have to worry that they are making themselves look bad, as both options are equally socially desirable. The total score on all 40 NPI items is most often used, though the NPI can also be broken down into seven subscales measuring authority, exhibitionism, exploitativeness, entitlement, self-sufficiency, superiority, and vanity.

There is no standard cutoff for high or problematic narcissism on the NPI other than comparison to the average, as every point on the scale tends to predict just a little more narcissistic behavior. People with high narcissism scores are not necessarily a different kind or type of person—just someone with more of a trait than others. Most people display at least a few narcissistic tendencies at times, but the more they display, the more narcissistic they are.

Most of the research on narcissistic personality uses the NPI, so the scale is an important part of the definition of narcissism. A narcissist will freely admit to these specific traits even if he or she denies being a narcissist. The use of a valid, reliable measure like the NPI also negates arguments about the items. You might not agree that feeling special, or living your life however you want to, or seeking attention is a narcissistic trait. That's irrelevant, however, because the scale score *itself* predicts specific behaviors and attitudes. When researchers find that narcissists show less empathy, it means that people who agree with more of the NPI items show less empathy. Regardless of whether the items fit your personal definition of narcissism, study after study shows that *these items* predict certain values and behaviors. It doesn't matter if you call it narcissism, confident ambition, specialness, or anything else—the scale is linked to these outcomes.

Another important issue is the difference between the personality trait of narcissism and narcissistic personality disorder (NPD). We see this confused all the time, so we want to be very clear: *Being highly narcissistic or a narcissist is not the same as having a diagnosed psychiatric disorder or a pathological level of narcissism.* To be diagnosed with NPD, someone has to meet at least five of nine specific criteria describing a long-term pattern of behavior involving grandiosity, a lack of empathy, and a need to be admired. The person must also be suffering some form of impairment, such as depression, failures at work, or very troubled close relationships. Only a trained professional can diagnose NPD. NPD is less common than narcissistic personality because narcissistic personality does not have to be as extreme as NPD or be associated with clinically significant problems.

The clinical definition of NPD has provoked debate among psychologists. Several researchers have argued that clinical NPD captures two different types of people: extraverted, outgoing, and exhibitionistic folks like those who score high on the NPI, and more introverted, depressed, vulnerable, and psychologically empty (but also grandiose) people who are sometimes seen in psychotherapy. A good example of a "vulnerable" narcissist is the comic book guy on *The Simpsons*, clearly different from the classic outgoing "cool" narcissist. A diagnostic manual used by some therapists breaks narcissism into these two types, a distinction that might appear in the next version of the *Diagnostic and Statistical Manual of Mental Disorders*, known as the DSM.

In this book, we focus on the more outgoing, exhibitionistic form of narcissism and not as much on the more vulnerable form (although we discuss the vulnerable form in some places, such as the growth in eating disorders). We also focus more on narcissistic personality than on NPD, because the epidemic of narcissism goes far beyond the 1 in 16 Americans who have been clinically impaired by NPD at some point in their lives. "Normal" narcissists are much more common and thus potentially more destructive. Most people at the 90th percentile on the NPI scale, for example, don't have diagnosed clinical NPD, but they cause plenty of trouble for the people around them—maybe even more than those with NPD, since they're still functioning well (at least for now).

One final but very important issue is the difference between narcissism as a personality trait and narcissism as a cultural condition. The narcissism epidemic involves two intertwined stories. One story is about the high level of narcissism among individuals. The other story is about a shift in our shared cultural values toward greater narcissism and self-admiration. These two issues are related, of course, but the cultural changes are even more dramatic than the personality changes. We discuss the issue of personality and culture in detail near the end of this chapter.

MYTHS SURROUNDING NARCISSISM

When we talk to people about narcissism, we always get lots of interesting questions. Many of them fall into what we like to call the Top Five Myths of Narcissism. (We cover a sixth myth, that you have to be narcissistic to be successful, in the next chapter, and a seventh, that you have to love yourself to love someone else, in Chapter 13.)

MYTH 1:
Narcissism Is "Really High" Self-Esteem

Narcissism is often confused with "really high" self-esteem. Narcissists *do* have high self-esteem, and in fact many techniques used to increase self-esteem might lead to greater narcissism. But narcissism and self-esteem differ in an important way. Narcissists think they are smarter, better looking, and more important than others, but not necessarily more moral, more caring, or more compassionate. Narcissists don't brag about how they are the nicest, most thoughtful people in the world, but they do like to point out that they're winners or that they're hot (like the teenage girls Jean overhead in a YMCA locker room, one of whom looked in the mirror, grinned widely, and declared in a loud voice, "Wow—I look hot!" She then proceeded to list all of the boys who thought so, too). People merely high in self-esteem also have positive views of themselves, but they also see themselves as loving and moral. This is one reason narcissists lack perspective—close relationships keep the ego in check. For example, if you beat a close friend in a tennis match, you typically don't scream, "In your face!" and do a happy dance. You say, "Good game." Narcissists are missing the piece about caring for others, which is why their self-admiration often spins out of control.

MYTH 2:
Narcissists Are Insecure and Have Low Self-Esteem

Many people believe that narcissists are actually insecure and "hate themselves deep down inside." Their self-importance, this theory goes, is just a cover for their deep-seated doubts about themselves. This idea can be traced back to some strands of psychodynamic theory, which speculate that narcissism is a defense against an "empty" or "enraged" self, hidden low self-esteem, or a deep-seated sense of shame. Psychologists sometimes call this the "mask model," because it suggests that narcissism is a mask for low self-worth. This argument is seductive in its convenience, allowing us to write off narcissistic people as flawed souls who just need to learn to love themselves enough—our culture's cure-all. We can believe that narcissists are actually suffering even when they look happy and self-satisfied. This view also fits with many psychodynamic explanations of behavior in which the conscious and unconscious are opposed, such as the antipornography crusader who secretly buys *Hustler* in a brown paper bag at the 7-Eleven or the gay basher who is really homosexual.

The "cover for insecurity" model of narcissism is pervasive in our culture. On TV's *ER*, a coworker confronts a mean, bitingly sarcastic surgical resident by saying, "What is it about your need to belittle other people? Does insulting someone make you feel like a man, bolster what little self-esteem you're clinging to? I can't even begin to imagine what happened in your life to make you the kind of person that everybody hates." The usually confident surgical resident looks flustered and promptly drops the papers he's carrying, which is nifty TV shorthand for "You're right. You discovered the hidden truth about my poor wasted soul." On *7th Heaven*, the unlikable character Rose suddenly decides to consider other people's feelings. "I've been completely self-centered and condescending," she admits to Annie, her fiancé's mother. "I think I started getting like this after my parents divorced. I blamed myself. The more I blamed myself the worse I felt and the less I thought of myself. To hide that, I started acting superior to everyone so no one would know that I feel like nothing." Annie not only believes her but decides that Rose is actually a wonderful person.

A lot of the available information about narcissism is based on the mistaken idea that narcissists have low self-esteem underneath. An online site notes that narcissists "actually have low self-esteem and experience a sense of insecurity around others. It is this insecure feeling that leads them to project a grandiose image of themselves as perfect in many ways." Celebrity life coach Patrick Wanis told MSNBC, "Paris Hilton is suffering from narcissism. Although she seems to be confident she is in fact insecure, arrogant, and has low self-esteem." Janice wrote on a *New*

York Times comment board, "In coping with narcissists, it helps to remember that the size of a person's 'ego' varies inversely with the level of self-esteem. Deep down, narcissists are very insecure and unhappy with themselves; those problems are what makes them narcissistic to begin with." Many people see insecurity as the crucial difference between narcissism and self-confidence. It's a way to have your cake and eat it, too: you can feel great by admiring yourself, but as long as you're secure, it's not narcissism.

However, there is no evidence that the extraverted narcissists we focus on in this book have low self-esteem or are insecure underneath—they like themselves just fine, and even more than the average person. Adults who score high on narcissism typically score high on self-esteem as well. The most common self-esteem measure has items such as "I feel I am a person of worth, at least on an equal basis with others" and "I feel that I have a number of good qualities." Someone who thought he was entitled to the best would find very little to disagree with here. To narcissistic people, these self-esteem items sound like a pale shadow of their own greatness. "You bet I'm a person of worth—more than most people!" they think. "I have *a lot* of good qualities, not just a number!" The subset of "vulnerable narcissists" do have occasional bouts of low self-esteem and can end up in therapy, but in this book we focus more on the socially savvy narcissists who have the most influence on the culture. Much of the confusion about narcissism comes from thinking that most narcissists are like these vulnerable narcissists, but they're not.

But what if these outgoing narcissists are just *saying* that they have high self-esteem? Maybe, deep down inside, they really do dislike themselves, and their narcissism is a defensive cover for their lack of true self-esteem. New methods in social psychology have made it much easier to answer such questions. The Implicit Association Test (IAT), developed by Tony Greenwald of the University of Washington and Mahzarin Banaji of Harvard, measures how fast people can associate two concepts. The IAT was first used to measure racial prejudice. In that version, pictures of white and black faces appear on a computer screen next to words like *good* and *bad*. In the first round, test takers press the key on the side of the keyboard under "good" if a white face appears and under "bad" if a black face appears. They then do the reverse, pairing white faces with "bad" and black faces with "good." The computer measures how fast people can press the key for each pairing; being able to pair white faces with "good" faster than black faces shows a preference for whites (try it yourself at https://implicit.harvard.edu/implicit/). Many people who express little prejudice in explicit surveys still show an implicit racial prejudice on this test. Author Malcolm Gladwell, who wrote about unconscious associations in his book *Blink* and who is biracial himself, was embarrassed to discover that he found it hard to pair black faces with "good" but easy to do the same for white faces. The test is an intriguing measure of our true beliefs—the unconscious feelings and associations we have absorbed from our culture.

Researchers have recently adapted the IAT to measure self-esteem, with respondents pairing keys for "me" and "not me" with positive and negative words. People with high self-esteem find it easy to associate themselves with positive words like *good* and *wonderful* but react much more slowly when trying to pair "me" with *awful* and *wrong*. Several researchers have used this technique to discover how narcissists actually feel about themselves "deep down inside."

It turns out that deep down inside, narcissists think they're *awesome*. Narcissistic people found it just as easy—or even easier—than non-narcissists to hit the key for "me" when they saw words like *good, wonderful, great,* and *right* and found it equally or more difficult to press the "me" key for words like *bad, awful, terrible,* and *wrong*. Narcissists also had higher unconscious self-esteem than non-narcissists on such items as *assertive, active, energetic, outspoken, dominant,* and *enthusiastic* (versus words like *quiet, reserved, silent, withdrawn, submissive,* and *inhibited*). Narcissists scored only average on words like *kind, friendly, generous, cooperative, pleasant,* and *affectionate* (versus *mean, rude, stingy, quarrelsome, grouchy,* and *cruel*), but even in this domain they showed no signs of low self-image. Thus narcissists have very similar views of themselves on the inside *and* the outside—they are secure and positive that they are winners, but believe that caring about others isn't all that important.

Another way to look at unconscious self-esteem is with the "name-letter task," in which researchers ask people to rate the letters in the alphabet according to how beautiful or likable they are. Rating the letters in your own name (especially the first letter) as more likable or beautiful is a good indicator of internal self-esteem. If we authors had high unconscious self-esteem, we would find the letters *j* or *k* to be particularly beautiful. Sure enough, narcissists think the letters in their name are powerful and assertive and a little more beautiful, but not more kind and nurturing. Again, narcissism is not about deep self-loathing or low self-esteem, but a confidence in individual achievement areas paired with a neutral to negative attitude toward closeness and emotional intimacy with others.

Narcissism as a cover for insecurity is an important issue, as many people assume that narcissism can be cured with even *more* self-admiration. It can't. "If Michael had more self-esteem, he wouldn't be so disrespectful," they'll say. The truth is that Michael might be disrespectful because he thinks he's better than you are and feels his needs are more important than yours. More self-esteem, especially if it crosses over into narcissism, might only make that problem worse. Thus it is very important that programs seeking to work with school bullies be very careful when trying to build their self-esteem, as narcissism might be an unintended consequence. Bullies need to learn respect for others. They already have too much respect for themselves.

MYTH 3:
Narcissists Really Are Great/Better Looking/Smarter

Maybe narcissists are justified in their beliefs that they are special because they really are special. It certainly would be easier to be narcissistic if you were actually beautiful or particularly talented at something, but there isn't much evidence that narcissists are any better on average. Two studies found that narcissists didn't score any higher on objective IQ tests, and another found no correlation between narcissism and performance on a test of general knowledge. Studies on creativity are mixed, with one finding a positive correlation and another finding no relationship. Narcissists also aren't any better looking: across two studies, strangers who rated head shots found narcissists no more attractive than others, even though *they* thought they were more attractive (one of these studies was cleverly titled "Narcissistic men and women think they are so hot—But they are not"). However, narcissists do know how to pick out a flattering picture of themselves (or take enough pictures so at least one of them is flattering). For example, the pictures that narcissists chose for their personal Web pages were rated as more attractive by observers. Overall, narcissists believe that they are smarter and more beautiful than they actually are.

MYTH 4:
Some Narcissism Is Healthy

Some people have asked us, "So should we all hate ourselves instead?" Of course not. Saying that hating yourself is the alternative to loving yourself is a false choice. Just as obesity researchers are not saying that Americans should all become anorexic, we're not suggesting self-hatred. A small number of people do hate themselves and could use some self-admiration. But you can like yourself just fine without loving yourself to excess. We believe that it would be better for everyone not to concentrate on self-feelings—positive or negative—quite so much. Instead, focus on life: your relationships with others, your work, or the beauty of the natural world. Think about the deepest joy you experience in life—it doesn't typically come from thinking about how great you are. Instead it comes from connecting with the world and getting away from yourself, as when you enjoy time with friends, family, and children, are engaged at work, or do all-absorbing tasks such as art, writing, crafts, athletics, or helping others.

Is some amount of narcissism healthy? The real question is, "Healthy for whom?" Selfishness, for example, might allow you to get a bigger piece of dessert after dinner, but will hurt your longer-term relationships with your companions and might cost you a dinner invitation in the future. A narcissist would probably be on the first lifeboat on a sinking ship—adaptive, yes, but not good if he's taking a place away from a child. Similarly, it's great to eat when you're hungry, but not that great if you're snatching food out of the mouth of a baby.

Hurting others is wrong, and that belief informs our stance on whether self-admiration is healthy. Narcissistic behavior that causes others to suffer isn't "healthy." Narcissism at the expense of one's own performance (for example, failing at a task as a result of overconfidence) is also not healthy. Getting a rush of excitement and self-esteem from being a legend in your own mind seems a tad unhealthy, but, hey, if it works for you and isn't adversely affecting others in your life or your own performance, we aren't going to make a big deal out of it. So narcissism that helps performance but does not hurt others, such as the confidence you might need before a big public performance, is the healthier aspect of narcissism, although there are probably other ways to get the same result without focusing so much on the self.

Myth 5:
Narcissism Is Just Physical Vanity

Although vanity is certainly one of the negative characteristics of narcissists (which we address in Chapter 9), it is far from the only one. Narcissists are also materialistic, entitled, aggressive when insulted, and uninterested in emotional closeness.

IS THE NARCISSISM EPIDEMIC GROWING?

Given the downsides of narcissism, we wondered if this negative personality trait was now more common than in the past. Self-esteem has risen among children and college students, as have several other traits correlated with narcissism.

So we set out to determine whether the pervasive trend toward self-admiration in America extended to narcissism. After many hours of searching psychology databases and research reports, we and our coauthors Sara Konrath, Joshua Foster, and Brad Bushman found 85 samples of 16,275 college students who filled out the Narcissistic Personality Inventory between 1979 and 2006. This allowed us to look into the past to see how previous generations responded to this questionnaire when they were in college and compare their responses to those of more recent college students.

We found that the move toward self-admiration has a dark side. College students in the 2000s were significantly more narcissistic than Gen Xers and Baby Boomers in the 1970s, '80s, and '90s. The Boomers, a generation famous for being self-absorbed, were outdone by their children. By 2006, two-thirds of college students scored above the scale's original 1979–85 sample average, a 30% increase in only two decades. One out

College Students' Narcissistic Personality Inventory Scores, 1982–2006, from 31 Campuses Across the U.S.

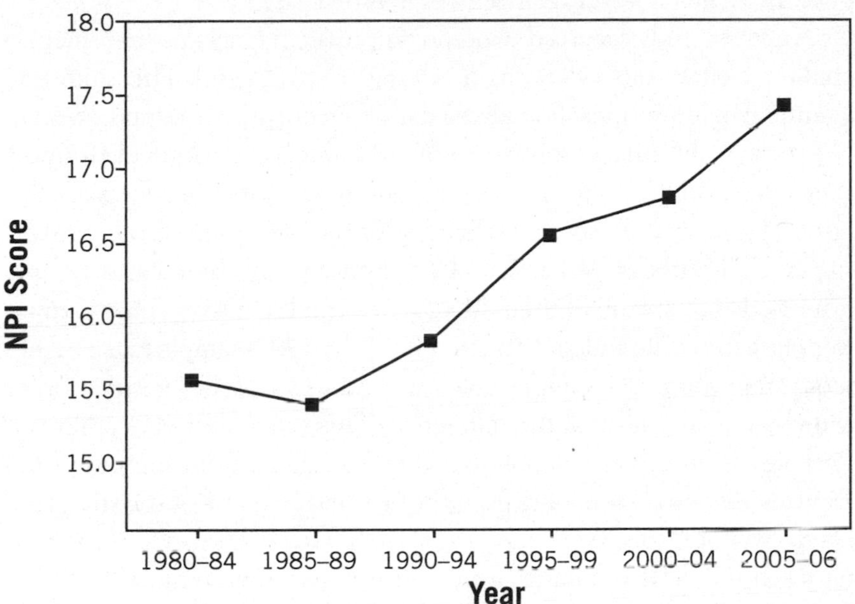

Source: Twenge, J. M., Konrath, S., Foster, J. D., Campbell, W. K., and Bushman, B. J. (2008). Egos inflating over time: A cross-temporal meta-analysis of the Narcissistic Personality Inventory. *Journal of Personality, 76*, 875–901.

of 4 recent college students answered the majority of questions in the narcissistic direction. The upswing in narcissism appears to be accelerating: the increase between 2000 and 2006 was especially steep. The changes were especially large for women; men still score higher on narcissism than women, but young women are closing the gap.

Over the last few decades, narcissism has risen as much as obesity. In other words, the narcissism epidemic is just as widespread as the obesity epidemic. It is also useful to consider what the increase in narcissism would look like if it occurred in some other familiar measurements: it's the same as an SAT score going up 75 points (out of 1600) or the height of all men going up by about an inch.

Of course, this study shows a shift in the average—plenty of college students are not narcissistic. But you will probably see it among more young people, because there are now more students with high levels of narcissism. A small to medium-sized change in an average score multiplies into a much larger change in high scores.

Another study received widespread press coverage, as it seemed to challenge our results by finding no change in narcissism. This study had a number of limitations. It analyzed data from only three campuses, all in Northern California, compared to the 31 campuses nationwide from 21 states in our study. It was also very difficult to separate the effects of campus and time in their study, as their 1980s sample was from the University of California at Berkeley and UC Santa Cruz, their 1990s sample from Berkeley, and all of their 2000s data from UC Davis. Thus campus was perfectly confounded with year—so if the 1990s sample had a higher score than the 2000s sample, there was no way to tell if generation or campus was the cause of the difference. This is a definite possibility, as Berkeley is an urban campus that draws students from big cities and Davis is very rural and draws from the agricultural parts of the state (the Davis mascot is the Aggies, and the campus is well-known for its veterinary school). These samples were also not very representative of U.S. college students; by 2008, 44% of their sample was Asian-American, though nationwide, only 6% of college students are Asian-American. Because Asian-Americans score lower on the NPI, these samples look very different from the rest of the country. When we examined these data within ethnic groups (for example, whites, Asian-Americans) and within campus (UC Davis, which had the most data), narcissism increased markedly. From 2002 to 2008, this sample's narcissism scores rose even faster than we found in our study. So even the study purporting to challenge ours actually found a striking increase in narcissism over time in recent years.

The trend toward narcissism in American culture has been building for a long time. The personality data we have from college students filling out the NPI goes back only to 1979. But the increase in narcissism probably began at least a decade earlier. It is relatively safe to say, for example, that the college Boomers of the late 1960s and '70s were more narcissistic and self-focused than the more staid college students of the 1950s and early '60s (now aged 65 or above). That's probably why advertisements for retirement planning services suddenly changed their approach in the last few years, focusing more on "dreams," fun, and

University of California at Davis Students' Narcissistic Personality Inventory scores, 2002–2007, Centered Within Ethnic Group

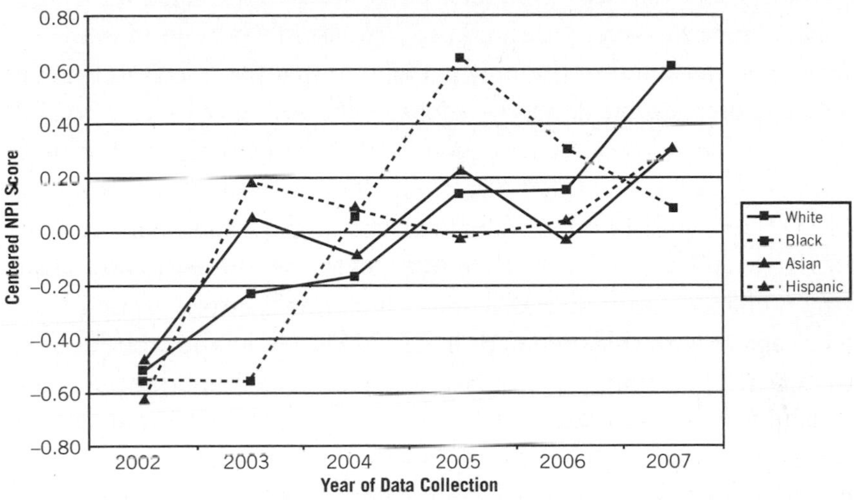

Source: Twenge, J. M., and Foster, J. D. (2008). Mapping the scale of the narcissism epidemic: Increases in narcissism 2002–2007 within ethnic groups. *Journal of Research in Personality, 42,* 1619–1622.

returning to childhood (the Boomer-laced Ameriprise ads with Dennis Hopper declare, "Dreams don't retire"). Almost every trait related to narcissism rose between the 1950s and the '90s, including assertiveness, dominance, extraversion, self-esteem, and individualistic focus. Even some older generations later turned to the modern way of thinking; one sample of women born in the late 1930s increased markedly in narcissistic and individualistic traits during the 1970s when they were already in their forties. These trends have continued their ascent, with the Boomers' children topping them on every measure—including narcissism. Although Boomers rebelled against their straightlaced parents in the 1960s, their own offspring are more than happy to continue their parents' focus on the self. However, our point in this book is not to single out one generation or another. Although young people are often the most affected by cultural change, there is plenty of narcissism among people of all ages. In addition—we can't stress this enough—young people didn't raise themselves. They got these narcissistic values from somewhere, often from their parents or media messages created by older people.

Both of the datasets on narcissistic traits over the generations used college students—every research psychologist's favorite (and free) captive audience, and thus the only population that has filled out the NPI for three decades. We don't know for sure if the change extends to children, younger adolescents, and young adults not in college, but other sources of data point in that direction. One study compared more than 11,000 teens aged 14 to 16 who filled out a long questionnaire in either 1951 or 1989. Out of more than 400 items, the one that showed the largest change over time was "I am an important person." Only 12% of teens agreed with this statement in the 1950s, but by the late '80s more than 80% of girls and 77% of boys said they were important. A study called Monitoring the Future found that the number of high school students who said that "having lots of money" was "extremely important" increased 66% between 1976 and 2006. A 2008 Harris Interactive poll found that 21- to 31-year-olds were voted the most greedy and self-indulgent—even by the twenty-somethings themselves, who were actually *more* likely than older generations to agree that the young generation had these narcissistic tendencies. (So much for the "narcissism in the young is only in the eyes of bitter old people" argument.)

Youth also have unrealistically high expectations for themselves. In 2000, 50% of high school students expected to attend law, medical, dental, or graduate school, double the expectations of students in the 1970s. However, the number of people who actually attain these degrees (that is, a measure of reality) has not changed. In addition, more than two-thirds of high school students now say that they expect to be in the top 20% of performance in their jobs.

It's difficult to say based on hard data whether older adults have shown the same trend toward greater narcissism, as people older than college age have not completed the NPI very often. Are, say, thirty-somethings today more narcissistic than thirty-somethings were 25 years ago? Our guess is a confident "maybe." For one thing, young adulthood looks more like adolescence now than it used to. Baby Boomers in the 1970s typically settled into employment, married, and had at least one child well before they turned 25. Today's average 25-year-old has not achieved any of these milestones; their lives more closely resemble those of adolescents, the time in life when narcissism peaks. So our best estimate is that adults in their twenties, thirties, and forties are more narcissistic now than they were a few decades ago. The movement into a less narcissistic adult life may now take longer—or not happen at all, a stark contrast with a few decades ago, when 26-year-olds didn't live with their parents and 45-year-olds didn't wear jeans and listen to hip bands. The study on women born in the 1930s suggests that even grandmothers might be more narcissistic now than grandmothers were a generation ago.

Alarmingly, Narcissistic Personality Disorder (NPD) also appears to be increasing.

The most comprehensive study of NPD ever conducted was released just as this book was going to press. Researchers at the National Institutes of Health asked a nationally representative sample of over 35,000 Americans if they had ever experienced the symptoms of NPD during their lifetimes (the interviewers asked only about symptoms and did not mention the name of the disorder). They found that 6.2% of

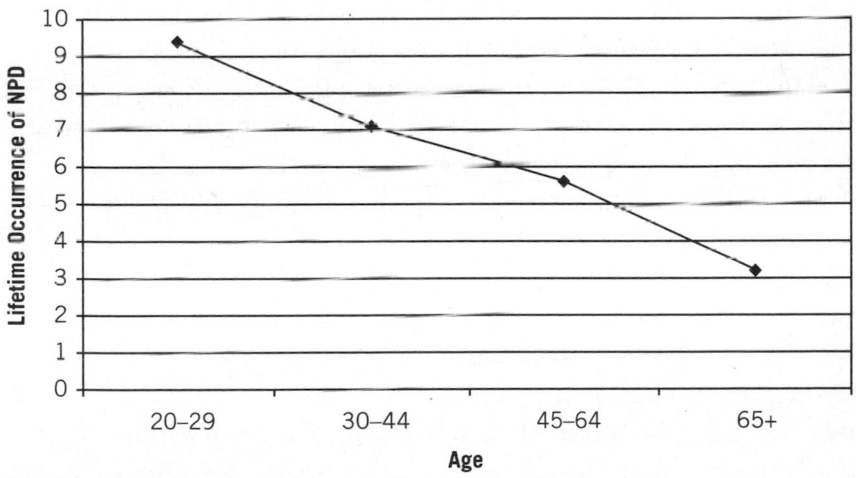

Source: Stinson, F. S., Dawson, D. A, Goldstein, R. B., Chou, S. P., Huang, B., Smith, S. M., Ruan, W. J., Pulay, A. J., Saha, T. D., Pickering, R. P., and Grant, B. F. (2008). Prevalence, correlates, diability, and comorbidity of DSM-IV Narcissistic Personality Disorder: Results from the Wave 2 National Epidemiologic Survey on Alcohol and Related Conditions. *Journal of Clinical Psychiatry, 69*, 1033–1045.

Americans—1 out of 16—had suffered from NPD at some point in their lives. Even more stunning, 9.4% of Americans in their twenties had experienced NPD (including an incredible 11.5% of young men), compared with only 3.2% of those over 65 years old. So nearly 1 out 10 Americans in their twenties has experienced NPD, versus 1 out of 30 of those over 65.

If rates of NPD were constant over the generations, there would be *more* older people who reported experience with NPD, because they had more years in which to develop the disorder. Instead, rates among older people are only a third of those among younger people. Although it is possible that older people forgot some earlier episodes of NPD, there would have to be a huge amount of forgetting to explain this large a difference, especially since a trained professional facilitated their recall.

A 25-year-old, for example, has had only seven years to experience NPD, as the disorder cannot be diagnosed until someone is 18. Someone who is 65 has had 47 years to develop the disorder. Thus if the 20–29 age group continues on the same trajectory, developing NPD at a rate of about 1.3% a year, 54% of them—more than half—will develop NPD by the time they are 65. We highly doubt the problem will ever get this bad, but even if the rate of development is half that, 26% of people now in their twenties—1 out of 4—will have experienced clinical-level NPD by the time they are 65. Even before the publication of these data, some therapists called the increase in narcissistic problems "epidemic" or even "pandemic." Along with the two datasets showing increases in narcissistic personality traits, this alarming rate of NPD, especially among the young, is strong empirical evidence for an epidemic of narcissism.

We are often asked if it's just the rich white kids who are narcissistic, but that doesn't appear to be the case. Author Jake Halpern found that twice as many black as white teens said they'd rather be famous than be smarter, stronger, or more beautiful. One social worker remarked to us that the inner-city youth he works with have "this overconfident attitude that isn't based on anything substantial. They believe they are great mainly because their teachers continue to tell them how great they are," a description that sounds pretty similar to some affluent suburban kids. In an Internet survey, young people who reported higher incomes scored slightly higher on the NPI, but the link between NPI scores and income was stronger for people in their thirties and especially forties. In other words, rich kids are only a little more narcissistic, but rich adults are significantly more so (or, at least narcissistic adults say they are richer—we have not seen their bank statements, so it's possible that this is just self-promotion). Privilege may lead to narcissism, but it's more likely to do so when it's earned rather than conferred by one's parents. Interestingly, rates of NPD are slightly higher among adults with *lower* incomes—possibly because NPD includes dysfunction in its definition. It might be more difficult to be narcissistic and poor than it is to be narcissistic and rich, leading to more problems. Alternatively, people with NPD might have lower incomes because they are difficult to work with, making it harder to hold down a good job.

Ethnic groups differ in levels of narcissism, primarily due to cultural issues. In particular, Asian cultures are more collectivistic and discourage individualism and narcissism. Overall, more traditional cultures—those that value family, duty, and obligation—are less narcissistic than more modern cultures like that of the United States. In one dataset, Americans scored in the top 10–20% of nations on narcissism. In another study, Americans obtained higher narcissism scores than people from any other country. Our students might not be the brightest, or our poverty level the lowest, but Americans do just fine on narcissism tests.

CULTURE AND NARCISSISM

Personality does not exist in isolation. This increase in narcissism in individuals is, we believe, just an outcome of a massive shift in culture toward a greater focus on self-admiration. (In the appendices to this book, available at www.narcissismepidemic.com, we describe a detailed model of the interplay between culture and the individual.) Narcissism has spread through the generations like a particularly pernicious virus—one with multiple means of entry and transmission. First, Americans' immunity to narcissism has weakened. At one time, strong social pressures kept people's egos in check. Mothers asked children, "Who do you think you are?" (instead of "What do you want for dinner, princess?") Religious leaders stressed humility and modesty. Strong communities and stable relationships discouraged arrogance and made it less necessary to meet and impress new people. Narcissism has also been transmitted as an unintended consequence of good intentions, as in the self-esteem movement and less authoritative parenting. Instead of creating friendly, happy children, however, these practices often produce self-centered, narcissistic young people.

In addition, norms for self-presentation have shifted with cultural trends and new technology. As we explore in the chapters to come, Internet social networking sites and celebrity culture have raised the bar for narcissistic behavior and standards. Using MySpace to post a picture of yourself half naked and posturing provocatively is now considered totally normal—even though it is also deeply narcissistic. Americans are being persuaded that becoming more vain, materialistic, and self-centered is actually a good thing. This can happen even if you're not particularly narcissistic but just get drawn into what everyone else is doing. Today, if you don't get your teeth whitened, everyone thinks you are either poor or an espresso-drinking, cigarette-smoking European. Ten years ago, nobody would have noticed.

THE NEW VIEWPOINT ON NARCISSISM

When the Associated Press covered our study on narcissism increasing over the generations in 2007, dozens of college students wrote news stories and opinion pieces in response. Very few college students disputed the notion that their peers were self-centered; instead, they argued that their generation's narcissism was perfectly acceptable. Interviewed in The *Daily Pennsylvanian*, University of Pennsylvania freshman Kyle Johnson said, "This extreme self-esteem [is] justified since this generation will be remembered as the greatest generation of all time." San Diego State University junior Camille Clasby protested in the *Daily Aztec*, "But we are special. There's nothing wrong with knowing that. It's not vanity that this generation exhibits—it's pride. And it's no wonder with all that we are accomplishing that we have a lot to be proud of." That might be true, but so did earlier generations, and they weren't as narcissistic. This statement resembles the classic narcissistic confusion between *thinking* you're great and actually being great. Some older folks agree with this assessment, however; *Generations* authors Neil Howe and William Strauss, both Boomers, call people born since 1982 "The Next Great Generation." An Austin, Texas, TV station did a Web poll asking people if they agreed that the younger generation was self-absorbed. One of the choices was "Yes, but it's OK because they're also the best generation ever." Although only 4% of respondents chose this answer, it's interesting that it was even included as an option. The most popular response, at 62%, was "Yes, and it's awful."

But *is* it awful? Or is narcissism necessary to succeed in today's competitive world?

CHAPTER 3

Isn't Narcissism Beneficial, Especially in a Competitive World?

Challenging Another Myth About Narcissism

Listen in on conversations these days, and a word you'll hear a lot is *competitive*. ("It's so competitive now." "If we do that we won't be competitive.") Sometimes it's even used as an adjective to describe style and quality ("Hey, that suit is competitive.") People talk about competition for jobs, for getting into college, in sports. There's worry that the United States won't be able to compete in a global economy, and that good-paying jobs will be outsourced, downsized, or otherwise canned. In some neighborhoods, winning and competing are emphasized beginning at age two, when parents try to get children into the best private preschools. Some parents start even earlier by buying Baby Einstein videos or playing classical music to fetuses presumably listening in pregnant bellies.

By high school, the emphasis on winning has reached a fever pitch. The competition for college admissions has grown so fierce that some students spend their high school years on a constant treadmill of Advanced Placement courses, SAT test prep sessions, and meetings with privately hired consultants, costing up to $40,000, who help them craft the perfect application essay. Even some state universities now reject three-fourths of their applicants. Some parents "help" their kids compete by doing their homework and projects for them, even through college. Doctors report that they are seeing more and more repetitive stress injuries among younger and younger children as kids play one sport for longer and much more intensely than in the casual pickup games of generations past. Parents fight with one another at children's sports games; in 2000, one father beat another to death at a kids' hockey practice.

In a convenient combination of the American core cultural values of self-admiration and competition, many people believe that always putting yourself first is necessary to compete. If it can help us get ahead, we're interested, and if it's something fun like self-admiration, sign us up. "Show me someone without an ego," opined Donald Trump, "and I'll show you a loser."

When our study on narcissism over the generations was covered in the press in 2007 and 2008, a large number of people responded by saying that narcissism was necessary, especially in an increasingly competitive world. This is yet another example of our culture's blurred distinction between self-worth and narcissism, and the increasing acceptance of doing whatever it takes to get ahead. A University of Michigan student wrote online, "The people conducting this research didn't have to deal with the amount of competition we face daily. We have to be confident and focused on ourselves in order to succeed. So if our generation seems a little more obsessed with the 'Me' than those before us, it is not our fault." San Diego State junior Camille Clasby wrote in the *Daily Aztec*, "Today's college students have more pressure and stress put on them than in past years. The way we're able to meet and exceed the challenges we face is by believing in ourselves. Feeling special is a great form of motivation." Lauren, 27 and from Atlanta, wrote in a *New York Times* comments section, "Aren't self-confidence and belief in oneself basic requirements for success in one's personal and professional life? If that's the definition of a narcissist, proud to be one. And a successful one, at that ;)."

Mike Nolan, a Purdue University engineering student, was even more direct in the *Exponent*. "The country I've grown up in rewards individuals who 'grab life by the balls,' " he wrote. "So for all you psychologists that believe this is some kind of mental disorder, perhaps you should take the stick-up-your-ass-ism inventory and then go cry about something stupid. Mike Nolan, for one, is going to continue working to achieve big things."

Some educators also agreed that self-admiration and even narcissism are necessary for success. "We have a society in which narcissistic behavior is a good quality to have," said Marc Flacks, a professor of sociology at California State University, Long Beach interviewed in the *Los Angeles Times*. "This is a bottom-line society, so students are smart to seek the most direct route to the bottom line. If you don't have a me-first attitude, you won't succeed." Bob Portnoy, director of counseling and psychological services at the University of Nebraska at Lincoln, noted in the *Lincoln Journal Star*, "In this country, the idea of valuing oneself is critical to success. And to me, that's healthy narcissism."

All of these well-intentioned folks take it for granted that a high level of self-confidence, even narcissism, leads to success. There's only one thing wrong with this popular, pervasive, and deeply rooted belief: it's not true.

NARCISSISM AND SUCCESS

Narcissists love to win, but in most settings they aren't that great at actually winning. For example, college students with inflated views of themselves (who think they are better than they actually are) make poorer grades the longer they are in college. They are also more likely to drop out. In another study, students who flunked an introductory psychology course had by far the highest narcissism scores, and those who made A's had the lowest. Apparently the narcissists were wildly unrealistic about how they were doing and persisted in their lofty illusions when they should have dropped the course (or perhaps done something radical, like study).

In other words, overconfidence backfires. This makes some sense; narcissists are lousy at taking criticism and learning from mistakes. They also like to blame everyone and everything except themselves for their shortcomings. Second, they lack motivation to improve because they believe they have already made it: when you were born on home plate, why run around the bases? Third, overconfidence itself can lead to poor performance. If you think you know all of the answers, there's no need to study. Then you take the test and fail. Oops.

In one series of studies, people answered general knowledge questions like "Who founded the Holy Roman Empire?" They then rated their confidence in their answers and were given the chance to place a monetary bet on the outcome. Unknown to the participants, these were "fair bets," so someone who was 99% confident of their answer would make less money than someone who was only 60% sure. This is similar to horse racing, where the favorites have smaller pay-offs (a 1-to-25 pony pays off more than the 1-to-2 sure thing), or football, where there is a "point spread" for each game.

Narcissists stunk at this game. Their performance on the questions was the same as everyone else's, but they were more confident of their answers and thus bet too much and too often. Narcissists also showed their trademark decoupling from reality: they started off saying they would do better than others, but they did worse. Undaunted, the narcissists continued to claim that they had outperformed others on the test and would do well in the future. At least for a short period of time, narcissists were able to live in a fantasy world where they thought they were successful. They were even able to maintain these beliefs in the face of failure. Narcissism is a great predictor of imaginary success—but not of actual success.

Narcissists also love to be know-it-alls, which psychologists call "overclaiming." You say to your know-it-all friend, "Have you heard of jazz great Billy Strayhorn?" or "Do you know Paul Klee's paintings?" or "Do you know when the Treaty of Versailles was signed?" and the know-it-all says, "Of course." You might be tempted to ask him, "Have you heard of jazz great Milton Silus?" or "Do you know John Kormat's paintings?" or "Do you know when the Treaty of Monticello was signed?" to see if he still answers "of course"—even though none of these things actually exists. That's overclaiming. One study had people answer 150 questions, including thirty made-up items. Narcissists were champion overclaimers—they were so smart they even knew things that didn't exist.

Narcissists have a high tolerance for risks, because they are so confident they are right and that things will go well. For this reason, narcissists are successful when investing in bull markets, when their overconfidence and willingness to take risks pays off. In a study using a simulated stock market, narcissists did better than others when the market was headed up. But their superior performance disappeared as soon as the market turned south—then narcissists lost their shirts due to their higher tolerance for risk. This, in part, is what happened in the mortgage market during the late 2000s: Both buyers and lenders were narcissistically overconfident and took too many risks. When many buyers couldn't pay their overly optimistic mortgages, the market turned downward, eventually taking much of Wall Street with it. In the short term, narcissism and overconfidence paid off in spades, but when failure came it was even more spectacular than usual. In the end, the financial crisis was the worst since the Great Depression.

It's tempting to believe that narcissism might still be beneficial when leading a large company. Not so, according to Jim Collins, the author of the bestselling business book *Good to Great*. In an exhaustive study, Collins found that companies that moved from being "merely good to truly great" did so because they had what he calls "Level 5" leaders. These CEOs are not the charismatic, ultraconfident figures you would expect. Instead, they are humble, avoid the limelight, never rest on their laurels, and continuously try to prove themselves. Collins profiles Darwin E. Smith, the former CEO of Kimberly-Clark, who wore cheap suits and shunned publicity. In his twenty years of service as CEO, Smith oversaw stock returns that bested the market four times over. Instead of showing in-your-face braggadocio, Smith quietly kept at his work. "I never stopped trying to become qualified for the job," he said.

Collins's study of companies did not originally set out to find a profile of CEOs; he had been looking for company characteristics that would explain business success. But the profile of the humble but determined CEO came up over and over. These CEOs were also excellent team players, something else narcissists aren't. "Throughout our interviews with such executives," Collins writes, "they would instinctively deflect discussion about their own role. When pressed to talk about themselves, they'd say things like 'I don't think I can take much credit for what happened. We were blessed with marvelous people."

In other words, Collins found that the best corporate leaders were *not* narcissistic or even particularly self-confident. Companies with short-term success, however, were often headed by attention-seeking, arrogant leaders. In these companies, Collins writes, "we noted the presence of a gargantuan ego that contributed to the demise or continued mediocrity of the company." This lines up well with the academic research on narcissism and judgment: in the end, narcissists' overconfidence undermines their performance.

Business professors Arijit Chatterjee and Donald Hambrick studied

CEO narcissism and company outcomes. In more than 100 technology companies, they found that the more narcissistic the CEO of a company was, the more volatile the company's performance. Apparently the narcissistic leaders were using dramatic, highly public corporate strategies. For example, they might buy up a smaller competitor or start a new "cutting-edge" business venture. When those strategic decisions paid off, the company did really well; when they didn't, it was a disaster. Less narcissistic leaders, in contrast, produced a more steady performance. Given that volatility in performance is considered a negative in the valuation of companies (in economics, volatility is seen as "risk"), the narcissistic CEOs were not ideal.

Narcissists are also not popular bosses. Employees rate narcissistic managers as average in problem-solving skills but below average in interpersonal skills and integrity, two qualities considered very important for management. Another study found that while narcissists saw themselves as excelling at leadership, their peers thought they were below average.

Despite the iffy performance record of narcissists in leadership roles, narcissists *are* more likely than others to emerge as leaders in an organization. In one study led by Amy Brunell, groups of previously unacquainted students worked together on a task. Narcissists quickly came to dominate these interactions; they saw themselves as leaders, and so did others in the group. A study of business executives found that narcissists emerged as leaders in these real-world contexts as well. However, narcissists' rise to leadership is short-lived. Over time, group members notice narcissists' negative qualities and stop viewing them as leaders. Unfortunately, by then they were the boss and the group had to listen to them.

Enron—the company made up of "the smartest guys in the room" that cooked its books and subsequently imploded—is a microcosm of the downfalls of narcissism. As Malcolm Gladwell argues in his essay "The Talent Myth," "Enron was the Narcissistic Corporation—a company that took more credit for success than was legitimate, that did not acknowledge responsibility for its failures, that shrewdly sold the rest of us on its genius." Gladwell argues that creating a great organization involves cultivating great teams of individuals who can work well together—not just individual superstars. This is yet another reason narcissists are often not very successful in the long run: they would rather take all the glory for themselves than share it with a team.

There is one exception to the rule that narcissism doesn't lead to success. Narcissists are good at individual—though not necessarily group—public performance. When narcissists can receive public recognition and admiration for their performances, they try harder and do better than non-narcissists. One lab study tested this by having a group of students write down as many uses for a knife as they could within twelve minutes (a common test of creativity). When individual performance was recognized by putting each person's name on the board with his or her number of creative uses, narcissists performed very well. When the credit went only to their group, however, narcissists didn't try very hard and performed fairly poorly. This lack of effort with a group will make a narcissist a liability in business, where much work is done in groups and individual work isn't always publicly recognized. But in acting and solo singing, narcissists feed on the glory of the spotlight. So narcissism might be beneficial in a situation like trying out for *American Idol* or a reality TV show. Notice we said trying out. Once narcissists have to work with other people—which in real life and even in most reality TV they almost always do—their performance tanks, and reality sets in.

SELF-ESTEEM AND SUCCESS

After our study on narcissism was released, a staff editorial in the *Reading* (Pennsylvania) *Eagle* argued that parents should continue to tell kids they are special, because it will "improve their self-esteem and give them the confidence they need to achieve their potential." If parents don't tell their children they are special, they opined, "the pendulum could swing too far in the other direction, creating a generation of children with alarmingly low self-esteem, a problem that would be just as bad as rampant narcissism." This editorial assumes, as most Americans do, that self-esteem is strongly linked to doing well in life. Our culture tells us it pays to believe in yourself as long as you aren't arrogant or narcissistic.

However, this isn't really true, either. A major review of the research on self-esteem and achievement found that high self-esteem does not cause better grades, test scores, or job performance. It's a problem of correlation not equaling causation. There is a small correlation between self-esteem and better achievement, but it is almost entirely explained by better performance causing higher self-esteem. Self-esteem comes *after* success, not before, because self-esteem is based on success (whether that's academic success or simply being a good friend to someone). Much of the rest of the already small link is due to confounding variables—rich kids, for example, have higher self-esteem and make better grades. Some children with low self-esteem do poorly, but it's because they were abused or had parents who did drugs—things that cause both low self-esteem and poor outcomes. On its own, self-esteem does not lead to success.

Think about it this way: if self-admiration caused success, American children, who have the highest self-esteem of children anywhere in the world, would also be the most successful. This simple prediction, however, doesn't match the data. In a recent study, 39% of American eighth-graders were confident of their math skills, compared to only 6% of Korean eighth-graders. The Koreans, however, far exceeded the U.S. students' actual performance on math tests. We're not number one, but we're number one in *thinking* we are number one.

Within the United States, the ethnic group with the *lowest* self-esteem, Asian-Americans, achieves the *highest* academic performance. So the group with "alarmingly low self-esteem" is actually doing the *best* in school and, in the words of the editorial, doing plenty "to achieve their potential."

U.S. high school kids have not improved in academic performance over the last 30 years, a time when self-esteem has been actively encouraged and boosted among American children. According to the National Assessment of Educational Progress (NAEP), 17-year-olds' math scores have risen slightly, from 304 to 307, but reading scores have stayed completely flat at 285. So, at best, there has been less than a 1% improvement in academic performance. At the same time, high school students' grades have inflated enormously. While only 18% of students said they earned an A or A- average in 1976, 33% said they were A students in 2006—a whopping 83% increase in self-reported A students. So, we have had less than a 1% improvement in actual learning over 30 years, but an 83% increase in A grades. Apparently, our culture has decided to go with the strategy of boosting the fantasy of success rather than success itself, similar to the amplifiers in the movie *Spinal Tap* that "go to eleven."

But perhaps self-esteem boosting still helps somehow. The best way to find out if one thing causes another is to turn to the gold standard of research methods, the scientific experiment. In a true experiment, people get a treatment, or don't in the control group, and it's random which group they end up in. For self-esteem, an ideal experiment would assign people to receive self-esteem boosting feedback (or not) and then see what their grades were.

Psychologist Don Forsyth and his colleagues conducted such an experiment. They were particularly interested in interventions for poor-performing students—those who needed the most help and presumably were the most in need of a self-esteem boost. College students in a psychology class who got D or F grades on the first test were sent an e-mail every week with a practice question from the class. That's all the control group students saw. Other students, though, got a self-esteem boost along with the practice question. For example, "Past research suggests that when students get back their tests, they tend to lose confidence: they say things like 'I can't do this,' or 'I'm worthless,' or 'I'm not as good as other people in college.' Other studies suggest, though, that students who have high self-esteem not only get better grades, but they remain self-confident and assured. . . . Bottom line: Hold your head—and your self-esteem—high."

What happened was remarkable. The people in the control group who only got practice questions did about the same on the final as they had on the first test. But the performance of the students who got the weekly boost to their self-esteem actually *declined.* Their average test score went from a 57 (out of 100) on the first test to a 38 on the final. Self-esteem boosting led to failure, not success.

But perhaps the students did poorly because they felt bad about themselves in spite of the self-esteem messages, or because they didn't believe the messages. After the final, students received a last e-mail asking them to rate their self-esteem by responding to two statements: "I feel good about myself as a student in Psychology 101" and "I feel good about myself in general." Even though their grades went down, the students who'd had their self-esteem boosted felt just as positively about themselves, and even a little more positively, than the control group. A full 70% of the self-esteem-boosted students reported the scale maximum for self-esteem, compared to 50% in the control group. So the students who got a self-esteem boost felt great about themselves even though they failed miserably. This is not good news for a culture that emphasizes self-esteem as the route to success.

Self-esteem also isn't a consistent predictor of status or leadership. When group members vary in self-esteem, high self-esteem people gain status in the group. But when most people in the group are high in self-esteem—which happens more and more with self-esteem on the rise—high-self-esteem people can't all attain the status they seek. At that point, those who are likable and care for others emerge as the group leaders. So when a group has lots of "sharp elbows," much like today's overcompetitive society, what counts for success is not caring for yourself but caring for others.

To be clear, we are not advocating underconfidence, hating yourself, or low self-esteem. If you don't think much about loving yourself, do work hard for the good of the group, and are more realistic about your abilities, that doesn't mean you hate yourself. It is very possible to do well without letting your ego get in the way. An open, nondefensive approach to learning is often best. One of Keith's graduate student friends was also a captain in the U.S. Army. When Mr. Army was fresh out of West Point and had his first command, a crusty old sergeant told him to keep his mouth shut and figure out what he was doing before he said anything. Instead of letting his ego get in the way and argue with the sergeant, Mr. Army shut his mouth and learned—a lot. He was able to become a better officer by knowing both what he knew *and* what he didn't know. The same is true of children in school and playing sports. When parents and teachers protect children from failure to cushion their self-esteem, kids may end up doing worse because they aren't learning from their mistakes. It is just fine to feel a little bad about yourself as you learn something. If you think about the experiences that have taught you the most, they probably involve times you failed or faced huge challenges. Having confidence in your true abilities includes knowing your weaknesses and learning from your failures, and that has nothing to do with hating yourself.

We also want to be clear that we are not arguing against passion for a career and "doing what you love." There is a big difference between "doing what you love" and "loving yourself." Being passionate about what you do can actually counter egotism. This is the idea of "flow"—

you get so absorbed in what you're doing that you forget about yourself. People who can do this, and draw joy from doing something they love, are less defensive in the face of criticism, perhaps because they don't feel the need to defend their ego. As long as your passion doesn't seriously interfere with your relationships, we are all in favor of passion for your work.

WHY DO AMERICANS THINK NARCISSISM IS SO IMPORTANT TO SUCCESS, EVEN THOUGH IT ISN'T?

Competition and Self-Promotion

When people say they need to be narcissistic because the world is increasingly competitive, they are half right: competition and status seeking have increased in American society. There is a growing perception that you have to claw your way into the upper classes or risk being mired in poverty. Economic inequality has risen sharply in the United States, with the top tier of workers earning more and more than the bottom tier. The Census Bureau's "Gini" index of income distribution shows economic inequality in the United States growing steadily between the 1980s and the present. The income level of the upper 1% of families has tripled while wages for most Americans have stayed stagnant. Even after accounting for inflation, the number of multimillionaires in the United States nearly doubled between 1998 and 2004. CEOs, who in 1982 made 42 times more than the average employee, now make 364 times more. Reaching the top level of professions has become more difficult as billable hours and limited partnerships squeeze lower-level lawyers, managed care saps doctors, and university budget cuts shrink the number of tenure-track professorships.

Some business researchers have argued that the social contract has broken down because the company will no longer take care of the worker as long as the worker does good for the company. For example, pensions are a thing of the past. Workers now fund their own retirement—perhaps with some matching funds from the company, but it's mostly up to them. Similarly, employees rarely stay at the same company for their entire careers anymore. Jobs are no longer stable; they can be outsourced, restructured, or simply eliminated. Employees have responded by job-hopping when times are good, always looking for the best opportunity for themselves as individuals.

Due to greater competition and the breakdown of this implied social contract, self-promotion is more necessary than it once was. When you switch jobs more often, you have to know how to polish your résumé and sound good in an interview. With college admissions more competitive, students must "package" themselves to get in. "Young people are taught every day (by politicians, news media, and our families) that you get nowhere in this world if you do not sell/promote yourself," wrote Zach in our online survey. "Name a politician or entertainer who doesn't talk about themselves constantly. Do you know anyone who just got into a good college or a good job without shamelessly selling themselves in résumés, personal statements, and interviews?" All of this makes it seem that being self-centered pays off.

We don't deny that self-promotion is now necessary in a world of increasing competition and decreasing loyalty. We have both advised some of our own graduate students to be more self-promoting in order to advance their careers. However, it is possible to be self-promoting when necessary without becoming completely narcissistic. To borrow a metaphor from psychologist Virginia Kwan, self-promotion should be just one tool in your toolbox—something that is useful "only under certain circumstances, not a defining feature of that person's personality." Polishing your college application, writing a good résumé, putting up a personal website, and making a good impression in a job interview are undoubtedly good skills to have. But it's not necessary for that self-promotion to become full-fledged narcissism. Narcissists do tend to be good at self-promotion, but so are non-narcissists who kick butt in an executive job interview and then come home and change their kid's dirty diaper without thinking such a task is below them.

Self-promotion can also be taken too far. For example, it's admittedly self-promoting to go on TV to sell your product, but if you come across as arrogant you won't sell much. Many people have very powerful radars for detecting displays of arrogance. Like most things in life, self-promotion is better in moderation—it is good when used sparingly and in the appropriate situations. If the narcissism epidemic is going to be contained, parents and teachers need to start telling young people (and themselves!) to use self-promotion selectively. That's a very different message from the now-common idea that it's right to "always put yourself first."

Narcissists' Greater Visibility

Another reason so many people believe that narcissists are phenomenally successful is that narcissists seek attention. In short, they're really good at getting on TV (or looking snazzy at the local bar, or showing off at the gym). It's a classic example of what psychologists call the availability heuristic—believing that things happen more often when they come to mind more easily. For example, many people think flying on planes is dangerous because they can easily remember the image of a horrific plane crash, even though driving a car is actually far more dangerous statistically. Successful narcissists are a little like plane crashes: they are spectacular, they get noticed, and they can be a disaster.

This phenomenon is easy to see in the media. Donald Trump, who puts his name on everything he builds, has his own TV show, named a university after himself (yes, there is a Trump University), and picks fights with talk show hosts, is a great example of someone who is both successful and appears to be narcissistic. We know about Donald Trump's success *because* he is relentlessly self-promoting. It is hard to miss The Donald in the media, and he *is* rich—but there are other real estate tycoons you've never heard of because they are not self-promoters and don't want to be in the limelight. Many other successful people are not self-promoting. For example, Warren Buffett, the billionaire investor, gave most of his fortune to charity and drives around Nebraska in a Lincoln with license plates that say THRIFTY. Tom Hanks, who has won two Best Actor Academy Awards, is known in the film industry for being a genuinely nice person, as was Paul Newman, who donated millions to charity. You don't have to be a narcissist to be successful, but Americans can think of lots of successful narcissists because they're always grabbing the limelight.

THE TRAP OF NARCISSISM

So if narcissism doesn't lead to success, and comes with so many costs, why is anyone narcissistic? In general, people do things—even really harmful and stupid things—for a reason. People cheat in relationships because they meet someone who looks desirable at the moment; they steal from their workplaces because they want the paper clips or the money and figure that the company owes them; they become problem drinkers not because they want to destroy their lives but because alcohol makes them feel really good.

Narcissism shares several things in common with other destructive behaviors. First, it feels good. It is fun to gamble, binge drink, have an illicit sexual relationship, eat glazed donuts, or take notepads from the office. Second, destructive behaviors usually have short-term benefits and long-term costs. When you gamble, you get the fun and excitement of going to the casino and playing cards. But you also risk the long-term costs of losing all your money, destroying your marriage, and losing your self-respect. When you binge drink, you have the benefit of giddy fun, but the longer-term costs of vomiting, a massive hangover, and the inability to show up at work. Last, destructive behaviors often make other people suffer. When someone cheats in a relationship, much of the cost is paid by the uninvolved spouse and children. Consumers all pay the cost of employee theft in terms of higher prices. The risky mortgage rewards the homeowner and the lender in the short term, but hurts both in the long run when the owner can't pay the bill.

Like other destructive behaviors, narcissism is a "time-delay trap"—it tempts you with some good outcomes up front and then hurts you in the end. Narcissists resemble fish that swim into deep-sea traps to eat the yummy bait—wow, a free meal!—but are unable to leave the cage and end up sautéed and a meal themselves (though usually not free). Just like a fish trap, narcissism offers short-term benefits but long-term costs.

Narcissism does have short-term benefits. It feels good. It's fun to look at yourself in the mirror and think, "I am so frickin' hot," and even better to post pictures of yourself online and have people comment, "You are so frickin' hot." It is exciting to be in the spotlight enjoying your fifteen minutes of fame. It feels good to be cool and hang out with cool people—it might even be fun to step on people on the way to success. And it's enjoyable to think you are a success—even when that means ignoring negative feedback and blaming others for your failures.

So far, so good, but then the trap springs shut. Vanity and self-centeredness eventually drive other people away. The cool people let you hang with them only as long as you are cool and good-looking, so you end up spending a lot of time, energy, and money staying cool and good-looking. The failure to take responsibility feels good in the short run, but eventually catches up with you as you fail to improve. In the long run, many narcissists end up depressed because they destroy their personal and professional lives through their self-centeredness. By then, though, narcissists are trapped. Imagine what a narcissist has to eventually acknowledge about himself: I am really not that special; I am not all that hot; I am pretty much average at my job; if I died, the world would just keep on going; Dean Martin and Miles Davis were cool, but I'm not.

Narcissism is also a social trap with large consequences for society. Social traps are reinforced because they have benefits for the individual, but the costs are borne by others. Consider the trap of SUVs. Before so many people drove SUVs in the 1990s, the SUV driver had some big advantages. She could see farther than people in other cars because the SUV rode so high, and, if she got in an accident, the SUV would cause more damage to the smaller car. Many of the costs of the SUV were paid by other drivers. Although the SUV driver could see, the vehicle blocked the visibility of the other cars behind it. The driver of an economy car was more likely to get killed in an accident with an SUV. But as the benefits of SUVs caught on, everyone bought them. After that, the benefits largely disappeared. The driver of an SUV no longer has a large visibility advantage because the vehicle in front of him is likely to be an SUV. Likewise, if he gets in a wreck, it is more likely to be with an SUV. Finally, with huge numbers of people driving SUVs, gas consumption went way up. Now we have more expensive gas and more air pollution. In short, our nation was trapped into driving SUVs because the costs—at least initially—were carried on the backs of other drivers and not by the SUV driver himself.

Narcissism functions a lot like an army of SUVs, with benefits to the individual narcissist paid by others. Narcissists can keep up their own positive self-views and emotions, but others suffer. A narcissist can keep his pride intact if he hits a person who insults him; he can uphold his positive self-image by stealing credit from his coworkers on a successful project; he can establish a favorable image as a "player" by dating multiple partners without their knowing about one another. A recent psychiatric study found that the biggest consequences of narcissism—especially when other psychiatric symptoms were held constant—was suffering by people close to them.

And, of course, those working with or living with the narcissist are often forced to fight fire with fire. They start stealing credit from coworkers or become players simply to keep up. To use an analogy, if one passenger on an airplane reclines his seat all the way back, the passenger behind him is forced to do the same and so on until every seat in the plane is back. This is a very important point—even a small number of narcissistic individuals can have huge effects on everyone else in a society. With 1 in 16 people suffering from full-blown NPD at some point in their lives, this is becoming a bigger and bigger problem. In America today, more and more of the plane seats are tilted back, and more and more people are tempted to do the same themselves.

In the next chapter, we explore how, exactly, we ended up on that plane, with the disease of narcissism spreading like a virus through the thin, recirculated air of modern American culture.

CHAPTER 4

How Did We Get Here?

Origins of the Epidemic

If you remember the 1970s at all, the very mention of the decade probably makes you smirk—or cringe. Everything was taken to excess—the colors, the abnormally wide ties, the gold disco chains, the stifling polyester. Of the two definitive books on the decade, one (*How We Got Here*) is Day-Glo orange, and the other (*The Seventies*) is pea green.

Both books make a similar argument: The unfortunate colors and regrettable fads of the 1970s are long gone, but other '70s trends have become the status quo realities of our time. The movement of the U.S. population to the South and West, women working, and the dominance of the service economy over manufacturing all started during the '70s, and all are here to stay. The '70s also play a starring role in the growth of the psychological trend of narcissism. In fact, if we had to place a date on the beginning of the narcissism epidemic, it would be sometime during the '70s.

But we have to go back farther than the '70s to discover how the United States became a place where mass murderers seeking fame and attention send press kits to TV networks and young girls think it's a great idea to have hundreds of "friends" looking at their scantily clad bodies on social networking sites. Somewhere along the line, American culture's core ideas and values were modified to include the idea of self-admiration.

SELF-ADMIRATION WAS NOT ALWAYS A CORE AMERICAN IDEA

A key element in solving the mystery of the narcissism epidemic is the value placed on self-admiration. Not that long ago, self-admiration was not a core cultural value in the United States. If the 2007 NBC public service announcement saying "everyone is born with their one true love . . . themselves" had been broadcast during an episode of *Leave It to Beaver* in the 1950s, viewers would have been baffled and perhaps even disturbed. Today, however, there is very little shock expressed when children sing about how special they are in preschool or when a TV character parrots the mindless psychobabble that you have to love yourself before you can love someone else. Most people do not see what a truly radical departure this is from the past, either because they are too young to remember or because the change happened too slowly for them to notice.

Just as Christianity merged the observation of Christmas with pagan winter solstice rituals and Santa Claus gradually got more press than Jesus, our core cultural ideas have been slowly co-opted to make room for the centrality of self-admiration. Since the beginning, America's two major core values have been freedom and equality. In the Declaration of Independence, these were mentioned in response to King George III's tyrannical acts against the American colonies, including the restriction of our free trade with other nations, taxation without representation in Parliament, and the requirement that Americans house British soldiers in their own homes. Unique for its time, the Declaration of Independence claimed that freedom and equality were inherent rights: "We hold these truths to be self-evident, that all men are created equal, that they are endowed by their Creator with certain unalienable Rights, that among these are Life, Liberty, and the pursuit of Happiness."

This recipe for American individualism—individual freedom tempered with equality—was soon after established in the Constitution. The government was explicitly constructed so no one institution got too much power, with three branches of government, checks and balances, and democratically elected leaders. Within a few years, the Constitution also included the Bill of Rights. Both carefully balance freedom of individual action and fundamental equality and tolerance for others.

The ideal of the United States as a place of equality is deeply ingrained. For example, one study found that subliminally flashing an image of an American flag reduces prejudice. However, being reminded of American ideals did not increase participants' self-esteem. This study and the words of the Constitution both show that equality and tolerance are the core ideas of American government, not self-admiration.

The United States was founded on several other values that are unrelated to self-admiration and even antithetical to narcissism and entitlement. For example, for most of our history Americans have adhered to a work ethic postulating that hard work demonstrates one's worth in the eyes of God and others. This value attracted millions of immigrants who pursued the American dream—freedom from persecution, a life of safety and security, and the ability to work and achieve prosperity, no matter your background, race, or religion. Americans were famous for their "can-do" attitude and their persistence in chasing innovation. The current ethic of self-admiration, in contrast, declares that it is not necessary to do anything to be special or to like yourself.

The United States has also historically valued self-reliance, which is quite different from narcissism. In his culturally defining 1841 essay "Self-Reliance," Ralph Waldo Emerson argued that individualism must be grounded in effort and responsibility. He praised young people who chose to work hard rather than show off: "A sturdy lad from New Hampshire or Vermont, who . . . always, like a cat, falls on his feet, is worth a hundred of these city dolls." In other words, repeated effort and hard work are what define you. If you are not successful, suck it up and try again. This would be a great public service announcement, but it is a little at odds with our current cultural values, which instead focus more on admiring yourself no matter how little effort you put in or however bad the result.

So if self-admiration wasn't there from the beginning, when did it become so central to American culture? Few people talked of self-admiration in the first half of the twentieth century, when the country was focused on overcoming two world wars and the Great Depression. After World War II, the country entered a period of domestic focus and Cold War nationalism that, if anything, discouraged self-admiration. As just one example, women's assertiveness—a personality trait related to standing up for one's individual rights that correlates with self-esteem—declined during the period from the 1940s to the mid-1960s. Although the 1950s weren't always as conformist as they are now portrayed, social commentators at the time noted the era's group mentality (William Whyte's *The Organization Man*, 1956), focus on others' opinions (David Reisman's *The Lonely Crowd*, 1950), and rigid views of women's roles (Betty Friedan's *The Feminine Mystique*, 1963). For the most part, postwar America emphasized fitting in and getting things done rather than admiring yourself.

THE 1960S

The American flag of self-admiration slowly began to unfurl in the 1960s. Many of the protests of the era focused on individual rights and liberties, though these movements were at first very group-oriented, with mass demonstrations aimed to gain rights for entire groups of people (for example, blacks and women). Although many remember the '60s as a narcissistic era of hippies and drug use, the culture of the time, both in liberal movements and in Nixon's conservative "Silent Majority," was highly collective and group-oriented. In addition to the civil rights movement, the decade was marked by other collective endeavors such as the founding of the Peace Corps (1961), the space program (*Apollo 11* landed on the moon in 1969), and the modern environmental movement that resulted in the first Earth Day (April 22, 1970).

Even the drug culture of the time promoted communal impulses. Keith remembers seeing a Jerry Garcia show in San Francisco in the 1980s that opened with the clown Wavy Gravy describing the acid tests twenty years before. Although taking a lot of acid and grooving to amazingly long Grateful Dead songs sounds like self-absorption, Wavy Gravy's description was very different. Acid tests, he said, were about reaching outside yourself to help someone who is in even worse shape than you. When you reached outside yourself, you passed the acid test. The 1969 Woodstock music festival is remembered and celebrated as a communal experience consistent with Wavy Gravy's acid test. Contrast this with Woodstock 1994, when the crowd threw mud at the performers onstage, and Woodstock 1999, which featured a rule against bringing in outside food and drink (thus forcing the purchase of $4 water in 100 degree heat), vandalism and looting (which accelerated after the band Limp Bizkit played their song "Break Stuff"), and arson-ignited fires that finally led to the concert's early end. Four rapes occurred during the concert, and police arrested several concertgoers for stealing. Although the '60s certainly had its share of riots and flames, they were usually incited by a cause greater than expensive bottled water.

One part of the 1960s did eventually transform into a source of self-admiration: the human potential movement. This movement didn't start out as a way to promote self-admiration, but its emphasis on introspection and self-improvement morphed over the years into a focus on self-admiration. In 1960, author Aldous Huxley (best known for writing *Brave New World* and *The Doors of Perception*) began to hold seminars at the Esalen Institute in Big Sur, California, which centered on psychologist Abraham Maslow's idea of self-actualization, originally defined as the experience of reaching one's full potential—being all that one can be. This concept in itself is not narcissistic: self-actualization includes sharing one's sympathy and benevolence with many people. Maslow placed self-actualization at the top of his famous hierarchy of human needs, and described it as very difficult to achieve—Maslow could identify only a few people who were truly self-actualized. Maslow also included self-esteem as an essential need in his hierarchy, one rung below self-actualization, and much easier for most people to achieve. In short, self-actualization is tough; self-esteem is relatively easy. Thus as the human potential movement evolved through the 1960s and into the '70s, the more difficult concept of self-actualization was eclipsed by the easier concept of self-esteem. Today self-actualization is very rarely discussed, but self-esteem appears in magazine articles, children's television, and numerous books.

THE 1970S

By the 1970s, the communal goals of the '60s had dissipated, and only the gaudy, empty shell of self-focus remained. While '60s gatherings aimed for group goals, '70s group meetings like est (short for Erhard Seminars Training, one of the many self-exploration turned self-expression fads of the decade) trumpeted individual self-discovery and success. Even

TIMELINE

1960–64	Peace Corps founded
	First Esalen seminar (Alan Watts)
	John F. Kennedy assassination
	First Baby Boomers enter college; Merry Prankster bus trip
1965–69	Watts riots in Los Angeles
	Summer of Love; Human Be-In
	Robert Kennedy and Martin Luther King, Jr., assassinations; riots at Democratic convention in Chicago; Woodstock (August 1969); Altamont (December 1969); Brandon's *The Psychology of Self-Esteem; Apollo 11*
1970–74	First Earth Day (April 22); *Phil Donahue Show* premieres
	Kohut's *Analysis of the Self, The American Family* (first reality TV show); est (Erhard Seminars Training) started
	Deep Throat in theaters
	CBGB club opens in New York
	Nixon resigns; *People* magazine started
1975–79	Tom Wolfe's "Me Decade" article appears
	Saturday Night Fever, Pumping Iron
	Lasch's *The Culture of Narcissism*
1980–84	Term "Yuppie" coined; Narcissistic Personality Disorder (NPD) in *DSM-III*
	MTV on air; IBM PC; *Entertainment Tonight* premieres
	Generation X first enters college
	Lifestyles of the Rich and Famous premieres
1985–89	California Task Force to Promote Self-Esteem; *Oprah* premieres
	Inside Edition and *Hard Copy* premiere
	First wave of Generation Me enters college
1990–94	Internet commercialized
	Jerry Springer premieres
	MTV's *Real World* premieres
1995–99	O. J. Simpson "Trial of the Century"
	Term *blog* coined
2000–04	*Survivor* premieres; Top of Internet bubble; those born after 1980 enter college
	Tyco CEO Kozlowski's $2 million party; Enron bankruptcy
	American Idol premieres
	MySpace begins; Second Life begins
	Facebook begins
2005–07	Top of housing bubble
	Time makes "You" Person of the Year; Paris Hilton biggest Google news search item
	Nearly 1 out of 10 people in their twenties have had NPD
	Steroid scandal in baseball
	Plastic surgery at all-time high
2008	Mortgage meltdown and credit crisis; possible to hire fake paparazzi

music and entertainment switched from communal experiences like Woodstock to disco and cocaine—both activities done in groups, but while dancing or getting high on your own (except for the Hustle).

The '70s brought unchecked inflation and high levels of unemployment, an abrupt shift from the stable economic expansion of the 1960s. When Christopher Lasch wrote *The Culture of Narcissism* in 1979, he subtitled it *America in the Age of Diminishing Expectations*. Lasch theorized that people turned to themselves when the economic machine faltered—an intriguing hypothesis, but one proven wrong by the subsequent decades. The economy improved significantly beginning in the mid-1980s, and narcissism, both individually and culturally, has been up ever since. The opposing view, held by author Tom Wolfe among others, is that *good* economic times lead to the excesses of narcissism. When children of prosperity get whatever they want, this theory goes, they learn that the world revolves around them. This theory also suggests that people raised in hard economic times should be less narcissistic—duty-oriented, good savers, unconcerned with seeking fame. And indeed they are—this is a spot-on description of the Greatest Generation who lived through the Great Depression and World War II, arguably the last non-narcissistic generation in American history.

Yet given that narcissism flourished in the economically unstable '70s, economics are clearly not the whole picture. The '70s had stagflation, but it also had the most attention-seeking wide lapels ever worn by men. So if it wasn't only the economy, what was it?

Three social trends seem to be the main culprits. The first catalyst was the movement toward self-esteem, which began with good intentions—wouldn't it be great if people felt good about themselves all the time? Nathaniel Branden's first book, *The Psychology of Self-Esteem*, published in 1969, got the ball rolling. Branden declares that loving yourself is crucial: "There is no value judgment more important to man—no factor more decisive in his psychological development and motivation—than the estimate he passes on himself. . . . The nature of his self-evaluation has profound effects on a man's thinking processes, emotions, desires, values and goals. It is the single most significant key to his behavior." As you know from the earlier chapters, little of this is true. However, research on self-esteem was in its infancy then, so Branden's claims were plausible given what was known at the time. The problem is that no one went back and revised the cultural script once research showed that self-esteem wasn't that important after all.

By the '70s, the '60s goal of self-exploration had begun to transition naturally into the goal of self-expression, in many ways the theme of our current age. The Baby Boomer idea of self-exploration and "finding yourself" sounds narcissistic and often is, but it can also lead to greater maturity and eventually a return to the community. Both Jesus and Buddha, for example, left home on journeys of self-exploration but eventually taught giving and caring to generations of people. Some forms of self-exploration are also difficult, involving introspection, discipline, and sometimes deep discomfort. Self-exploration sounds similar to self-expression—both, for example, emphasize individuality. Self-expression, however, is much easier to do. All you have to do is talk about yourself, draw attention to yourself, and sometimes promote yourself.

"Express yourself" also makes a simple yet effective advertising slogan, and has been used to sell everything from customized coffee mugs to Botox. Over the last few years, technology has allowed Americans to take self-expression to new heights with personal websites, Facebook pages, videos, and blogging. The media has also shifted toward self-expression because opinion is a lot cheaper to obtain than actual news. All this self-expression would be fine if what was expressed had some value, but that is often not the case. We all know people who, in person or online, talk because they want to, and not because they actually have something meaningful to contribute.

At the same time that the interest in self-esteem and self-expression ramped up, the culture began to move away from community-oriented thinking. As Robert Putnam showed in his bestseller *Bowling Alone*, memberships in groups such as Kiwanis, the PTA, and even bowling leagues began to decline in the '70s. Personal relationships showed similar trends. The divorce rate skyrocketed, young people began to marry later, and the birth rate plummeted. Singles culture, practically nonexistent in the 1950s and '60s, was all the rage, with singles-only apartment complexes springing up and disco rooms full of gold-chain-wearing bachelors and young bachelorettes trying not to sprain their ankles dancing to "Stayin' Alive" in four-inch platform heels.

A few other authors have also pegged the roots of the narcissism epidemic to the '70s, which gives us further confidence in the date. In 1976,

Tom Wolfe accurately labeled a decade that was only half over with his groundbreaking *New York* magazine article, "The 'Me' Decade and the Third Great Awakening." The article opens by describing a woman at an est session. "The trainer said, 'Take your finger off the repress button.' Everybody was supposed to let go. . . . Then the trainer told everybody to think of 'the one thing you would most like to eliminate from your life. . . . ' 'Hemorrhoids!' blurts out one woman to the room of 250 other people. Before long, she and everyone in the room are moaning, and then screaming, to rid themselves of whatever they find objectionable in life." Wolfe argued that Americans abandoned the vision of themselves as part of an interconnected social system—a connection of parents to children and grandchildren and of community to community—and instead turned to the narcissistic pursuit of the self as a source of value, almost like a religious experience. The quest for the self is in some ways the misguided quest for the divine spark within.

Psychological therapy also underwent a shift during the '70s. Before then, most therapy clients were treated for repressed desires (for example, sex, aggression) in the classic Freudian model. In other words, they weren't expressing themselves enough. Beginning in the late '60s, however, psychotherapists saw more and more patients whose problems were caused by too *much* self-expression and too much self-centeredness. Psychoanalytic theorist Heinz Kohut first identified narcissistic personality disorder (NPD) in 1971. By 1980, NPD was officially included in the

Psychology Publications on Self-Esteem and Narcissism

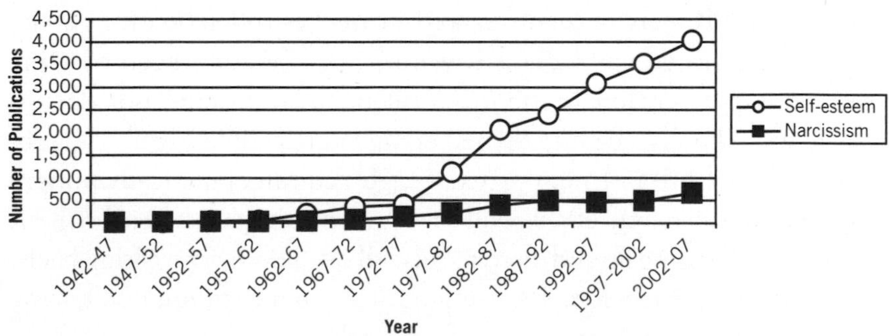

Source: PsycInfo database of journal articles in psychology and related fields, American Psychological Association.

Education Publications on Self-Esteem and Narcissism

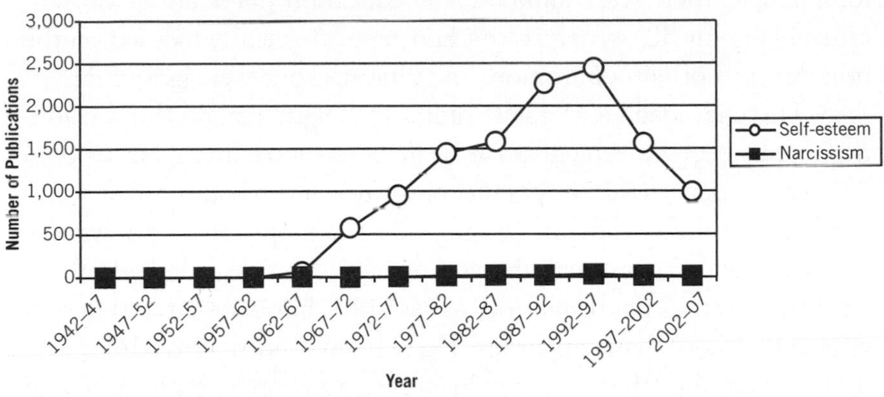

Source: ERIC (Educational Resources Information Center, U.S. Department of Education) database of journal articles in education and related fields.

DSM-III (the official handbook of psychiatric disorders). In other words, by 1980, disorders of narcissism were officially acknowledged in the United States—another indicator that the '70s was some kind of inflection point or origin source of the epidemic of narcissism.

Even with all of the signs pointing to the '70s as the origin of the narcissism epidemic, we authors are still researchers at heart, and we wanted to see some numbers that provided proof. It is sometimes difficult to quantify a cultural shift—how do we know what people were talking about and when? We don't, but we do know what people were writing about.

We began our search with academic journals, which told us when psychologists and education experts began to be interested in self-esteem and narcissism. As you can see from the graph on page 64, psychology researchers' interest in self-esteem really took off in the late '70s. Interest in narcissism has lagged behind, but seemed to get going during the late '70s to the '80s.

Education researchers are more likely to be interested in practical implications, and to focus on consequences for children. Educators began to discuss self-esteem fairly early, beginning in the late '60s (when the Baby Boomers were leaving school) and peaking in the '90s (when today's twenty-somethings were in school). However, almost no research in education has explored the effects of narcissism. From 1992 to 1997, for example, there were almost 2,500 education publications on self-esteem but only 30 on narcissism. Educators are clearly focused on the brighter sides of self-admiration, and almost completely ignore narcissism. This one-sided view of self-admiration might explain the continuing popularity of self-esteem-boosting programs and curricula in schools.

Of course, articles in the popular press are an even better gauge of cultural change than academic journals. As the graph below shows, the popular media's interest in both self-esteem and narcissism lagged behind academic interest. By the late '80s to early '90s, however, interest in self-esteem had more than caught up. There has not been as much interest in narcissism, but that is slowly beginning to change, with more and more articles on the topic every five years beginning in the early '90s. In 2002–2007, popular media interest in both self-esteem and narcissism reached all-time highs.

Because of the unbelievable amount of news coverage of self-esteem today (almost 40,000 articles between 2002 and 2007), it is difficult to identify exactly when interest in self-esteem really took off. To examine this, we calculated the *change* in coverage from one five-year period to the next—in other words, how much coverage increased or decreased from the previous time period. These data show that the largest change occurred during the late '70s and early '80s. Just as the other cultural

Publications in Major News Outlets on Self-Esteem and Narcissism

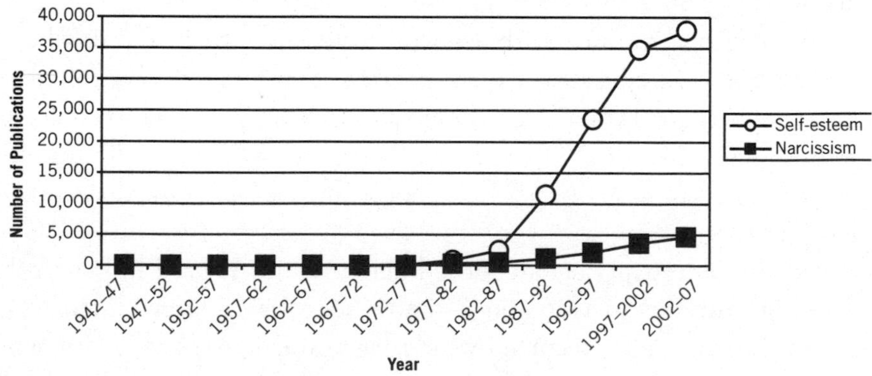

Source: LexisNexis database of newspapers and magazines.

Percent Change in Articles on Self-Esteem and Narcissism

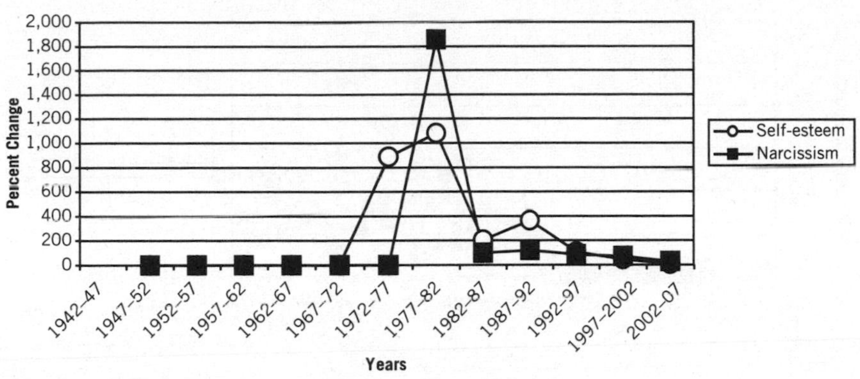

Source: LexisNexis database of newspapers and magazines.

markers suggest, something shifted in American culture in the '70s, and we live with those changes today.

Finally, we looked at the number of books published in the United States every year. This graph looks very similar to the others, with an inflection point in the '70s. Until 1976, fewer than five books a year addressed self-esteem or narcissism. In most years before the mid-1970s, there were none. Interest steadily grew through the '80s, peaking with the 28 books on self-esteem published in 1994. Books on narcissism have held fairly steady between five and ten a year since the late '70s.

Thus an array of sources, both empirical and observational, point to the '70s as the beginning of the narcissism epidemic. As our data on individual-level narcissism show, narcissism only grew after the '70s. Orange polyester pantsuits came and went, but narcissism has persisted, growing more widespread every year.

THE 1980S AND BEYOND

No single event initiated the narcissism epidemic; instead, Americans' core cultural ideas slowly became more focused on self-admiration and self-expression. At the same time, Americans' faith in the power of collective action or the government was lost.

America has always been an individualistic nation, but it was

Books Cataloged in Library of Congress on Self-Esteem and Narcissism

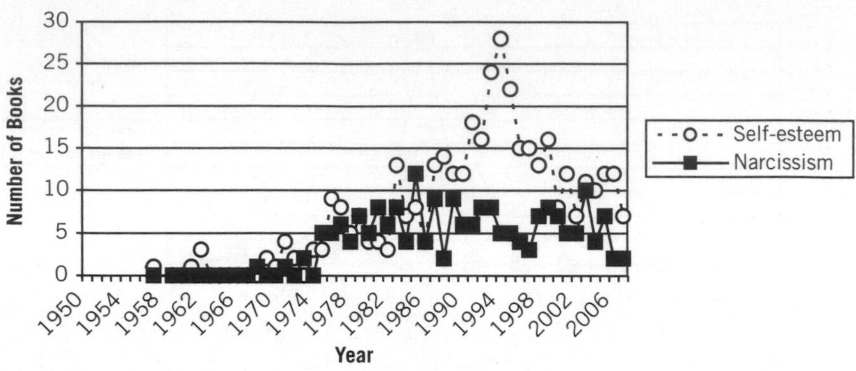

Source: United States Library of Congress database.

founded on ideas of individual liberty, freedom from tyranny, and fundamental equality—values that emphasized independence, not narcissism. But when these powerful ideas were supplemented by the new values of self-admiration and self-expression, the results were ugly. In the 1970s, self-indulgence and self-absorption were rampant, as was a sense of malaise. Once these new values took hold in the '80s and beyond, the malaise of the '70s faded, replaced by a more extraverted, shallow, and materialistic form of narcissism. The culture ended up with a self-perpetuating cycle in which social beliefs and behaviors changed to fit the new cultural idea of self-admiration. Parents began to raise their children to think highly of themselves, and educational practices began to emphasize self-admiration and self-expression. The media focused on celebrities more than in the past, as our timeline clearly shows. *People* magazine's first issue appeared in 1974, and the first episode of the *Lifestyles of the Rich and Famous* aired in 1984. By the '90s, celebrities were covered in mainstream news outlets and everyday people began to seek fame (even if it was infamy) on daytime talk shows such as *Jerry Springer*, which first aired in 1991. Reality TV soon followed, pioneered by *The Real World* in 1992 and *Survivor* in 1999. The Internet has taken this to a whole new level—Americans can now broadcast themselves 24/7 on YouTube and promote themselves on Facebook and MySpace.

Although it's too early to tell, the advent of MySpace, Facebook, and

YouTube in 2005–2006 may prove to be a second inflection point for the growth of the narcissism epidemic. And 2008 will be remembered as the year when credit-fueled, entitled dreams finally hit the wall of reality. It is difficult to say where the history will go from here. Even with talk of penny-pinching in an economic crisis, the cultural value of self-admiration is deeply ingrained, as is the materialistic narcissism that flows from it. Becoming a nation of no-nonsense savers again is going to be difficult—partially because our parents have treated us as royalty since before we were born.

SECTION 2

ROOT CAUSES OF THE EPIDEMIC

CHAPTER 5

Parenting

Raising Royalty

On a recent trip to Babies R Us, Jean stood in the checkout line doing her best to prevent her daughter from running for the hills (or wherever toddlers go when they don't want to stand still). This became more difficult when Jean was distracted by the display of bibs at the checkout counter. In large white letters on pink and blue, they announced: "Chick Magnet," "Supermodel," "Princess," and—available in both colors—"I'm the Boss."

This is just a glimpse into the new parenting culture that has fueled the narcissism epidemic. It says a lot about our culture that people think a six-month-old wearing a "Supermodel" bib is cute. It is increasingly common to see parents relinquishing authority to young children, showering them with unearned praise, protecting them from their teachers' criticisms, giving them expensive automobiles, and allowing them to have freedom but not the responsibility that goes with it. Not that long ago, kids knew who the boss was—and it wasn't them. It was Mom and Dad. And Mom and Dad weren't your "friends." They were your parents.

This sea change in parenting is driven by the core cultural value of self-admiration and positive feelings. Parents want their kids' approval, a reversal of the past ideal of children striving for their parents' approval. At least in the short term, children love parents who give in to their demands. It doesn't feel great when you don't give your child what she wants and she says, "I hate you" (or Keith's personal favorite, "I just don't love you as much as I love Mommy"). Until recently, parents considered it their responsibility to deal with these emotional storms by standing their ground. Many of today's parents instead seek to raise children high in self-admiration and self-esteem, partially because books and articles have touted its importance. Unfortunately, much of what parents think raises self-esteem—such as telling a kid he's special and giving him what he wants—actually leads to narcissism.

Parents do not consciously think, "Wow, wouldn't it be great to raise a narcissistic child?" Instead, they want to make their children happy and raise their self-esteem but often take things too far. Good intentions and parental pride have opened the door to cultural narcissism in parenting, and many parents express their love for their children in the most modern of ways: declaring their children's greatness. A remarkable percentage of clothing for baby girls has "Princess" or "Little Princess" written on it, which is wishful thinking unless you are the long-lost heir to a throne. And if your daughter is a princess, does this mean that you are the queen or king? No—it means you are the loyal subject, and you must do what the princess says.

More than at any time in history, the child's needs come first. Parents routinely ask their children—even those too young to answer—what they want ("What do you want for dinner?" "Do you want to talk to your grandma?" "Do you want to go to the park?"). On one airplane flight, a preschooler was happily occupied watching his DVD player. When his mother put on her own headphones, the child grabbed them and protested loudly, "No—you're not supposed to do that." The mother's response was breathtaking. "I'm sorry," she said to the three-year-old.

Parents who want to stick with the older model of child rearing that downplays materialism and emphasizes politeness and discipline are swimming against the cultural tide. If you don't let your children do something, but every other message that your children hear—from the media, friends, the school, and other parents—tells them it's OK, your resistance only lasts so long. We know—we've been there. Many parents' resolve has crumbled in the face of permissive norms. Parenting is always a struggle of one sort or another, and these days it's often the struggle of concerned parents against an overwhelming tide of narcissistic values.

HOW PARENTING HAS CHANGED

When a group of 1920s mothers listed the traits they wanted their children to have, they named strict obedience, loyalty to church, and good manners. In 1988, few mothers named these traits; instead, they chose independence and tolerance. A larger nationwide study that traced parental attitudes through 2004 found similar results. It asked, "If you had to choose, which thing on this list would you pick as the most important for a child to learn to prepare him (or her) for life?" The five choices are "to obey," "to be well-liked or popular," "to think for himself or herself," "to work hard," and "to help others when they need help." Some things are constant: American parents have always ranked "to think for himself or herself" as the most important. Back in 1958, however, people said that the second most important thing a child could learn was "to obey." Not anymore. Throughout the 1980s and '90s, the importance of obedience steadily declined until it was ranked second to last. The ranking of obedience reached an all-time low in 2004, the last year for which data are available.

These surveys shore up the feeling many Americans have about mod-

Change in Parents' Valuing of Obedience in Children

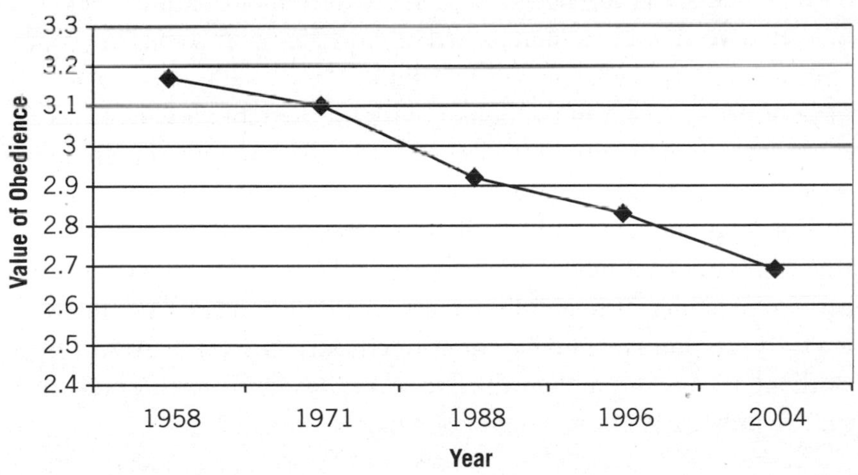

Source: Alwin, D. F. (1988). From obedience to autonomy: Changes in traits desired in children, 1924–78. *Public Opinion Quarterly, 52*, 33–52; and General Social Survey data, 1988, 1996, and 2004.

ern parenting: that we have become too indulgent, that we praise children too much, that we treat our children almost like royalty. You'd be hard-pressed to find anyone in America who believes that parents are now more strict than they were thirty years ago. Virtually everyone agrees that parents are now considerably more lenient. "Too many [modern] parents have innocently made the mistake of idealizing their children instead of truly loving them," writes psychologist Polly Young-Eisendrath. It's good that we don't always expect blind obedience anymore, but we may have veered too far toward obeying our children instead of them obeying us.

You can buy your daughter a T-shirt that says "Spoiled Rotten" or clothe your son in a shirt that says "Sorry, girls, I only date models." One bright red shirt declares "I'm in Charge." Another line of T-shirts allows you to announce that your child is the "Future Leader of the Free World" or a "Future Reality Show Contestant." You can even buy your newborn baby a "Bling" brand pacifier decorated with rhinestones, complete with a tote that says "Princess" or "Rock Star." These days, even when you're just a few weeks old, it's important not to leave the house without your bling.

In his prescient 2001 book, *Too Much of a Good Thing*, child psychologist Dan Kindlon argued that modern parents too often spoil their children. "Compared to earlier generations, we are emotionally closer to our kids, they confide in us more, we have more fun with them," he wrote. "But we are too indulgent. We give our kids too much and demand too little of them. I see it in the homes I visit, at the schools where I speak, in the family counseling I've done, and in the parents and children I encounter in shopping malls, supermarkets, and video stores." Kindlon concentrated on upper-middle-class children in his book, but much of the overindulgence he documents seems to be trickling down the socioeconomic ladder. When children are overindulged, Kindlon argues, it leads to outcomes resembling the seven deadly sins: pride, wrath, envy, sloth, gluttony, lust, and greed. The seven deadly sins are, of course, a succinct summary of the symptoms of narcissism.

In the '90s, two authors developed a name for these modern sprites: Indigo children. They argued that these children are the next step in the spiritual evolution of mankind. It seems more likely to us that the type of child they describe is instead the product of overindulgent modern parenting. Indigo children, the authors write, "come into the world with a feeling of royalty (and often act like it)," "seem antisocial," "have difficulty with absolute authority," "see better ways of doing things, which makes them seem like 'system busters.' " For them, "self-worth is not a big issue," and "they simply will not do certain things; for example, waiting in line is difficult for them." (It is for us, too, but then again, we're not the Princess, the Future Leader of the Free World, or even a Future Reality TV Contestant). More and more parents and teachers, the authors report, see kids who can't or won't listen to adults. "You cannot 'talk down' to these children. They will spit in your eye if you talk down to them. . . . From birth, Indigo children have a need for recognition and status. They really can be like royalty, with all this attention!" The authors consistently describe these children as "special."

They're special all right, but perhaps not in the way those authors mean. In 2001, a *Time*/CNN poll found that 80% of people thought kids were more spoiled than they were in the '80s and '90s. In the same poll, two-thirds of parents described their *own* kids as spoiled. As the accompanying *Time* cover story explained, "Go to the mall or a concert or a restaurant and you can find them in the wild, the kids who have never been told no, whose sense of power and entitlement leaves onlookers breathless, the sand-kicking, foot-stomping, arm-twisting, wheedling, whining despots whose parents presumably deserve the company of the monsters they, after all, created."

Well, maybe. Certainly there has been a shift in parenting away from rules and limit setting, and toward the child getting what he or she wants. But many parents do set limits and try very hard not to overindulge. Then the kid sees endless plastic devices on TV and wants them all. Or he notices that his friends at school get to eat ice cream for dinner and he never does. Or she sings "I am special / I am special / Look at me" at preschool. Eventually, she gets a little older and wants to wear a bikini on her MySpace page, stay out all night, and, oh, yeah, for my birthday can you get me a Fendi handbag, modeling lessons, and a $50,000 car just like that girl on *My Super Sweet 16*? Thanks, Mom.

As a parent, you could easily exhaust yourself saying no all day, so occasionally you say yes. Kids have always begged their parents for stuff—what's new is that parents are now more likely to say yes (perhaps from indulgence, perhaps from a greater willingness to go into debt).

What you might not realize is that you're in the same battle as parents all around the country, fighting against an increasingly narcissistic culture. "This is a war waged block by block, house by house," writes Nancy Gibbs in *Time*. "If it is too much to try to battle the forces of Hollywood or Madison Avenue or the Nintendo Corp., at least you can resolve that just because the kids down the street watch unlimited TV doesn't mean your kids should, too. You can enforce a curfew, assign some chores and try hard to have dinner together regularly." Or you can give in, because, let's face it, that's easier.

Even apart from the societal pressure, some parents have trouble setting limits, in a way that would have been unimaginable a few decades ago. Sitcom star Leah Remini's daughter Sofia, almost four, sleeps in her parents' bed and demands up to eight bottles a night. "It's a vicious cycle," says Sofia's father, Angelo Pagan. "The pee wakes her up, and then she needs more water bottles to go back to sleep." They let this go on for years. "We didn't even know we were doing the wrong thing," Remini said. "Pediatricians told me, but I didn't believe them. She kept waking herself up for water, so I'm thinking she must be dehydrated." The leniency extends to food during the day as well. "She wants a Popsicle for breakfast? She gets a Popsicle for breakfast," says Remini. "We acknowledge we're being completely railroaded by our child."

HOW DID WE GET HERE?

Like so much of the narcissism epidemic, modern parenting began with good intentions. The parents of the 1950s, who raised the Baby Boomers, might have had too many rules and limits. "Because I said so" was supposed to be enough of an explanation. "Just wait until your father gets home" meant that you would be on the receiving end of a belt. Parents were often emotionally distant authority figures who rarely got down on the floor to play with their children. It was more common then than it is now to hear a parent tell a child he was "no good" or a "bad boy."

We now know better, which is a good thing. It's better to explain the reasons behind the rules than just say "because I said so." Children behave better when their actions are redirected ("No hitting; play nicely") rather than being labeled with a self-fulfilling prophecy ("You're a bad boy"). A definitive review of the research on spanking showed that children who are spanked comply with immediate requests, but are actually *less* likely to behave on their own in the future. They are also more likely to be aggressive toward other children. Parents now interact with their children and play with them intently. And the advances in child protection and health are remarkable—car seats, safer cribs, and the advice against pregnant women smoking and drinking have all saved little lives, bodies, and minds. Much of the emphasis on specialness and self-esteem began with good intentions as well—parents were told that kids who felt good about themselves would do better in life. Yet in many cases, the emphasis on good feelings has turned into overindulgence.

The movement toward parental involvement—for example, knowing your child's teachers—has now turned into overinvolvement. Popular media reports coined the term "helicopter parenting" for the moms and dads who hover close to their children, protecting them from everything. You can now buy a helmet for your toddler just in case he falls while walking. Afraid that children would be upset if they lost, parents encouraged children's sports leagues to stop keeping score—and if the league is radical enough to keep score, everyone gets the same size trophy whether they win or lose. (And this resembles real life *so* much.) In other leagues everyone gets a trophy just for being on the team. Jean's nephew has one that says "Excellence in Participation." What does that mean—I'm good at showing up? Honor rolls are not published in the local newspaper for fear of hurting the feelings of the lower achievers. Parents argue with teachers over the child's grade instead of leaving that task to the child himself (or sometimes the adult himself; colleges have begun to report parents calling to complain about grades). And of course the whole idea of arguing over grades smacks of narcissism: That teacher doesn't know what she's talking about! I'm the greatest—that D can't be right!

When Jean gives talks to corporate executives, she hears some amazing stories about how parents are now reaching into the lives of young workers as well. Some newly minted college graduates have brought their parents to their job interviews. One twentysomething young woman, on the job for a year, brought her dad to her employee evaluation meeting with her boss.

CREATING A NARCISSISTIC CHILD

Some early psychodynamic theorists believed that narcissism resulted from cold, neglectful parents, but empirical data has not supported that conclusion very strongly except in some forms of vulnerable or covert narcissism. More modern behavioral theories argue that narcissism instead arises from inflated feedback—if you're told over and over that you are great, you'll probably think you are great.

Four psychology studies have examined the relationship between parental styles and children's narcissistic personality traits. In one study, 9- to 13-year-old children completed a measure of narcissism and reported their parents' behaviors once and then again 12 to 18 months later. Children whose mothers were both warm and psychologically controlling—in other words, like a helicopter parent—later scored the highest on narcissism. In another study, narcissistic young adults reported that their parents were indulgent. Narcissists were more likely to agree that "Looking back, I feel that my parents sometimes put me on a pedestal," "When I was a child my parents believed I had exceptional talents and abilities," "When I was a child my parents praised me for virtually everything I did," and "When I was a child my parents rarely criticized me." Two other studies asked teens and young adults to report how closely their parents monitored them as adolescents. The narcissistic respondents were more likely to say that their parents didn't really know where they went at night. These studies aren't perfect—some rely on small samples, others ask adults to report on the parenting they received years ago, and the results contradict each other in places (for example, psychological control is linked to narcissism, but controls such as curfews guard against it). Yet the general picture of parenting that leads to narcissistic kids closely resembles the modern parent: overindulgent, praising, and putting the child in charge. None of this is good news for the parent whose kid wears a bib saying "I'm the Boss."

ROLE REVERSALS

A generation or two ago, the roles of parent and child were well defined, and the parent was the one in charge. Period. Today, however, many parents are uncomfortable being authority figures. They would rather have their child like them than respect them, and would rather be the child's friend than a stern parent. This trend began in the '70s with books like *PET: Parent Effectiveness Training*, which argued that parents didn't really know more than their kids—saying adults know more, they wrote, is akin to the belief that some racial groups are superior to others. Although the book clearly states that parents should not let their children do whatever they want, it was the first among many parenting manuals that encouraged equality between parents and children.

Many children now make household decisions, something that was unheard of just a few decades ago. Eighteen-year-old Nikki Fatigati, from Woodridge, Illinois, helped her father decide to take a new job, including running down the differences in salary and signing bonuses. Her father, Jim, says that when he was a teen his parents would never have shared the details of such a decision. "I was deathly afraid of my father," he said. "Deathly." David Zapata was surprised when his two daughters announced that the family needed a second car. "In my family, my dad was the boss," he said. But they bought the car. A survey found that more than 40% of teens see their opinions as "very important" in making family decisions, a trend the polling firm says only began to show up after 2000.

Even preschoolers help make family purchasing decisions—and we're not talking about a 50-cent candy bar. At a recent trip to a furniture store, Jean saw a young mother ask her two-year-old son which bed he wanted. Sure, he's the one who would sleep in it, but he was unlikely to know what would fit the family budget and which bed was the best made. Karen Hill Scott, an educational consultant, knows a family in which the five-year-old boy chose the family's new car. "This really is the era of the weak parent," says Hill Scott. No kidding. Giving this much power to children teaches an entitled view of life, with all of the fun and choices but none of the responsibility. This is different from giving your children choices so they can learn to be independent. Asking a child "Would you like to wear your blue coat or your red coat?" when it's cold out is very different from asking "What would you like to wear?" and risking that the child will answer, "My swimsuit." When psychologists originally suggested letting children make decisions, they meant between two reasonable alternatives, and on small things—not furniture and cars.

When these children grow up, it's a fair bet that their parents will be reluctant to use their authority—assuming they have any left—to set curfews or tell them they can't go to parties with alcohol. When a parent sees herself as her child's friend, it's tough to insist on a bedtime or make strict rules. And the teen who decides on her dad's job might have a hard time listening when he tells her he's the boss of when she gets in at night. In the studies on parenting and narcissism, this kind of lax parental monitoring was one of the strongest correlates of narcissism in teens. It's also a good predictor of teen drug and alcohol abuse and crime.

And then there is the stuff. As Nancy Gibbs writes, "In New York City it's the Bat Mitzvah where 'N Sync was the band; in Houston it's a catered $20,000 pink-themed party for 50 seven-year-old girls who all wore mink coats, like their moms." Adjusted for inflation, kids in the 2000s spend 500% more than their parents did at the same age. The equipment required to be cool seems to cost more and more every year. As kids get older, the demands grow larger for expensive iPods, cell phones with every feature, and front-row concert tickets. Many kids don't earn the money to pay for such things, instead expecting they will just be given to them. This is the very definition of entitlement, one of the central facets of narcissism.

The 1971 film *Willy Wonka & the Chocolate Factory* featured four children whose excesses, then ridiculous, now seem commonplace: Mike Teevee, who is obsessed with appearing on television; Violet Beauregarde, who wants to win at all costs; Augustus Gloop, who presages the child obesity epidemic; and Veruca Salt, who demands every material thing she sees . . . *now*. Back in the early '70s, everyone knew that the fifth child, Charlie Bucket, was the good kid because he was poor and refused to cheat. Now that just means he's not cool.

OVERPRAISING

One of the studies on parenting found a link between narcissism and parents putting kids on a pedestal—praising them for everything and rarely criticizing. It's hard to find a more succinct definition of parenting in the modern era, where kids get sports trophies just for participating. Most parents think this will help children. Parents believe that praise builds self-esteem, which, in turn, builds success. Parents also think that praise encourages performance and assume that higher levels of praise encourage higher levels of performance. Finally, parents believe that praise is an alternative to feelings of shame as a motivator for children's behavior. The threat of shame is a powerful motivator, but not a pleasant one.

Praising children when they do good work or behave well is fine—in fact, that approach works better than punishing children for behaving badly. But in the last few decades, American parenting has moved to a different model, heaping on praise for the littlest achievements and even, sometimes, for poor performance. Thinking that you're great when you actually stink is a recipe for narcissism, yet this is what many parents and teachers encourage in children every day in the name of self-esteem.

Excessive praise has even been built into our education system. Although 20% fewer students in 2006 (versus 1976) did 15 or more hours of homework a week, twice as many reported earning an A average in high school. In other words, students are now getting better grades for doing *less* work. Extracurricular activities have similar policies. Michelle, a 45-year-old alumna of Indiana University who responded to our online survey, returned recently to judge IU Sing, a university-wide singing contest. She was surprised to discover that the competition now awards first through fifth place in two divisions, five specialty awards, and Best Overall. "There are so many awards given, it seems difficult for an act to NOT receive something," she said.

Unfortunately, overpraising is not the solution it seems to be—it not only may lead to narcissism, but to failure. After doing well at a task, some children in a study were praised for how smart they were. Others were told that it was good they worked so hard. Later on, those praised for hard work did much better—this was something they could do again. Those who had been told they were smart were afraid to try—what if they did badly? That would mean they weren't smart anymore. This study suggests that it is better to praise a child for working hard, rather than giving the overly general way that has become so popular—telling a child she is special, great, and smart.

In her recent book *The Self-Esteem Trap*, Polly Young-Eisendrath describes how treating children as "special" leads to young adults who are self-absorbed but fragile in the face of hard work and negative feedback. They feel entitled to high-status occupations but quickly become discouraged when they aren't highly successful right away.

When Keith brought this up in one of his graduate seminars, most of the students reported having similar feelings or knew these were common feelings among their peers. Keith then gave the class the standard "how to be successful in academics" lecture (the same one he got not that long ago). In short, to master any semicomplex profession takes at least ten years of effort. The usual formula for success in academics (and many other fields as well) is to 1) find the best person in the field who is willing to let you work with him or her, 2) do whatever that person says for five years and work your butt off, 3) and finally, after you have earned that person's confidence and respect, you establish yourself in the field over five or more years with that person's support. Then 4) return the favor by mentoring newcomers to the field. Being successful is a "war of attrition"—you get rejected a lot, but if you keep plugging away you will likely move ahead.

Many of the students, however, weren't very pleased with the idea of a 10-year career path. They thought success should come quickly and didn't like the idea of learning from people smarter than them. In other words, they thought they were special. They would do better, instead, to focus on learning, developing skills, and slowly becoming successful at a career.

BE A WINNER, NOT A LOVER

Parents have also been whipped into a hypercompetitive frenzy by a wave of new baby products that promise to "promote cognitive development!" or "develop thinking skills!" Baby Einstein videos are the most famous example, the title seeming to suggest that they will help your child become a genius. Parents buy Baby Mozart tapes believing they will make their children smarter; in 1998, then-governor Zell Miller of Georgia put $105,000 in the state budget to buy a classical music CD for every newborn. As Dave Walsh puts it in his book *No*, "a lot of parents worried about their babies falling behind other babies who were listening to *The Magic Flute*." Although on the surface it's a good thing that parents care about their children's learning, these products can promote the narcissistic values of hypercompetition and winning at all costs, while not considering the values of caring and consideration for others. Parents buy Baby Einstein videos, not Baby Mother Teresa videos.

Many parents continue this attitude when their children become teenagers and young adults, telling them to get an education and succeed in a career before they get involved in an emotionally close relationship. Laura Sessions Stepp, a *Washington Post* reporter and the author of *Unhooked*, writes, "Several of the young women I was observing labored under [the] impression that they couldn't love deeply and passionately . . . and live the independent, meaningful lives their parents told them they wanted, and many of them did, in fact, desire." In a column in the Duke University student newspaper, Anne Katherine Wales wrote, "At Duke, we're on a fast-paced track . . . getting internships with big companies. . . . But somewhere along the line most of us have gotten really close to someone, maybe even fallen in love. For some reason, this scares us beyond belief. Somehow this doesn't fit with our plan of achieving our dreams. . . . We have career counselors telling us how to get that internship, get accepted to med school and get that high-paying job. But no one is telling us how to work our feelings into this equation for success." A focus on individual achievement that leaves out feelings, love, and caring is a recipe for narcissism. The missing piece of caring for others cascades into many of narcissism's negative outcomes, such as lack of empathy, incivility, entitlement, and aggression. In raising superachievers, today's parents may have, perhaps unintentionally, raised super-narcissists.

TREATMENT FOR THE EPIDEMIC

Parenting is an incredibly powerful force for spreading cultural values. From our parents, we learn right and wrong, how to treat others, political and economic beliefs, prejudice or tolerance, and manners (or lack thereof). Parenting has such a big impact on children because parents are the first ones there.

It is unlikely American culture will ever go back to the earlier model of the authoritarian parent. In some ways, this is a good thing—spanking leads to more aggression, and requiring unquestioned obedience fails to help children develop an internal guide for behavior. Yet many parents have clearly swung too far in the direction of putting their child in charge. Here are a few steps parents can take to temper narcissistic impulses in their children:

• *Say no, and mean it.* There's nothing wrong with saying no to your child. But you have to stick to it. If you say no and your child whines and screams and then you give in, you've just taught your child that whining and screaming is effective. For more on this, we highly recommend David Walsh's book *No: Why Kids—of All Ages—Need to Hear It and Ways Parents Can Say It.* It is an excellent guide to striking a balance in parenting: showing lots of love, but also the right amount of parental guidance.

• *Don't give your child too much power.* Five-year-olds should not be picking out the family car, their bed, or even their own clothes all the time. A mother on a message board about preschoolers said, "I actually encourage my daughter to pick out clothes she likes. Winters are always hard because the girl wants to wear skirts and flip-flops year-round." Yes, preschoolers love having a say in what they wear, and giving them some power prevents too many morning battles. The key is *some* power. Like the child who wants to wear flip-flops in the winter, most young children can't yet make good decisions if they are given too much say. Instead, it works best to give the child limited choices. In the winter, you might ask, "Would you like to wear your gray corduroy pants or your black corduroy pants?" This way, the child still gets to choose but doesn't end up freezing.

The same goes for food. If you ask a two-year-old what he wants for dinner, the answer is likely to be "cookies." So provide limited choices between a few healthy options. Similarly, if you ask a three-year-old, "Do you want to go to bed now?" the answer is often "no." But limited choices can work here, too. Jean tried this with her then three-year-old niece. "Alex," she said, "Do you want to go to bed now, or in five minutes?" Alex thought it over and said "Five minutes." After five minutes, Jean said "OK, Alex, it's been five minutes. Time to go to bed." To Jean's pleasant surprise—who knows if this psychology stuff actually works?—Alex said "OK," and went to bed with no protest. If she had protested, the key would have been to follow through. The child who wheedles you into giving in and wins has just learned that he doesn't have to do what you say.

Be sparing with how often you ask a young child, "Do you want . . ." Parents often ask this when the child really has no choice. Jean saw a father in an airport ask a three-year-old, "Do you want to fly on an airplane?" More than likely, the child was going to get on the airplane whether she wanted to or not. Even when the child might have a choice, this question puts the child firmly in charge. If you, as the parent, have decided to go to the park, it's up to you to gauge whether the young child is in the mood to do so, instead of asking, "Do you want to go to the park?" She might not know exactly what she wants—predicting whether one will like an activity in the future is a hard task even for most adults. Instead, say, "We're going to the park." But avoid falling into the trap of saying "OK?" and making a statement into a question ("We're going to the park now, OK?"). If you're worried that you're forcing your child to do something he doesn't want to do, don't—if he really doesn't want to go, he'll let you know. But it should be up to him to say that spontaneously, rather than you giving him the opportunity to control the situation. At that point you can decide whether to honor his wishes. If everyone else in the family wants to go, you'll probably all still go. And then your child will learn that he doesn't always get what he wants—not so terrible a lesson to learn. He'll also learn that it's sometimes necessary to compromise for the good of others, a useful skill in friendships and relationships.

It's fine to let older children and teens make more decisions. But make sure that they aren't making too many of the family purchasing choices. If they have the fun of making the choice but don't have to pay for it, they might develop an entitled attitude that they deserve to get everything they want. When they're on their own and paying off their college loans on their tiny starting salary, they may be shocked to no longer have the resources to buy the best. It's fine to get kids' input on things like where to go on vacation, but the final decision has to rest with you as the parent. You've got years more life experience and know what is best for your whole family, including your budget.

• *Carefully consider the messages you are sending to your children about competition and winning*. Yes, it's a dog-eat-dog world out there, but teaching winning at all costs is not going to work out well in the long run. Cheaters are usually caught eventually, and even if they aren't, they shortchange themselves by not learning material or doing something on their own.

It's a harder call to decide what to tell teens and young adults about boyfriend/girlfriend relationships. It's tempting to tell them to achieve their career goals first, but the truth is that most young people will still have sex. If they believe that a relationship will slow them down, they'll still have sex, but won't form emotionally close relationships. Friendships can't really replace this—they do teach emotional intimacy, but of a different sort than a romantic relationship. Nevertheless, it's true that many teens are hurt by early relationships that go badly. Within reason, these can be a learning experience—the classic "better to have loved and lost than never to have loved at all" (and, instead, hooked up with the whole fourth floor of the dorm).

• *Think twice before you buy your kid something that announces how great he is*. A shirt that says "Spoiled Rotten" is cute until the kid does something bratty—which, let's face it, is going to be about three minutes for most kids. Unless you're Prince William or Harry, don't dress your daughter in an outfit claiming she is a "Princess." She's not. Get over it. Similarly, putting a bib on your child's neck that announces "I'm the Boss" is likely to be a self-fulfilling prophecy. Sure, kids change our lives, but there's no need to announce that they now run the household. And please don't buy them something that announces how great *you* are, like the "My Mom is Hot" shirt worn by Tori Spelling's son, or the "I'm marvelous and so is my Mommy" shirt Jean saw in an Old Navy store. Some people have protested that these shirts are "cute." Our question is, why is this cute? Our culture is increasingly accepting—even encouraging—narcissistic behavior, which looks "cute" until it gets obnoxious. And the interval between the two is often very, very short.

Speaking of cute but sometimes obnoxious, we look next at America's most revered, most admired narcissists: the gods and goddesses we know as celebrities.

CHAPTER 6

Superspreaders!

The Celebrity and Media Transmission of Narcissism

Americans know a lot about celebrities. We read magazines about them, so many that the weekly gossip mag is one of the few areas of print journalism that is actually growing. We watch TV shows about them such as *Access Hollywood* and get updates on their antics through mainstream news outlets like CNN and the *Today* show. *People* Mobile, which debuted in 2007, delivers "up-to-the-minute celebrity news . . . on your phone" (because think of how horrible it would be if you were a minute behind on Britney's latest child custody news). In 2006, the most popular Google News search was for Paris Hilton, and that was *before* she went to jail. In 2007, the top three Google news searches were for *American Idol*, YouTube, and Britney Spears.

Despite this constant stream of celebrity news, most Americans don't know what celebrities are "really" like—we don't see them in their private moments or hear their personal conversations (although TMZ.com is doing its best to change that). There's not a lot of research on celebrities. It's not as if we can go up to them and have them fill out personality questionnaires.

Except that Dr. Drew Pinsky did. The host of the nationally syndicated radio show *Loveline*, Pinsky cornered 200 of his celebrity guests and gave them the Narcissistic Personality Inventory, the same questionnaire used in almost all of the research on narcissism. Pinsky and his coauthor Mark Young found that celebrities scored significantly higher on narcissism than the average person. "This is like you found out Liberace was gay," deadpanned Pinsky's cohost, Adam Carolla.

Obvious or not, the study was the first proof of rampant celebrity narcissism. The study also found that there was no correlation between narcissism and career length, suggesting that celebrities' narcissism was there *before* people gave them special treatment for being famous. Young and Pinsky also looked at different types of celebrities to see who was the most narcissistic—was it actors, comedians, or musicians? Nope—it was reality TV stars. So the programs that show real people doing real things—not acting out a fictional story from a script—feature even *more* narcissistic people. Reality TV shows, often the majority of the highest-rated shows, are a showcase of narcissism, making materialistic, vain, and antisocial behavior seem normal. Fictional TV shows already have a large impact on children and teens, shaping how they view the world. This is even more true of reality TV, with no fiction and no script to stand in the way of undeveloped minds' belief that this is the way everyone behaves in real life.

Reality TV stars and other celebrities have an important role to play in the spread of narcissism. In the epidemiology of viruses, some people are known as "superspreaders." The historic prototype of the superspreader is Typhoid Mary, the cook who gave more than 50 people typhoid fever between 1900 and 1915. Celebrities and the media they dominate are the superspreaders of narcissism. Through gossip magazines, movies, commercials, and reality TV, Americans get a regular infusion of the narcissism virus. As Pinsky and Young's study shows, Americans are obsessed with people who are obsessed with themselves. In this new world, being narcissistic is cool.

Not all celebrities are narcissistic, of course. But unfortunately the ones we hear about the most often are. Narcissists are masters at staying in the spotlight; they love attention and will do almost anything to get it. This is also one of the few realms where narcissism is helpful—narcissists thrive on public performance. Unlike many people who find it extremely anxiety-provoking to be in front of a crowd, narcissists love it. With the advent of reality TV, nonstop celebrity coverage, and instant fame, more and more narcissistic people are spreading their disease far and wide.

The queen of narcissistic celebrity superspreaders just might be Paris Hilton. In May 2007, Paris was sentenced to 45 days in jail because she drove with a suspended license after being convicted of driving while intoxicated. She immediately protested that it wasn't her fault, claiming her publicist didn't tell her she wasn't supposed to drive. Before long she was meeting with California governor Arnold Schwarzenegger, hoping for a pardon, and hundreds of people signed a "Free Paris" petition declaring that Paris should not be sent to jail because "she provides beauty and excitement [in] our otherwise mundane lives." As one commentator put it, "the people who wrote the petition aren't saying Paris is innocent. They're just saying they want Paris free because she's fabulous." While in jail in June 2007, Paris said, "I received so many letters from girls who look up to me. It made me realize that I have a responsibility, so I'm going to be the best role model I can be." She talked about becoming a philanthropist and changing her ways. A month later, she was photographed wearing a shirt with a silk-screened image of . . . herself. If she became a philanthropist, she's kept it quiet. And Paris keeps virtually nothing quiet.

Lindsay Lohan, who made the news with numerous trips to rehab, isn't exactly humble, either. "I have such an impact on our younger generations, as well as generations older than me," she wrote in a letter that appeared in the *New York Post*. Complaining about an unflattering magazine article, she wrote, "I am willing to . . . use my celebrity status to move the focalpoint(s) of the press to the real issues that we have going on as we speak." She signed the letter, "Your entertainer." To round out the triumvirate, Britney Spears reportedly has ended up lonely because she has alienated her friends with her extreme self-centeredness.

Pinsky and Young's study found that female celebrities were more narcissistic than male celebrities—the opposite of most samples, where men are usually more narcissistic. Of course, narcissistic male celebrities aren't hard to find, either. When Nicole Richie was pregnant with his baby, Joel Madden said he hoped it was a boy because "a world can use another Joel." (We hope he wasn't too disappointed by instead having a daughter, Harlow.) Justin Timberlake complained that "the Grammys used me for ratings. And look at it—they were up 18 percent!" Before premiering a song at a show, he said, "If you don't like it, fuck you." One woman who dated former *Late Late Show* host Craig Kilborn told *Us Weekly*, "He took me to his house and made me watch his show on TiVo. And then he pulled out magazines of himself."

One journalist wrote in our online survey, "I interviewed hundreds of well-known actors and actresses over a 10-year period, and this, basically, is how the interview went: 'I think . . . I believe . . . I am . . . My passion is . . . I'd like to think what I do makes a difference to the world . . . Me . . . Me . . . More Me . . . Major Me . . . did I mention Me? I am a role model to so many . . . I am, in fact, God incarnate. [They], and not only the mega-stars, were so self-absorbed, so self-obsessed, that my attendance at the interview wasn't totally necessary. They blurted out their Me-ness unprompted." More Americans are keeping up to date on celebrity me-ness. The circulation of newspapers and traditional women's magazines is steadily falling, but the circulation of the celebrity magazine *Us Weekly* was up 10% in 2007 (to 1.9 million), and tabloid competitor *OK! Weekly* was up 23% (to 935,000).

Sports are another headline-making realm with more than its share of narcissists. When Barry Bonds broke Hank Aaron's record of 755 career home runs, the victory celebration was muted due to allegations of Bonds's steroid use. But even if Barry hadn't been hitting the juice, the adulation would still have been tempered due to Bonds's arrogant and combative attitude. "Even his teammates don't like him," said one sports commentator. Skier Bode Miller, who failed to finish in two events and nearly fell in a third one in the 2006 Winter Olympics, said, "I just did it my way. I'm not a martyr, and I'm not a do-gooder. I just want to go out and rock. And man, I rocked here." He admitted that he might not have trained as much as he should have, but he claimed he had a good reason: "My quality of life is the priority. It's been an awesome two weeks. I got to party and socialize at an Olympic level." Too bad they don't give medals for drinking.

THE QUEST FOR FAME

Fame is not all it's cracked up to be—the loss of privacy and the constant scrutiny can get old very quickly. But tell that to the people camped out at *American Idol* tryouts.

An increasing number of Americans not only admire fame from afar but fervently wish to enter the circle of celebrity themselves. In 2006, 51% of 18- to 25-year-olds said that "becoming famous" was an important goal of their generation—nearly five times as many as named "becoming more spiritual" as an important goal. A 2006 poll asked children in Britain to name "the very best thing in the world." The most popular answer was "being a celebrity." "Good looks" and "being rich" rounded out the top three, making for a perfectly narcissistic triumvirate. "God" came in last. A friend of Jean's once asked a teenage girl, "What do you want to be when you're older?" "Famous," she replied. "For what?" the older person asked. "It doesn't matter, I just want to be famous," said the teen. As the Counting Crows presciently put it in their 1993 song, "When I look at the television / I wanna see me starin' right back at me / We all wanna be big stars / But we don't know why and we don't know how."

Kendall Myers, of Austin, Texas, hired the company Celeb 4 A Day to send three "personal paparazzi" to follow her and her friends around on a girls' night out. People on the street began taking pictures of them with their cell phones, clearly thinking she actually was famous. Celeb 4 A Day also offers a megastar package (cost: a mere $3,000 in New York) that includes six paparazzi, a publicist, a limo, a bodyguard, and a mocked-up "celebrity" tabloid (the fake *MyStar* magazine) with your picture on the cover. The fake publicist, Celeb 4 A Day explains, "will escort you into your event fielding questions from your Personal Paparazzi, making sure you look and sound your best," and six photographers will be ready for "The Star's (that's you!) arrival." The fake paparazzi package includes them "asking questions, vying for coverage, shouting your name and everything else you've seen on T.V. and want to experience for yourself!" Celeb 4 A Day started in Austin and became so successful that it expanded to New York, Los Angeles, and San Francisco within a year. "Our belief is that the everyday person deserves the attention as much, if not more, than the real celebrities," the Celeb 4 A Day website notes. "You deserve it—we know it."

"It's as if being famous has become a right," says Joshua Gamson, a sociology professor at the University of San Francisco. "One of the rights to being American is the right to become famous—at least for an hour, maybe a day. If you don't have people asking who you are, you're nobody." Philip Barker, who hired a personal paparazzi to follow him and his friends around on a night out in Chicago, says that his group was moved to the front of the line at several clubs. "People thought, these guys are important people," Barker said. "Celebrities are always whining about people following them around. We're like, Are you kidding? That's our dream!"

A recent article in the American Airlines in-flight magazine, of all places, asked, "So, you wanna be famous?" and detailed all the ways regular people can achieve "overnight celebrity." "If you're ready to take the world by storm, then heed the following advice, and worldwide renown will be just a click away," it promises, suggesting people self-publish books, distribute their own podcasts, and upload their first films to YouTube. There's nothing wrong with doing any of these things, but it's interesting that the focus is not on creative output but on the ultimate goal of fame—and not just for talented artists or musicians, but for everybody sitting in a cramped coach seat who's bored enough to read the in-flight magazine. Their kids can practice for fame, too: a preschool in Atlanta encourages three-year-olds to use their Wee TV studio, which they boast "builds self-confidence and self-esteem."

For some young people, fame is not just a goal but something they've actively made part of their future plans. In 2005, 31% of American high school students said they expected to become famous someday. Underprivileged kids buy into this dream just as much or more than those with more money; just as many kids from poor neighborhoods as from middle-class ones were sure they would become famous. As communications researcher Danah Boyd puts it, for "working class kids . . . the only path out [is] the 'lottery' (a.k.a. becoming a famous rock star, athlete, etc.). Over and over, working class kids tell me that they're a better singer than anyone on *American Idol* and that this is why they're going to get to be on the show." When asked whether they would rather become famous, smarter, stronger, or more beautiful, 42% of black teens said famous, as did 21% of white teens. Even being *near* fame is appealing: 43% of middle school girls said they wanted to become a celebrity personal assistant, twice as many as chose "the president of a great university like Harvard or Yale," three times more than chose "a United States Senator" and four times more than "chief of a major company like General Motors." So just being close to a celebrity is now considered more desirable than being a public servant, a successful businessperson, or a university president.

Magazines and TV shows allow adults to fantasize about what you could do and buy if you were only famous enough. Brands of jeans have become breakout sellers simply because the right celebrity wore them. Gossip magazines regularly mention the bars and restaurants currently in vogue with young Hollywood, and travel stories showcase how you can do what famous people do if you spend gobs of cash. A recent cover story of *Spirit*, the Southwest Airlines magazine, was called "Famous Vegas." The city is becoming popular with stars again, the magazine explained, "But why let the celebrities have all the fun? We've supplied everything but the entourage to help you see the city like an A-lister." It details a day of activities like "pick up your Ferrari 360 Spider ($1,500/day)."

Little girls can now own a famous pet. Pawparazzi became an overnight hit in 2006 with their line of six small stuffed dogs and cats complete with their own bling, celebrity magazine, and gossip magazine bio. There's a movie star dog, a supermodel cat, and a feline pop star. The idea is that kids can carry around their famous pet wherever they go, just as Paris Hilton does. As the toy's website explains, "Pawparazzi are celebrity pets, living big lives of glamour, fashion, and travel. They are actors, musicians, athletes, writers, and other fascinating personalities. They are adored by their fans and followed by the press, especially *Pawparazzi Magazine*, which always seems to get the latest gossip!" The website gives the backstory for each star toy, complete with wry references to real-life media and products: "From humble beginnings, Powder was discovered when she was climbing trees in her front yard. Her meteoric rise to super model began with her first magazine cover in *Pounce Illustrated*'s fashion edition. She is the cover cat for the Cats Factor cosmetic line." The website also includes "Star Snippets" such as "Friends say rock singer Kyra is expecting a litter of kittens in May. She will interrupt her 'Stalking Birds' concert tour for the birth. . . . Kyra says she'll be working with a personal trainer to get in shape after the birth. 'In the meantime, I'm styling my fur.' " Although the Pawparazzi are intended as fun fantasy play, the values they teach kids are disturbingly narcissistic: fame is the ultimate virtue, right after looking good; the best thing in the world is to lead a "big life" centered on glamour and fashion; the way to be a "fascinating personality" is as a celebrity actor or musician. The line was so successful that Pawparazzi added six new toys within a year (announced as "a new litter of celebrity pets").

Millions of people cannot wait for their chance to become a narcissistic celebrity superspreader, and the narcissism part starts early. While researching his book *Fame Junkies*, author Jake Halpern attended a conference of the International Modeling & Talent Association, where children who want to be "discovered" pay $3,000 and up for the privilege of possibly meeting agents and casting directors. What he noticed the most about the children he met at the convention, Halpern writes, "was their apparent sense of entitlement." This was especially true of a kid Halpern calls Ariel Barak, one of the few attendants who received some recognition from agents, even getting named "Best Pre-Teen Actor of the Year." Ariel and his father were living in Los Angeles while the rest of his family was in Virginia, and Ariel's father found the time difficult. "It's very hard for me. I miss my neighborhood, my family, even my obnoxious dog. Basically, I try to shut my emotions down totally, and I become a soldier in duty of my son," he said. After hearing this, Ariel leapt to his feet, pointed at his father, and yelled, "Drop down and give me twenty!" As Halpern observes, "Although he had not yet landed a big part, Ariel Barak was already a star in his own mind."

And it helps: narcissists do better than other people when bathed in the limelight of public competitive performance, so narcissism *is* useful in these narrow circumstances, such as when auditioning for a part. In show business—at least when it comes to getting a spot on a reality show—it pays to be narcissistic. Of course, 99% or more of people will not make a living as an actor or entertainer, but with half of young people saying becoming famous is an important goal, many more people aspire to these dreams. And many of the rest read the celebrity magazines, tune in to *Entertainment Tonight*, or troll the Web for news about their favorite starlet—a starlet who is probably more narcissistic than your average girl on the street. Maybe that's why American culture finds narcissism acceptable and even laudatory: it is a trait displayed in abundance by the modern equivalent of royalty—a royalty of fame that so many aspire to enter.

SUPERSPREADING IN POP CULTURE, AND HOW IT GETS INTO YOUR HOME

In a suburban kitchen, a teen boy talks to his friend's mother. "So . . . Ms. Kelly, how are things—everything good?" he asks. "Yeah—thanks," she replies. "Must be lonely, now that Mr. K left," he says, studying her appraisingly as she looks quizzically back. "I'm *reallllly* good company," he offers with a leer. The scene then cuts to the teen nodding approvingly at himself in the mirror, with the tagline, "Clearasil. May cause confidence."

In another Clearasil ad, a teen girl looks bored as her mother shows her date her baby pictures. "Here's her first tooth . . . And aw, here she is naked in the bath," intones Mom. The girl looks up with a sultry pout. "You should see me now," she says silkily. "No," protests Mom. "Oh, yeah," replies the girl with emphasis. After the tagline about confidence, she too is nodding at herself in the mirror.

The tagline really should be "May cause *over*confidence"—or actually, narcissism—given the boy's zero chance of making it with his friend's mom (or even being asked back to the house) and the girl's likely grounding (possibly until she's 35). It also shows what "confidence" is good for, at least in these portrayals—it aids 15-year-olds in their quest for casual sex (which, interestingly, it does: narcissistic people have more sex partners than those not so high on self-admiration).

Although these ads are meant to be funny and improbable, they shape the picture of reality for teens who are still learning about social roles and sexuality. The young people who commented on the commercial on YouTube identified with the characters and referred to them as if they were real people. Several male posters detailed exactly what they wanted to do with (or, more accurately, to) the girl ("I would stuff that bird"; "Id tap that"; "Id beat") and wished they were the girl's boyfriend in the ad ("my god, that girl is fine! I'd love to see her naked, and I'd love to be that kid"; "damn! that bitch is fine! . . . luckyass guy"). One guy with the username "PoopPoopFart" (ergo, likely a 13-year-old boy—or younger), wrote, "THIS SHIT IS HOT. *FAP FAP FAP FAP*." (*Fap* is slang, based on the similarity of the sound, for masturbation. Yes, we had to look that up, and yes, we know: ewwww.) Older people and parents weren't amused by the ads. The spots are "appalling, disgusting, and gave me the creeps," said Mike Galanos on CNN's Headline News, noting that "an ad is worse than a show—an ad is an ambush. I don't know it's coming, and then I have to have a talk with my 12-year-old."

One YouTube poster sarcastically noted, "great moral values . . ." His comment promptly got rated a negative 5 by other users. Many of the younger posters didn't understand why anyone was offended by these ads. "What you mean by that? I think theres nothing moral or immoral in this add, whatsoever"; "If you or your kids are offened then move to the Middle East. Sex is not a bad thing even among teenagers"; "for all you losers that are like 'well i don't think this is very appropiate blah blah blah' . . . wel shut the hell up . . . stupid fagget adults." These young people saw nothing wrong with teen sexuality being expressed in front of parents—or even *with* someone else's parent. That's confidence, they seemed to be saying, and the only thing more important is looking hot.

A Kohl's department store ad features a band singing a song called "Because I'm Awesome." As the clothes on the band members change every second or so in the ad, the singer declares "I'm a leader / I'm a winner" and "I don't need you / and I beat you / cuz I'm awesome." The rest of the song includes lyrics such as "Gonna make lots of money / And bought a self-tan." For those keeping score at home with the list of narcissistic traits: interest in leadership and power, check; competitiveness, check; saying one does not need other people, check; overinflated view of self, check; materialism, check; and vanity, check. A psychologist couldn't have written a more thoroughly narcissistic song. According to a YouTube poster who works at a Kohl's, "this song is played once every hour" in the store. Its fans have taken the song's message to heart. GuitarHero22, who posted the song's lyrics to a website, commented, "I was the one who got to upload these lyrics! Metro didn't have them before I put them up. Yeah me!"

Marketing and advertising in general discovered the trend toward self-admiration several years ago and helped it swell even larger. From 2001 to 2006, the U.S. Army—of all things—recruited soldiers with the slogan "An Army of One." Time Warner cable's slogan is "The Power of You." You can customize your own shoes at the Nike Store, choose your own ringtone for your phone, and mix your own music for your iPod. (It can't be a coincidence that the *i* in *iPod* and *iMac* can stand for the first-person singular.) A common advertising slogan is the entitlement-themed "You Deserve the Best." As Siva Vaidhyanathan wrote on msnbc.com in December 2006, "Notice that *Time* framed the Person of the Year as 'you.' That should sound familiar. Almost every major marketing campaign these days is about empowering 'you.' "

In between the commercials, many TV shows portray narcissism as normal, acceptable behavior. Reality shows are a process of self-selection—narcissists love the spotlight so much they seek it out by trying out for these shows. They might be more likely to make the cut because of their outsize personalities, and they stick around because they love public performance. Most reality shows are singing and dancing competitions. Those that deal with social and business challenges don't always crown narcissists as their winners, but the unlikable narcissistic character is often the most remembered (for example, Omarosa on the first season of *The Apprentice*, Jerri on the second season of *Survivor*, or Puck from *The Real World: San Francisco*).

One of the most common traits displayed on reality shows is excessive overconfidence combined with an aggressive competitiveness. On one episode of Cycle 8 of *America's Next Top Model*, Renee says, "I've got this in the bag. That was my first impression of the other girls. I just don't feel like they have the amount of character and determination that I have. I do want these girls to know that if they get in my way I will plow them over. No prisoners." A few minutes later, Sarah claims that she's the best: "None of these girls can hold a candle to what I have. I'm fierce. When I want something I go and get it. That's my entire personality." Natasha says, "Those girls are really masculine, and they're just not supposed to be here. Why are they here? But I don't care. There is no competition for me because I can beat them all." Kathleen says, "Of course I'm going to win this competition. I'm not a girl who gives up." Although it's great to have confidence in yourself, this kind of over-the-top self-inflation, combined with the derogation of others, teaches a narcissistic outlook. And none of these contestants won.

Perhaps the most egregious example of reality TV narcissism is the MTV reality show *My Super Sweet 16*, which features rich teens planning their extravagant 16th-birthday parties. Each episode features almost every facet of narcissism: materialism, overcompetitiveness, appearance obsession, the quest for fame, manipulativeness. One girl's father hires a director to film his daughter acting out scenes from movies (she was, of course, no Meryl Streep). Several girls in these shows command their friends to change their hair, makeup, nails, or even their boyfriend so they will make a better impression at the all-important party. Said one, "If I don't approve of what they're wearing, then I will personally take them to pick out another dress. If I don't approve of their escort, I will pick someone for them. I don't care if they're insulted by my critiques, because it's my party. My friends have really bad tan lines, and they need to fix them before the party. It's my party and I want things to go my way." Later, as she makes her grand entrance, she says, "I looooove having all eyes on me. It's amazing—I feel like I'm celebrity status."

As *Time* columnist Ana Marie Cox writes, "Their blingy flings are not celebrations of accomplishment; they're celebrations of self. . . . Each guest of honor is really after only one thing: 'I feel famous. I love it,' says one. . . . Far from joining polite society like the debutantes of the past, the kids gleefully rip through social graces, alienating friends and sacrificing tact." Adults who don't find the show nauseating may find it funny. Many teens, however, think it's really cool that the kids get whatever they want. If they feel a negative emotion at all, it's jealousy. When Priscilla gets a $100,000 car, her friends say things like "I want that car" and "Not fair." At least in the parts shown on MTV, no one comments on how the money might have been better spent on education or charity toward others (settle for "only" a $50,000 car, for example, and you could support an entire family for a year). Priscilla does note how outsized her gift is, but seems to view that as exciting: "I'm like, amazed, that I'm going to be, like, driving a car that's more than a lot of people's houses." It is also a way to win the competition with another girl: "My car is way hotter than Nikki's car," she says. And clearly that's more important than helping someone else.

Earlier in the episode, Priscilla tries on a dress for her party and says, "Everyone's going to be jealous of me when I wear this dress, because I look so good." Her mother warns her, "You're acting so conceited now." Priscilla replies, "I've got a reason, right?" A hip-hop song Priscilla has clearly heard then plays—a song that could be the theme song of narcissism: "I'm so outstanding / . . . Don't care if they can't stand me. I'm conceited I got a reason." In the next scene Priscilla "auditions" young men to be her escort, asking each to "lift up your shirt so we can see your abs." She decides to pick two escorts instead of one because, as she remarks to her friend, "Wouldn't it look good with two guys—one on each side?"

Even almost sociopathic narcissism feels right at home on *My Super Sweet 16*. Atlanta teen Allison tells a party planner she wants to block off part of Peachtree Street so there can be a parade for "my grand entrance." Peachtree is a major thoroughfare, the planner reminds her.

She responds, "My sweet 16 is more important than wherever they have to be." But there's a hospital across the street, the planner cautions—what if an ambulance can't get to the hospital? "They can wait one second. Or they can just go around," she says cavalierly. Amid all of this, Allison's mother just listens. When the planner finally turns to her in exasperation, she says, "If Allison wants it, make it happen." So much for that dying person in the ambulance.

YOU'RE NEVER TOO YOUNG FOR NARCISSISM

Shows for younger children actively encourage narcissism in a different but equally effective way. One PBS show proclaims, "You're Special Just for Being You!" An animated movie for preschool kids called "The Sissy Duckling," narrated by Sharon Stone and written by Harvey Fierstein, was meant to teach kids that it's OK to be different. But as happens all too often, a positive individualistic message goes too far and lands squarely in the world of narcissism. "I'm so hot, can't you see?" sings Elmer, the main character. "I'm unique and perfectly me."

Very young girls now watch TV shows like *Hannah Montana* and *High School Musical*. Even though these shows are about teens, their biggest fans are elementary school and even preschool kids as young as three. Girls are now exposed to the culture of "tweens"—a label applied to ages nine to twelve—at age four, eschewing *Sesame Street* and *Dora the Explorer* for *Hannah Montana*, *The Suite Life of Zack & Cody*, and other preteen shows. Although these shows are free of inappropriate sexuality and crass language, they are unfortunately not free of narcissistic attitudes. "You get the limo out front," sings Hannah Montana in the show's theme song. "Yeah when you're famous it can be kinda fun." She then goes on to sing about going to movie premieres, buying lots of shoes, and getting your face in magazines. Hannah Montana draws more viewers age six to fourteen than any other show on cable, reaching 164 million viewers around the world.

Girls dress up like Hannah Montana in makeover parties like those at Club Libby Lu, a mall-based chain that hosts makeovers for girls age six to eleven. Girls mimic their idol by donning blond wigs and concert costumes. (Some girls even post videos of themselves made up as Hannah Montana on YouTube.) They can also mix their own lip gloss and skin lotions. The website suggests, "Take your Sparkle Spa creation home and enjoy a relaxing evening pampering yourself or create a fun spa party for all your friends. Visit our V.I.P. area for super spa party ideas." (V.I.P. stands for "Very Important Princess," the chain's frequent visitor program.) Club Libby Lu hosted about a million makeovers in its 90 stores nationwide in 2007, despite the irony of face masks on skin that's only 6 years old (as one party planner put it, "Sometimes I want to ask, 'makeover what?' ")

Sweet & Sassy, a Texas-based salon for girls, offers a package in which the girl is picked up at her door by a pink limo. Some girls go to adult salons and have manicures and pedicures—at age seven, sometimes as a birthday party event. First- through third-graders are also wearing makeup more often: in a 2007 survey, 55% of six- to nine-year-old girls said they used lip gloss or lipstick, and 65% said they used nail polish. Cosmetics companies now refer to this age group as "the starter market." "We live in a culture of insta-celebrity," said marketing executive Samantha Skey. "Our little girls now grow up thinking they need to be ready for their close-up, lest the paparazzi arrive."

Entertainment for boys isn't much better. In August 2007, the number one show watched by two- to eleven-year-olds was World Wrestling Entertainment's *SmackDown*. This is disturbing enough given the violence and aggression showcased in this program (cartoonish to an adult, but real-looking to the younger end of this age group), but the aggression is done for show with dashes of vanity, exhibitionism, and grandiosity thrown in. The rest of the top ten programs for that age group included two episodes of *Family Guy* (a cartoon, but one with consistently adult themes), three episodes of Mexican telenovelas (soap operas known for short skirts and steamy plots), and four reality TV shows, such as *So You Think You Can Dance?*

Even when kids are watching informative adult programs, such as the news, the emphasis on narcissism and celebrity comes through. As Jake Halpern documented in *Fame Junkies*, the three network news programs spent more time on the Michael Jackson sexual molestation trial in 2005 than they did on the conflict in Darfur. The most-viewed stories on cnn.com—a rough gauge of what people find interesting in the news—are regularly topped by celebrity items.

Kids are even learning narcissism while reading. The series titles say it all: *The A-list, The It Girl, Gossip Girl, Poseur, The Clique*. Now a TV show, *Gossip Girl* focuses on the exploits of a group of superrich and sometimes supermean New York City high school students. *The Clique* doesn't even wait that long—the first book in the series begins the August before seventh grade as a group of girls prepares by going to a spa to get spray tans and eyebrow waxing. They are *12*. Later they wear three-inch high heels, buy $780 shirts, text one another constantly, and carry Prada bags, all while excluding those who aren't as cool as they are. *The Clique*'s readership of seven- to twelve-year-old girls now thinks it's normal (or at least desirable) to do these very adult things. Poppy, the publisher's imprint for the series, says it "takes the real world and makes it a little funnier, a little more fabulous." And a lot more narcissistic.

Young adult novels weren't always this way. Jean read scores of them in the 1980s—back then, novels for this age group focused on annoying younger siblings (*Tales of a Fourth-Grade Nothing*) or the trials of getting your period (*Are You There, God? It's Me, Margaret*). One series (*Dicey's Song*) was about a homeless family. Books about young people and their horses were also popular, such as *The Black Stallion* series. These books emphasized universal themes, such as family, the awkwardness of adolescence, dealing appropriately with conflicts or problems, caring for others, and friendly competition. Fortunately, some recent books have carried on this tradition in children's literature—most notably the *Harry Potter* series, which focuses on courage, teamwork, and friendship.

Not all teen pop culture is so relentlessly narcissistic. The smash hit TV movie *High School Musical*, which premiered in 2006 and spawned two sequels, features teens who tout teamwork and wholesome goodness. The rousing final number, joyfully performed after both the basketball and academic teams have triumphed over their rivals, is called "We're All in This Together." Dig a little deeper, however, and the movie fits perfectly into the rest of our self-focused culture. The finale song continues, "We're all stars . . . everyone is special in their own way." No unifying cause or deed is mentioned, so it's unclear just what "this" refers to in "We're All in This Together," other than "high school," "awkward adolescence," or maybe "getting into college." It's simply an extension of the self-esteem movement idea that we're all winners, and we're all special. The movie's plot centers around the not-exactly-humble theme that it's possible to be extraordinarily talented at *two* things, not just one (the basketball player makes a mean crème brûlée; the brainy girl is also a gifted singer).

The movie's highly rated 2007 sequel, *High School Musical 2*, contained similarly mixed messages. On the surface, the movie is a critique of narcissism—its villain, Sharpay Evans, is a spoiled rich girl who carries a small dog à la Paris Hilton, loves being on stage, and declares that she wants only "fabulous" things and will "bop to the top." Although teens understand that Sharpay is an example of how not to act, this flies over the heads of many of the three- to seven-year-olds who also watch and instead think Sharpay is great. Troy, the movie's hero, is clearly on a self-admiration trip: "The answers are all inside of me / All I gotta do is believe," he sings. Most Americans wouldn't see the self-admiration and teamwork messages as contradictory; after all, one of our core cultural beliefs is that you have to love yourself before you can love someone else. When that self-admiration becomes narcissism and specialness, however, relationships suffer. So even in shows like *High School Musical* that presumably promote teamwork, the emphasis on the narcissistic self comes through.

TREATMENT FOR THE EPIDEMIC

The American obsession with celebrities is probably here to stay, as is celebrity narcissism. *Us Weekly* is going to continue to sell millions of copies (including to Jean, who used to buy it at the grocery store but now has a subscription: it's for research—really). Still, it is worth making the effort to minimize the harmful impact of celebrity and media narcissism on society.

One place to start is with parents, who can play a big role in changing what children and teenagers view as normal. Shield them from shows like *My Super Sweet 16* that showcase narcissism. If they do watch, help them see that this behavior is deplorable instead of normal. You can have a similar talk with your kids when you watch such shows as *American Idol* or *America's Next Top Model*, helping them see that overconfidence doesn't help people succeed—even in these realms. Talk to them about adult jobs and how being arrogant and rude might get you fired, or at the very least, never promoted. Keith regularly uses the example of the narcissistic character London from the Disney show *The Suite Life of Zack & Cody* when he talks to his daughter about being spoiled. Parents can learn a lot about the child's perspective from these conversations. Often, parents will see the problems with the narcissistic character in the show, but the children will identify with these characters because they are confident, extraverted, and "edgy." (One three-year-old said she liked Sharpay, the narcissistic character in *High School Musical*, because "she's pretty.") A parent can help the child see that self-centered behavior doesn't pay off.

We also hope that writers and producers will get the message that excessive self-admiration is not praiseworthy but dangerous. You do not need to encourage children to feel special and proclaim that they are hot. You don't need to convince teenage boys that they should be confident enough to hit on their friend's mom. Songwriters, when you convince us that being conceited is OK because you "have a reason," realize you are teaching narcissism. And if you'd like to write something with a good message, such as the importance of teamwork, it's not necessary to muddy the waters by also including a self-admiration message or by telling kids they are all special. American culture is obsessed with getting across the message that we are all different and all unique. Why not emphasize instead what makes us all *similar* as human beings? That message promotes the good side of individualism: tolerance of all people, regardless of race, sex, sexual orientation, or background.

One of the best counterexamples to the narcissism epidemic in the media is Harry Potter, one of the highest-grossing book/movie series ever that also manages to skip the self-admiration message altogether. Instead it focuses on the classic themes of love, family, courage, and strong friendship (while keeping the narcissism with the bad guys where it belongs, such as the narcissistic and uncool Gilderoy Lockhart and the selfish and evil Lord Voldemort). More than anything else, Harry wants to be normal; he'd rather not stand out the way that he does. The *Lord of the Rings* series emphasizes similar values. Clearly, you can make a very large buck without resorting to self-admiration and over-the-top individualism.

And celebrities, we know you're fabulous, and we love you for it. But you don't have to wear a T-shirt with a picture of yourself on it, and we'll be fine with your self-promotion if you don't act like a jerk. Take some direction from George Clooney, whom *Time* magazine calls "The Last

Movie Star"—a guy who laughs at himself ("Before they could kill me on *Batman & Robin*, I said, 'It's a bad film, and I'm the worst thing in it' "), eats undercooked lamb at *Time* reporter Joel Stein's house, and even tries to help Stein by identifying the source of a mysterious beeping (after an extensive search including the attic, he finds it's the carbon monoxide alarm: "Either it needs a battery, or we have six seconds to live"). He turns down swag bags, noting that "rich famous people getting free shit looks bad. You look greedy. And I don't need a cell phone with sparkles on it." Clooney's smooth, he's a good performer, and he's definitely confident, but he's somehow managed to avoid the blatant narcissism of so many famous people. As a result, people love him, and he's even more successful than he would have been if he were a jerk. Like Tom Hanks before him—another movie star with a nice-guy reputation—Clooney shows that success, even in Hollywood, doesn't have to mean being an overly competitive, self-centered narcissist.

CHAPTER 7

Look at Me on MySpace

Web 2.0 and the Quest for Attention

Jennifer is a polite, soft-spoken teen who is close to her parents and active in her church. But as Candice Kelsey notes in *Generation MySpace*, Jennifer's MySpace page paints a much different picture. "Suck it slo, Ho!" reads the headline. In her bio, she warns "all you bitches" not to bother her because she knows "a lot of big ass [guys], ya'll!" The wallpaper background of the page is a picture of the singer Beyoncé with bulging cleavage. Another female student, only 14, uses a pink glittery backdrop with the Playboy bunny symbol for her wallpaper. Her page includes a picture of herself in a low-cut dress and several pictures of Victoria's Secret models, all set to a song called "Give It Up to Me." One boy posts on her page, "I really want you to come [to the party] . . . you've got boobs and know how to use them!"

The post-2004 Internet—the user-focused sites some call Web 2.0—is the new Wild West. Instead of rewarding gunslinging, it rewards narcissism. Web 2.0 and cultural narcissism work as a feedback loop, with narcissistic people seeking out ways to promote themselves on the Web and those same websites encouraging narcissism even among the more humble. The name "MySpace" is no coincidence. The slogan of YouTube is "Broadcast Yourself." The name "Facebook" is just right, with its nuance of seeing and being seen, preferably looking as attractive as possible. In December 2006, *Time* magazine officially made you—yes, you—their Person of the Year for promoting Web 2.0. So: the founders of Google, LonelyGirl15, the nutty guys with the Mentos and Diet Coke, and *you* are responsible for the success of the Internet. The cover came complete with a mirror, allowing you to gaze at yourself and think about how important you were for blogging about your lousy day at work and buying a vintage T-shirt on eBay. "Well, thank you, *Time*, for hyping me, overvaluing me, using me to sell my image back to me, profiling me, flattering me, and failing to pay me," wrote Siva Vaidhyanathan in an msnbc.com commentary. "As soon as I saw myself on my local newsstand, I had to buy a copy of *Time*."

Internet domain names beginning with *my* nearly tripled between 2005 and 2008, and trademark applications with *my* quintupled in the ten years between 1998 and 2008. MySpace is the most prominent example, but there's also mycoke, My.Subaru, My IBM, myAOL, My Yahoo, and My Times (a customized version of the *New York Times*). Myfuture.com, owned by the U.S. Department of Defense, encourages young people to enter military service. Mycokerewards.com, one of the company's most profitable segments, offers new content and rewards based "on what was created by you." Using *my* creates the impression that the company is interested in your personal opinion—like so much of our culture, it's all about me.

In her eye-opening book *Generation MySpace*, high school teacher Candice Kelsey lists four messages young people absorb from social networking sites like MySpace and Facebook:

1. I Must Be Entertained All the Time
2. If You've Got It, Flaunt It
3. Success Means Being a Consumer
4. Happiness is a Glamorous Adult (with adulthood defined primarily in terms of sexuality)

All of these messages are consistent with a growing culture of narcissism, with its rampant materialism, aggression toward others, vanity, shallow sexuality, and rabid desire for attention and fame. Some MySpace and Facebook pages contain a seemingly endless list of likes, dislikes, opinions, and so on in the conveniently titled "About Me" section. The first MySpace page Jean ever saw featured a graphic that read, in large black and red letters, "I ❤ ME." Web entrepreneur Andrew Keen argues that "MySpace is creating cultural narcissism in our young," and even some young people agree. "Sure, our generation seems more into ourselves than ever before, but that is from an older (and outsider) perspective," wrote a University of Michigan student in 2008. "Previous generations weren't given the same tools as us. We can't be blamed for growing up in a time when outlets (MySpace, Facebook, blogging . . .) were created specifically for us to talk about ourselves."

SOCIAL NETWORKING FOR NARCISSISTS

Many people use sites like MySpace and Facebook as a time-saving way to keep in touch with their friends. It allows them to have their own personal Web page complete with pictures, party invitations, and daily updates on their lives. This is clearly not a bad thing. Less positive, however, is the sizable number of people who apparently use MySpace and Facebook to seek as much attention as possible for wearing as little as possible. With the amount of young skin on display, it is no surprise that the sites have gotten bad publicity for attracting sexual predators, despite the rarity of that occurrence (teens are adept at spotting predators and rarely "friend" them). But that doesn't stop them from displaying their bodies to their peer group to gain attention. "Any teenager that claims he is on MySpace to talk to his friends is a liar. It's only about showing off," says Jack, 13, in *Generation MySpace*. "I am constantly broadcasting who I am," Indigo Rael, 22, told *USA Today*. "The Internet is just a way for me to reach more people with who I am."

"Is there narcissism [on Facebook]?" asked college student Caitlin Mueller in a 2008 column in the *Stanford Daily*. "Yes, duh! Like that eternally distracting reflecting pool of Greek lore, the Facebook profile can become an abyss of self-love that consumes one entirely . . . [E]ven the most socially competent among us tend to enjoy photo-documenting our social successes, so that those poor souls who are less gifted might at least witness our revelry. Facebook turns out to be the perfect venue for such showcasing. ('Caitlin is completely exhausted from a more awesome weekend than you'll ever have')." However, she writes, most people are still more interested in "stalking the profiles of others than in primping their own." Students want to know "who drunkenly disrobed at which party and who undeservedly landed which swanky new job, and we'd prefer the evidence complete with photos and links. Facebook is an incredibly efficient machine for such discoveries." In other words, Facebook allows you to become obsessed with other people's narcissism, too.

Social networking sites are extremely popular. In 2006, MySpace was the most frequently visited site on the Web, with 90 million users per month. By 2008 the site claimed 300 million members. Facebook, which began as a college-only site and then opened its doors to the general public in 2006, had 100 million members by September 2008.

Narcissists thrive on social networking sites like MySpace and Facebook. The structure of the sites rewards the skills of the narcissist, such as self-promotion, selecting flattering photographs of oneself, and having the most friends. Laura Buffardi, a graduate student working with Keith, did one of the first studies of narcissism and behavior on the social networking site Facebook. She found that college students who scored high on narcissism were masters at promoting themselves, gathering friends on the site, and highlighting their best qualities. When this study was released in October 2008, some bloggers responded with headlines such as,"Facebook a narcissist haven, say shrinks specializing in obvious" and "Today's lead story in 'Duh' magazine: Facebook profiles can be used to detect narcissism." Apparently Facebook users have noticed other users' more solipsistic tendencies. But if it is obvious that social networking sites project narcissism, that does not bode well for a society with so many people using social networking sites.

Narcissists often have problems getting along with others—something we explore more fully in Chapters 13 and 14—but of course online "friends" are often different from friends in real life. For one thing, friending (ah, the verbs of the modern age) someone on Facebook should really be called "acquaintancing" (or perhaps "networking"). Being someone's friend on Facebook does not necessarily mean that you have a deep, emotionally close relationship with him or her. It's more a sign of how many people you "know," or how many people want to say they "know" you. Having more friends is a status symbol, and it's embarrassing to only have five friends on MySpace or Facebook. In real life, of course, you are a truly lucky person if you have five true close friends. On MySpace, that's pathetic—because it's about quantity, not quality. For narcissists, it's a competition to see who can get the most and "hottest" friends, and narcissists love competitions.

Social networking sites reinforce narcissism in an endless loop. Narcissists have more "friends" and connections on these sites, and narcissistic behavior and images are rewarded with more comments and more "adds." Thus users are more likely to be connected with people who are more narcissistic than the average person. So in addition to the site structure facilitating narcissistic self-promotion, the way users are connected may pull the norm for behavior and self-presentation toward narcissism. If aliens landed on our planet and had to judge the human condition by popular social networking sites, the aliens would think that humans are more narcissistic than they actually are.

Even when your MySpace friends are your real-life friends, interaction online is not the same as in-person or even phone interaction. It facilitates the kind of superficial, emotionally bankrupt relationships favored by narcissistic people. A Carnegie Mellon University study found that in online discussion forums, posting frequently is related to acceptance, but actually helping others or asking questions leads to rejection. The researchers concluded that online communities are based on "superficial exchanges instead of meaningful conversations." Ashley, 21, answered our online survey and is not so sure that social networking sites are all that social. "Facebook and MySpace sell themselves as social networking sites, but I think they actually do more to keep people apart then unite them," she says. "Why bother calling a friend when you can just post on their wall? There's no need to visit a friend to catch up when you can just check their profile to see what's new." Josh, 23, agrees. "I guess it's like those machines that pet your pets for you. It sort of makes having friends pointless if you don't need to see or talk to them."

Almost everyone with a MySpace or Facebook page can tell you exactly how many friends he or she has. If it's fewer than 50, you must be lame. If it's over 300, you might be a "MySpace whore," those who do anything they can to add friends to their pages, from posting revealing photos to saying racy things on their blogs. It's all about the number. As Kelsey puts it, "Rarely do two people friend each other out of a sincere desire to relate, grow in intimacy, and strengthen a bond . . . [M]any of the friending exchanges reek of social climbing, posturing, self-aggrandizement, or accumulation." Some teens are smart enough to know this. Grayson, 17, told Kelsey, "You cannot connect with someone by exchanging stupid comments like 'Dude, love the layout. It's the bomb,' instead of calling them up and hanging out. Since the communication is so meaningless, it makes relationships meaningless."

Friending is also inherently competitive, as each user has to decide whom to put in their "Top 8" (since 2007, one can instead have a "Top 24"). Friends must be ordered and ranked, a squeamish bit of social rejection no matter how it's done. Friendship is now a competitive sport. J.D., 24, told Kelsey that two spots in his Top 8 will always be reserved for "the two most attractive female photos from my list of friends." J.D. is onto something: a research study found that Facebook page owners are considered more attractive when the friends on their page are more attractive. In a self-promoting age, it pays to make a calculated decision, as J.D. does, to screen your friends for physical attractiveness.

Most teens have their profiles set to private, meaning that the random Internet users cannot see their profile. However, many high school students have 300 or more "friends," all of whom can see their profile. So although most are not showing off to the world at large, they *are* displaying their assets to their peer group.

The point is to look popular and important by posting pictures. "What's the point of taking pictures with your friends if you don't post them on MySpace?" asks Karina, 16, in *Generation MySpace*. Jessica, 26, who teaches in New Jersey, wrote in our online survey, "Most of my high school students have MySpace pages and the kids who have the most 'friends' on the site are the ones who have the craziest blog stories or the most pictures or the most risqué wallpapers. The cooler you appear to be, no matter how truthful it is in reality, the more people will read your profile and 'request' your friendship. It's all about being recognized and having adoring fans."

Even e-mail addresses help narcissistic people show off. A research study found that narcissists are more likely to choose e-mail handles judged by others as "self-enhancing" and "salacious." So observers were able to tell from people's e-mails if they were more likely to be narcissistic. With every e-mail they send, some self-absorbed people are announcing how great they are. As the researchers put it, "Judging thefascinatingking@gmx.net to be narcissistic might [be] a pretty good guess."

THE MYSPACE PERSONALITY

Social networking sites encourage users to highlight only certain aspects of themselves. First, users can choose to present only the most attractive or cool pictures of themselves—some people call this "the angles" (for example, you show your good side, or if you're overweight you only show your face). "The vast majority of the women on MySpace try to look as sexy as possible by any means necessary," wrote Brian, 25, in our online survey. You can also highlight only the life events that make you look good and delete negative comments. "My MySpace profile contains only the good stuff that happens. Somehow the bad gets left out," admits Brittany, 23. Self-presentation on the Internet usually means looking better and cooler, as a *New York Times* article sums it up: "improving one's standing by linking to high-status friends; using a screen name like 'Batman' or '007' when in reality one is more like Austin Powers; referring to one's gleaming head as 'shaved' not 'bald'; listing one's almost-career as a D.J. or model rather than the one that pays the bills; making calculated decisions about what to list as interests or favorite books." In other words, social networking sites make it possible to open the gap between fantasy and reality.

Second, the sites emphasize only certain aspects of people's lives and only certain aspects of their personalities. Almost invariably, these are the behaviors and traits consistent with narcissism, such as partying, looking hot, having a good-looking boyfriend or girlfriend, or winning a competition (preferably a modeling or singing contest). It's very rare to mention how much you like history class on MySpace. And under "Who I'd Like to Meet," no one ever puts "Bill Gates" or "Benjamin Franklin." Teens try to look cool here by listing "hot" celebrities, popular athletes, or even porn stars. Many teens' MySpace pages are so shocking that Kelsey warns parents not to view their child's page right away. Instead, she advises that they cruise around the site for a full week looking at other teens' pages. After that they won't be as surprised by the beer bottles, scanty clothing, and attention-seeking images so common on the site.

Social networking sites shape the ways teens and twentysomethings view their worlds, and mold the malleable personality of young people like clay. Just as animals evolve and change to fit into their environments, young people are becoming more narcissistic to fit into the demands of the new digital world. As Kelsey puts it, "Because screen culture is . . . rooted in a peakaboo mentality anchored in images, today's teens are expert exhibitionists, vigilant voyeurs, and novice narcissists." To fully participate on these sites and get a lot of comments, you have to continually update your page and send out "news feeds" announcing new pictures or material. The sites actively encourage people to do the digital equivalent of yelling "Look at me!" One young woman posted 257 pictures of herself on her Facebook page, including one in which she sports an annoyed smile over a typed-in caption that reads "Damn paparazzi."

Generation MySpace's chapter on creating a MySpace page is called "Pimped Out," as that's how teens refer to particularly cool pages. Kelsey presents a sample "About Me" page typical of those she's seen from high school girls. "I love 2 Chill With my friends and ParTAYYY ON TEH WEEKEND!!!! . . . i love whip cream lol I love having fun and just being stupid and wild!! Hehe I luv 2 ShoP so Maybe one of you guys can take me shopping sometime! well if you really want to talk to me about me . . . ill be glad to tell you!" The "survey" responses include "Right Handed or Left Handed: both hehe"; "Your bedtime: whenever you put me to bed"; "Do you Swear: hell no." As Kelsey explains, "Here you'll notice the tendency to exaggerate desires and personality traits; the flashier you sound, the more interesting your online self may seem to other members." "Flashy," is, of course, just another name for narcissism on MySpace.

In spring 2008, Jean's graduate student Leah Bonds analyzed 200 MySpace pages of San Diego State University students. Let's just say they could not be described as modest. One said, "Fuck princess! I'm the queen." Another featured 21 pictures of herself in various sultry poses. "Yes im SMART, yes im FUN, yes im WILD! And yesss I LOVE TO PARTY. U think u can dance better than me . . . UR MISTAKEN!" noted another. Under "who I'd like to meet," one said "Someone who will take me to New York City" (because, of course, who you are doesn't really matter—it's just about what you'll do for me). Even those talking about their friends on their pages were oddly competitive about it; one young woman wrote, "My friends are better than yours and I would do anything for them." Jean's favorite page was the guy whose headline was "I wake up and piss excellence." (He wasn't even being original: The line is from the movie *Talladega Nights*.)

Some young people say that their MySpace page "isn't really me" (though they are more likely to say this to a parent than to a friend). But adolescence is a time to try out different identities, so their MySpace me could easily become part of their "real me" as their narcissistic self-portrayal on the site is rewarded. Narcissistic traits like attention seeking, retaliation, and looking hot lead to success on these sites—more friends and more comments. People tend to repeat behaviors that are rewarded.

In *Generation MySpace*, Colin, 15, echoes the sentiment of many teenagers that their MySpace page is centered on self-expression (one of the precursors to the epidemic of narcissism). "This is MY page which I put MY time into. And it is an expression of me and who I am. No one can make me get rid of it," he says.

SCREW YOU, BUT THANKS FOR THE ADD

The sexual aspects of MySpace have drawn lots of attention, but the aggressive and antisocial attitudes often expressed there are almost as shocking— and just as consistent with a culture of narcissism. Of course, plenty of MySpacers talk about how much they love their friends, but the "don't screw with me" attitude is also very common. "Baseball is my life. if you dont enjoy sports I probably wont like you and if you think baseball is easy or boring then FUCK OFF," wrote Matt. One young man's username is "salute me bitch" and another's is "$you just do you and imma do me$." One teen girl wrote, "If you don't lyk me for me, then fuck youu, your NOT worth my time." (Two sentences later she adds, paradoxically, "I am easy to get along with.")

Even the symbols and words people use on MySpace in their usernames promote such narcissistic values as a fascination with celebrity (***, which means starstruck) or an interest in money ($). Online slang often refers to risk taking, like "crunk" (crazy drunk), "blazed" (high), or "fade" (fight). 26Y4U means "Too sexy for you," %\ is hungover, >U is "screw you!" and :- d~ is "getting high." BOHICA is Bend Over, Here It

Comes; GYPO is Get Your Pants Off; GNOC is Get Naked On Cam. When Kelsey searched MySpace in 2006 for mentions of the word *fuck*, she got 13.7 million hits. *Porn* got 2.4 million hits.

Crass commercialism is also rampant on social networking sites and often overtakes any real friendship that was there to begin with. MySpace began as a place for bands to build a fan base, and many bands send out "friend" comments about their latest album—actually just a form of advertising. As MySpace evolved, spam postings from businesses became very common. Virtually every MySpace page has been hit with postings advertising ringtones, porn sites, prescription drugs—anything that can make a buck.

Tila Tequila, the so-called queen of MySpace, embodies the values and personality traits encouraged by social networking sites. Her MySpace page, on which she posts many revealing pictures of her hot body, quickly became a venue for self-promotion, which paid off in 2007 when she scored her own show on MTV. On *A Shot at Love with Tila Tequila*, 32 men and women competed for Tila's affections (she's bisexual). Tila has used several other websites to promote herself, mostly through nude or close-to-nude photos. In 2005 she launched Tilafash ion.com, a clothing line with the slogan "So hot you'll just want to take it all off!"

Tila is also known for her assertive, perhaps even aggressive, attitude. "I hate to say this but I will fucken slam you if you fuck with me. Give me respect, I give you yours . . . got it?" she wrote on her MySpace page. She has also expressed her desire for true love, both on her Web pages and on her show, although it seems unlikely that her current approach will pay off. In her song "I Love U," she raps, "I think I love you . . . But if you ever hurt me / I'll fuckin kill you." Her songs include modest, understated titles such as "Fuck Ya Man" and "Stripper Friends."

BLOGS, COMMENT SECTIONS, AND THE VALUING OF EVERYONE'S OPINION (EVEN IF IT'S STUPID)

The narcissistic culture of the new Internet goes far beyond social networking sites. There and elsewhere, it has become popular to publish one's thoughts in a blog. The 1970s self-expression craze has nothing on the millions of people of all ages who broadcast their every thought to the world. Some blogs are great, of course—interesting, informative, even addictive (Keith's current favorite is Surfysurfy, which is a journal of hand-shaped surfboards from the good folks at Moonlight Glassing). But many are vapid exercises in self-expression and attention-seeking. If you just wanted to record your thoughts, you'd keep a private journal, perhaps in a spiral-bound notebook. Today, many people now keep a detailed accounting of their every move online. It's clear that they're thinking, "It's about me, so of course it's interesting!" Reacting to *Time* magazine's "Person of the Year: You" cover, George Will wrote, "It's about narcissism, which is why a mirror is absolutely perfect. So much of what is done on the web is people writing their diaries as though everyone ought to care about everyone's inner turmoil." Kevin, 35, was even more direct in our online survey: "Here's what drives me crazy about blogs: Just because you CAN create a blog, doesn't mean you SHOULD. Suddenly everyone is an expert on everything and feels the need to publish their opinion to the world. Credibility has become meaningless."

Many blogs are shared only among friends—it's a convenient way to update people on your life by writing one posting instead of making 15 phone calls. Blogging does this beautifully. But the system of comments, responses to comments, and so on encourages argument—and often one-sided argument. It's not a true dialogue, as a verbal conversation would be, but one diatribe followed by the response to the diatribe. Doing it all onscreen also takes out the human element of empathy, nuance, and face-to-face-interaction.

Similar problems occur in the now-ubiquitous comments sections on newspaper, video, and other sites. On newspaper sites, comments sections allow—in theory—a community of people to exchange ideas on a topic. In practice, they often descend into uninformed thirdhand banality reminiscent of the way urban legends get started: "That can't be true, because my friend's hairdresser heard . . ." No, journalists aren't always right, but they've at least been trained to consider issues with a degree of objectivity. Our modern culture instead says, "Everybody's opinion is just as valid as everyone else's," and now backs up this notion on the Internet with the proliferation of blogs and comment sections. The problem is that most of the people who leave comments have no earthly idea what they are talking about. They think they do—common among people with a tendency toward narcissism—but they're clueless. The comments that do say something intelligent are often lost in the mountain of ignorance.

Comments also invite conflict. As we'll detail in chapter 13, the comments sections on sites like YouTube descend into hostility remarkably quickly. Perhaps because they can be anonymous, people say things on these sites that they would never say to someone's face. Political arguments on newspaper comment sites get contentious quickly, and it's very difficult to separate truth from opinion. Web 2.0, says Andrew Keen in *The Cult of the Amateur,* is "ignorance meets egoism meets bad taste meets mob rule."

In a sense, blogging has a difficulty faced by all forms of communication: the signal/noise problem. In engineering, a signal is important information coming through; noise is interference, static, and irrelevant sounds. On the Web, there's lots of good stuff (signal), but there is also a tremendous amount of useless noise. The minimal filtering of blogs lets in lots of information—lots of noise, but also some interesting signal. But this lack of filtering serves as a gateway for lots of narcissistic noise masquerading as signal. In some instances, the blogs are self-policing, as in the cases where self-important, conflict-inducing posters are labeled as "trolls" and shunned. But the very nature of the blogging world makes this difficult, as these trolls can often simply pick another identity and start posting again.

I'M MUCH MORE ATTRACTIVE IN MY SECOND LIFE

Virtual worlds such as Second Life also play a role in the narcissism epidemic. Virtual worlds are entire online communities where individuals can pick out identities, or avatars, and interact with others. (*Avatar* is an interesting term for this—the word was originally used to describe the human form of a deity, especially Hindu deities that often took various earthly forms.) These virtual communities allow people the freedom to create another identity: you can pick your name, your sex, and your physical appearance. You can even have a nonhuman form if you would like. You also have the freedom to change. If your virtual life turns into a disaster, you can pick another identity and start again. Of course, all of us have the option of abandoning our families, changing our names, and running off to Costa Rica to live on the beach, but it would not be an easy task—you don't want to ruin the lives of your real kids. In the virtual world, being whoever you want to be is much easier.

Not surprisingly, people in virtual worlds tend to pick identities that are better than they are in real life. Second Life avatars, for example, include few ugly, old, or overweight people. The clothing is usually attractive and looks clean and pressed. Does this change in virtual identity influence people's virtual behavior? One fascinating study randomly assigned people to an avatar in a virtual world. In the first experiment, some individuals were given attractive avatars and some unattractive avatars. The attractive avatars were more socially confident; they walked closer to the other avatar and talked about themselves more. In the second experiment, people were assigned either a short or tall avatar and completed a negotiation task. People with a tall avatar were more competitive in the negotiation. The researchers concluded that the type of avatars people use actually change social behavior in a virtual world, which they called the Proteus Effect. It's noteworthy that the attractive avatars' behavior was consistent with greater narcissism—they talked about themselves, were more socially confident, and were more competitive.

The other important question is, Does behavior in a virtual world actually change behavior in the real world? It seems to. For example, virtual worlds can be used to treat real-life phobias. People who are afraid of flying, or have social phobias, or are scared of spiders can learn to overcome these fears in a virtual environment. The general social practices and self-beliefs learned in virtual worlds might also carry through to real life, whether this is increased narcissism or greater tolerance for different types of people.

As is the case with much of the Internet, virtual worlds both promote narcissistic behavior and have benefits for society. With Second Life, people who are housebound due to illness, are socially phobic, or socially isolated due to physical circumstances can actually have an active social life of sorts. This seems very useful, and, for shy people, this might actually be therapeutic if the confidence they gain from Second Life can make their "first life" better. Likewise, people who are trying to figure out identity issues such as sexual orientation can experience these issues in a relatively safe environment. At the same time, however, Second Life's focus on looks and somewhat shallow relationships may promote narcissism.

BROADCAST YOURSELF

The founders of YouTube originally intended it as an easy way to share video—for example, post a video of your kid walking so your relatives can see it. (Jean did, prompting her brother to observe of his one-year-old niece's wobbly steps, "She looks a little drunk.") But most of YouTube—the videos that get viewed over and over—are either broadcast TV clips (*Saturday Night Live* is popular) or people looking to promote themselves or get attention. There are a lot of YouTube videos of teenage girls singing in their living room hoping to get discovered, and almost as many of people doing something really stupid in an attempt to get attention or fame. In a culture obsessed with fame, YouTube is a new way to seek it.

Andy Warhol's idea that "in the future, we will all be famous for 15 minutes" has come true—sort of (some have commented that it should be amended to "famous for 15 seconds" or even "famous to 15 people"). Anyone with a computer and an Internet connection can gain some amount of fame. You can review a book on amazon.com, write a blog entry, comment on a blog, put up a website, or film yourself doing something stupid, violent, funny, or pornographic.

YouTube is ground zero for many of these attempts to gain fame. By one day in 2007, 264,244 people had viewed a video of someone singing the phone book, 256,450 saw a dance called the Cosmonauty, and 787,151 watched a killer tortoise. By September 2008, 210,353 had watched a video with the intriguing though grammatically garbled title "My Love Secrets to Seduce Me." Compare this to the average daily viewership of CNN, which is around 500,000—50% fewer than were gazing at the evil reptile, and only twice as many who saw the Cosmonauty dance. However, YouTube fame is more fleeting than the usual news cycle. One day the video of you doing the chicken dance while wearing a panda outfit is everywhere; the next, a guy doing a headstand on a basketball has taken your place. Warhol, clearly, was a genius.

Other people use YouTube as a way to break into Hollywood without the usual gatekeepers of producers and studio bosses. In some cases this rewards genuine (if misleading) talent, such as that of Miles Beckett, who dropped out of a surgical residency in 2005 because he wanted to be a filmmaker. He posted a series of videos on YouTube about, as he put it, "a home-schooled girl preparing for a mysterious ceremony. That girl is Lonelygirl15." Beckett's Web serial (fictional, as it turned out) continues to garner more viewers than many cable TV shows. For every Lonelygirl15, though, there are hundreds upon hundreds of YouTube videos of what amount to the rejected singers at the initial tryouts for *American Idol*. This new technology has done more than democratize entertainment—it has given millions of people the opportunity to seek the attention and fame that they crave. As YouTube cofounder Chad Hurley says, "Everyone, in the back of his mind, wants to be a star."

At least they do now. Celebrity and fame has become an equal-opportunity dream; why just read about celebrities in a magazine when you can post a video and become famous yourself? "For all the talk about coming together, Web 2.0's greatest successes have capitalized on our need to feel significant and admired and, above all, to be seen," writes Lakshmi Chaudry in the *Nation*. "The latest iteration of digital democracy has indeed brought with it a new democracy of fame, [leaving] us ever more in the thrall of celebrity, except now we have a better shot at being worshiped ourselves."

A FEW LAST THOUGHTS

We do not want to appear too simplistic or negative in our discussion of the Internet. The Internet plays many roles in society, most of which are very positive. For example, e-mail makes it possible for us authors to constantly communicate with researchers from around the world whom we have never met. This leads to the type of international collaboration that would never have been possible pre-Internet. With one of us in Georgia and the other in California, writing this book would have been very difficult without e-mail. Likewise, the Internet allows us to stay in touch with old friends and colleagues. Our friends from grad school have dispersed to jobs all over the world, but we are still able to keep in touch using e-mail (and, if we were younger, Facebook). The vast amount of information available online is also extremely useful (though only when it's correct, but that's a whole other story).

Narcissism sneaks into the picture, however, in many ways. First, the Internet allows the fantasy principle to trump the reality principle. The Internet makes it very easy to be someone you're not, and that alternative persona is usually better, or cooler, or more attractive. Second, most Internet communication is through images and brief self-description, placing attention on the shallower aspects of the person: your (carefully selected) photo, your amusing quips, your blurbs. Third, people who are desperate for attention have access to a huge potential audience on the Web, via sites such as YouTube, blogs, newspaper comment boards, and photo-rating sites. All of this encourages narcissism, and, while we like an idiotic YouTube video as much as anyone, an Internet without rampant narcissism would be a much better place.

CHAPTER 8

I Deserve the Best at 18% APR

Easy Credit and the Repeal of the Reality Principle

The man in the commercial smiles as he describes his lifestyle: a four-bedroom house, a new car, even a riding lawn mower. How does he do it? "I'm in debt up to my eyeballs," he says with a fake, forced grin.

This little ad makes an enormously important point: The boom in easy credit, which began in the 1990s and (at least for mortgages) ended spectacularly in 2007–2008, allows people to pretend they are better off than they actually are. The inflation in credit leads to inflation in self-image, helping the narcissism epidemic spread far and wide. Take a culture that promotes self-admiration and material goods, add the ability to realize this self-admiration through buying things you can't really afford, and many people live the narcissistic illusion that they are wealthy, successful, and special. Although stricter standards for mortgages have now made it more difficult to perpetuate this illusion by buying a house beyond your means, credit cards are still fairly easy to come by.

Like many of the outcomes of narcissism, the spillover from the spending binge has negative effects on other people. Everyone has to pay more when prices of goods that can be bought with easy credit—most notably houses—rocket up. The narcissist who financed a million bucks on his granite-and-stainless castle with a no-documentation loan in 2003 drove up the cost of homes for John and Suzy Saver and the property tax of Sally Senior Citizen. Pretty soon anyone who simply wanted a house in a decent school district had to be "in debt up to his eyeballs." Without easy credit, the narcissistic binge that started the process would never have happened.

Even when mortgage lending tightened after people learned the hard way, credit card debt was still easy to get. In 2005, for the first time since the Great Depression in the 1930s, Americans spent more than they earned. It wasn't always this way—in the early 1980s, Americans saved about 12% of their earnings. Now people under the age of 35 spend 16% *more* than they earn. Consumer debt has risen an average of 7.5% every year since 1997, almost twice the rate of change in the 10 previous years. Average credit card debt now exceeds $11,000, triple what it was in 1990. This adds up to a total debt load for Americans of $2.5 trillion (yes, that's a *t*). Of this, almost $1 trillion is revolving debt such as credit cards, usually considered "bad debt." Much of the rest is in home mortgages, traditionally considered "good debt." However, even this "good debt" proved not so good in 2008 as risky mortgages failed and foreclosures soared. In 2006, *before* housing crashed, the bankruptcy rate in America was still ten times what it was during the Great Depression. Many of these people, of course, were blindsided with unexpected essential expenses, often medical bills. But many others got caught up in consumer culture and easy credit.

No matter how you look at the credit picture, it isn't pretty. The first figure (on page 125) shows the outstanding U.S. consumer credit (in millions of dollars) over the last several decades. These numbers don't control for increases in population, but it's clear that credit has risen much faster than the population.

The same pattern appears in changes in the personal financial obligation ratio, which is the percentage of people's disposable income eaten up by debt payments. Again, the increase over the decades is obvious.

Harvard law professor Elizabeth Warren, an expert on credit and bankruptcy, gave a presentation at Citigroup a few years ago. She emphasized that if the bank wanted to cut their losses from people who stopped paying their credit card bills, all they had to do was stop lending to people who couldn't afford to pay. Then one of the senior executives stood up. "If we cut out those people," he told her, "we're cutting off the heart of our profits. That's where we make all of our money." In other words, banks profit when people can't pay their credit card bills and rack up lots of late fees and interest charges. This is yet another example of the cultural and macro nature of the narcissism epidemic. People didn't just wake up one day and decide they would look rich by charg-

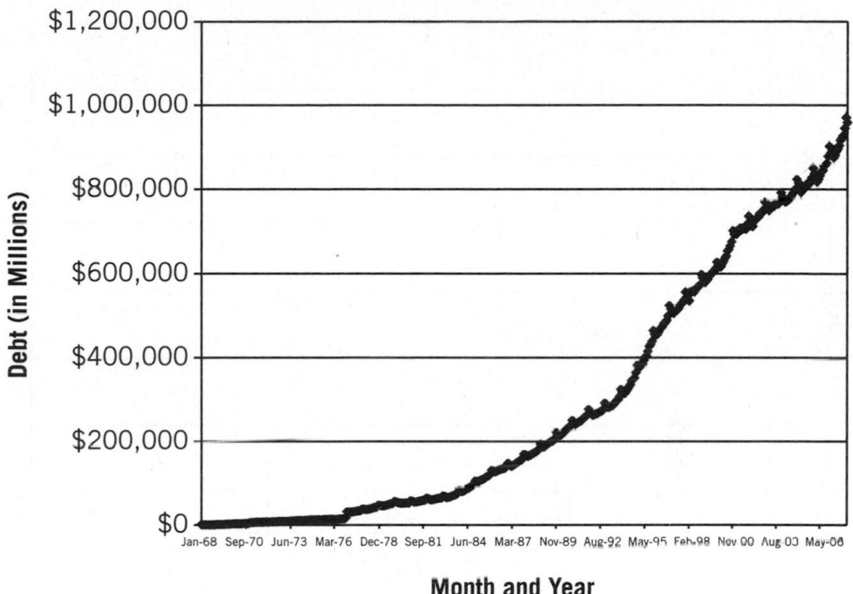

Source: United States Federal Reserve, http://www.federalreserve.gov/releases/G19/hist/cc_hist_r.html (viewed online June 8, 2008).

ing everything—banks realized they could make more money if credit was easy to obtain.

Of course, debt is not always a bad thing, especially in the short run. For several years, the debt in the economy worked out fine—consumers were spending money and banks were happy and making lots of cash. People felt like winners, started calling themselves "investors," and talked at cocktail parties about how much their homes were worth. But credit got out of hand and prices inflated too much. Then the mortgage crisis hit, housing prices began to plummet, foreclosures spiked, and suddenly the whole economy was in trouble.

This scenario could not have happened a few decades ago. Back then, credit and lenient mortgages were more difficult to come by. If you wanted to buy an expensive house but didn't make enough to afford it on a 30-year mortgage and didn't have 20% to put down, too bad—you couldn't buy the house. If you wanted a flashy car but didn't have the

Percentage of Disposable Income Going to Debt Payments, 1978–2008

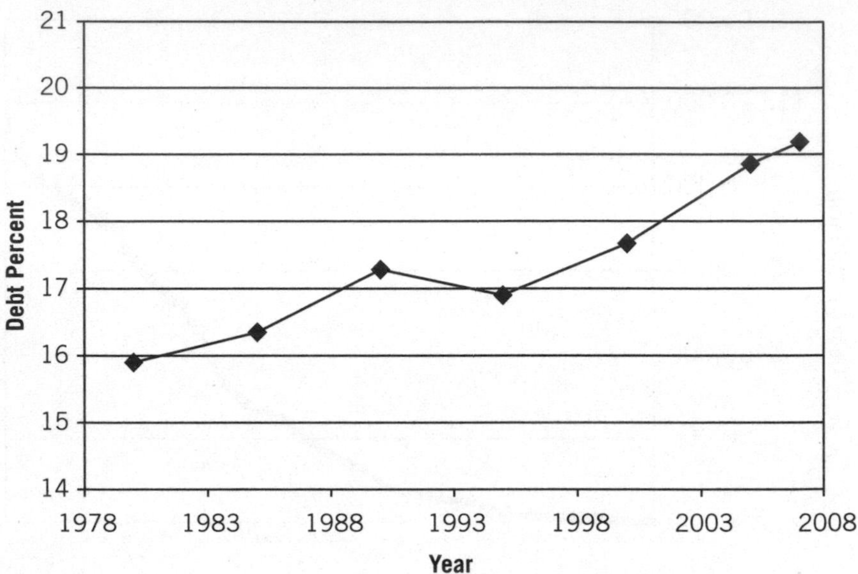

Source: United States Federal Reserve, http://www.federalreserve.gov/releases/housedebt/default.htm (viewed online June 8, 2008).

money, no go. Your lifestyle, and the image you presented to other people, was held in check by your actual wealth.

Then came interest-only loans, 0% down mortgages, car loans, and credit cards for everyone. It seemed great—everyone could get all of the expensive toys and houses they always wanted and felt entitled to, and didn't have to wait. It allows people to live like the royalty they think they are, even if they don't make enough to pay for it—at least they don't right now. Next month you'll pay off the credit card bill. OK, maybe next year. "But I really *wanted* that TV," you protest. "*Everyone* has a big flat-screen."

The availability of easy credit—in other words, the willingness and ability of some people to go into tremendous debt—has allowed people to present an inflated picture of their own success to themselves and to the world. This, of course, encouraged others to go into debt simply to "keep up." Unfortunately, buying flashy consumer goods on credit in order to look and feel like a winner is similar to hitting the crack pipe in order to improve your mood. Both are initially cheap and work really well—but only for a very short period of time. In the long term both leave you penniless and depressed. Even bankruptcy no longer offers much relief: in 2005, Congress passed the Bankruptcy Reform Act, which made discharging debts much more difficult. As getting credit got easier, the end reality got tougher.

At base, much of the economic meltdown of 2008 was caused by overconfidence and greed, two key symptoms of narcissism. Lenders, drawn by the lure of high fees, were overconfident and took the risk of writing mortgages too expensive for people to pay, and some homebuyers were overconfident in taking out those mortgages—plus, they really wanted that McMansion. Builders borrowed big and constructed acres and acres of subdivisions and condominiums, many of which now sit empty. Investment banks borrowed 30 to 40 times their available capital, using mortgages 10 times the size of homeowners' incomes as the supposedly reliable collateral. Everyone was on a narcissistic risk-taking binge and failed to anticipate the downside. As we discussed in Chapter 3, narcissistic thinking works very well in a rising market as risks pay off—banks got lots of mortgage money, and people got their houses. But narcissism is inherently an unstable, short-term strategy. When things went south, the crash was larger than usual because the risks were bigger, and narcissistic thinking was proven spectacularly wrong. Goodbye, fantasy; hello, reality! That, in a nutshell, was 2008.

THE PLEASURE PRINCIPLE

As psychologists, we authors read a lot of Freud when we were getting our degrees. Today, Freud is considered old-school—he was wrong about a lot. Nevertheless, Freud was among the first to talk about many very useful psychological principles, such as the workings of the unconscious mind. In some of his early writings, Freud described the psyche as a battle between infantile wishes, which he termed the *pleasure principle*, and the demands of the adult world, which he termed the *reality principle*. The pleasure principle appears in dreams, fantasies, and behaviors, but the dictates of reality must be heeded if the person is to function and thrive in society. Freud didn't see the reality principle as somehow better; rather, it was just reality. It had to be obeyed. Someone could have a grand fantasy life, but reality just doesn't allow those fantasies to actually occur in, well, reality.

Writer and satirist P. J. O'Rourke humorously captured this conflict in a description of God and Santa Claus. According to legend, Santa Claus buys you toys if you are good. But apparently, everyone is good (because everyone gets toys), so Santa Claus doesn't set a very high bar for behavior. Santa Claus also doesn't accept anything at all in return for the gifts he bestows. God, on the other hand, especially the Old Testament version, has a set of rules for belief and behavior. If you don't follow them, you suffer in life or burn in hell. (Even if you don't believe in God or an afterlife, you can see that bad or stupid behavior is often—maybe not often enough, but often—punished in earthly life as well.) God and earthly reality aren't always easy. Clearly, Santa Claus is far better than God in all respects. The difference, O'Rourke points out, is that Santa Claus isn't real.

The same is true of the pleasure principle. It would be great if we could live as eternal children, having our every need met and wish fulfilled. Unfortunately, this doesn't, and more importantly, can't, happen.

The image of ourselves we create by indulging the pleasure principle isn't real, but that doesn't stop us from believing in it. In a recent ad, a kid drives a soapbox racer shaped like a Hummer. All the other racers take off in front, but the kid in the faux Hummer cheats by going off-road and subsequently wins the race. This ad evokes the pleasure principle in viewers, calling to mind the childhood fantasy of vanquishing one's opponents in a soapbox derby. Try cheating like this in real life, however, and you end up being publicly humiliated. But in the fantasy world, this behavior makes sense—you win and don't get caught cheating. It's an appropriate ad for a vehicle like a Hummer, whose massive size appeals to the pleasure principle and whose massive gas bills are a drag on the reality of the pocketbook (and the planet).

We're not saying people shouldn't have dreams and fantasies. Imagining something is the first step toward making it happen. Many times, the goals we imagine become those we actually achieve, though usually after a lot of hard work. Today, however, the distance between fantasy and reality has been shortened. The reality principle has been repealed, at least temporarily, allowing people to make their fantasies become reality with little actual effort. Easy credit is the secret elixir that makes this possible.

NINJAS IN MCMANSIONS

If you want to drive a BMW, you don't have to come up with cash anymore. You can simply stroll down to the local BMW dealership and lease a car for a few hundred a month, even putting the first payment on your credit card. Rather than earning wealth, people today can borrow it and simply pretend to themselves and others that they have made it. Narcissism is linked to this quest for material goods and a "beat the Joneses" lifestyle. For narcissists, material goods such as a Rolex watch, a luxury car, and a huge kitchen with granite countertops are signals of status. Unfortunately, this type of materialism is eventually self-destructive; people who value being wealthy as an end in itself (rather than as an outcome on achieving other life goals) are less happy and more prone to depression.

As the 2007–2008 mortgage mess showed, the greatest growth of easy credit happened in home mortgages. Buying a home used to be a difficult-to-earn responsibility that involved saving up for a down payment and convincing the bank that you had more than enough to pay off the house over time on a 30-year fixed-rate loan. Not that long ago, mortgages resembled Henry Ford's statement about the Model T: you could have any color you wanted as long as it was black. Now you could have any mortgage you wanted as long as it was a 30-year fixed. That changed during the last few decades, with the array of loan products growing even more creative since 2000. First, down payments dropped from 20% to 10% to 0% or, our favorite, -2% (where you not only skip the down payment but got cash out of the house right away, often to finance the loan costs). Many mortgage lenders wrote mortgages for more than the homeowner could afford by traditional calculations. When Jean and her husband were looking to buy a house in 2005, a mortgage lender in San Diego told her they would loan her any amount of money that she "felt comfortable with."

In *Maxed Out*, James Scurlock tells the story of the cashier at Home Depot who got a mortgage for a $400,000 condo in Los Angeles, even though the monthly payment was more than twice her income. This was a "stated income" loan (otherwise known as a "liar loan"), in which "the Home Depot cashier writes down whatever income my friend tells her the bank needs to see on her application (wink, wink) and both the broker and the bank promise not to verify it (nudge, nudge)." Until things began to crash in late 2007, people were able to get loans with bad credit, poor documentation of income (no-doc loans), or so-called NINJA loans (No Income, No Job, No Assets). Both banks and homebuyers made the narcissistic assumption that home prices never go down—but even if that were true, these loans never sounded like a good idea. As Andy Serwer and Allan Sloan wrote in *Time* in September 2008, bankers were whining, "How were we supposed to know that people who lied about their income and assets would walk away from mortgages on houses in which they had no equity? That wasn't in our computer model." But it was common sense, if one backed away from the epidemic of overconfidence.

Many potential homeowners also took out risky, nonstandard loans. Adjustable-rate loans were common—pay a low interest rate for three, five or seven years, and then the rate adjusts, usually to something higher. Others were interest-only loans, allowing homeowners to pay interest but not actually pay off any of the house. Then there were the truly frightening negative amortization loans, where the initial payments were set very low, but the amount you owed actually *increased* over time. In 2004, Jean's husband polled 10 of his work colleagues and found he was the only one with a 30-year fixed mortgage. Everyone else had an adjustable or an interest-only loan. Jean and her husband felt like morons. In 2005, nearly half of new mortgages in California were interest-only, and the average down payment had fallen from 20% to 3%. Jean and her husband bought a new house at the peak of the market in late 2005, and came very close to getting an interest-only mortgage. That would have been a disaster, as home prices fell $100,000 in their neighborhood between 2005 and 2008. In other words, even psychologists who study narcissism are not immune to the modern desire for a large, comfortable home paid for with a funky mortgage.

In Southern California and other expensive housing markets, unusual loans are often used by people who just want to buy a house—even if it's a small condo. But it's also very common for middle-class people, convinced they must have 3,500 square feet and granite countertops, to use easy credit to achieve their material dreams. The standards for what material goods are deemed necessary for daily life seem to grow every year. For example, the size of new single-family houses rose from 1,905 square feet in 1990 to 2,227 in 2005. "My parents raised six children in a 1,200 sq. ft., 3 bedroom house with only one bathtub," wrote Atlanta resident Linda, 56, in our online survey. Now, of course, most suburban homes have at least two bathrooms, if not three or four, and many families with just two children would consider 1,200 square feet far too small. Just owning a home isn't good enough; it has to be a large home, preferably over 2,500 square feet and big enough so each child can have his or her own bedroom—and maybe even bathroom. At least in most middle-class families, the days of kids putting tape down the middle of the room or yelling at their sisters to get out of the one bathroom are long gone. Lots of bathrooms and chrome fixtures are great things to have, but the epidemic of narcissism has convinced us that we deserve them, and right now—and easy credit has made what should have remained a grandiose childish fantasy into a reality.

Data from the National Association of Home Builders show that over

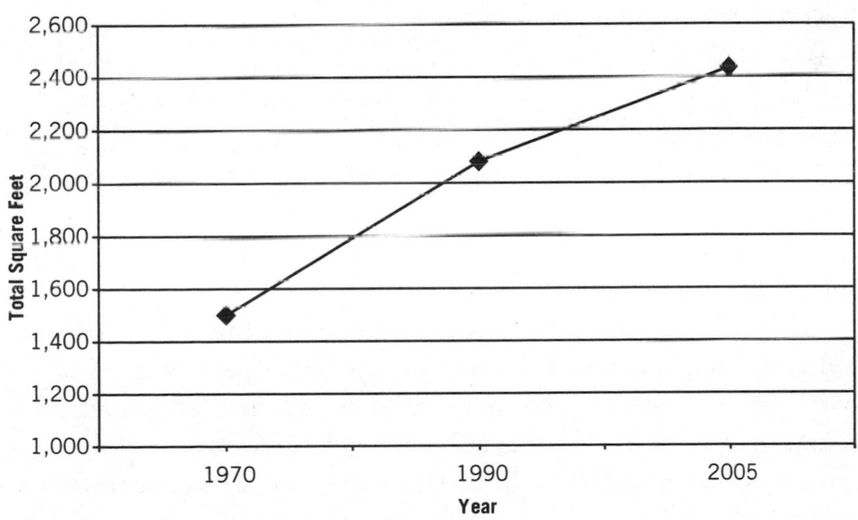

Source: National Association of Homebuilders, http://www.soflo.org/report/NAHBhousingfactsMarch2006.pdf (viewed online June 8, 2008).

Percentage of U.S. Homes 2,400 Square Feet or Larger

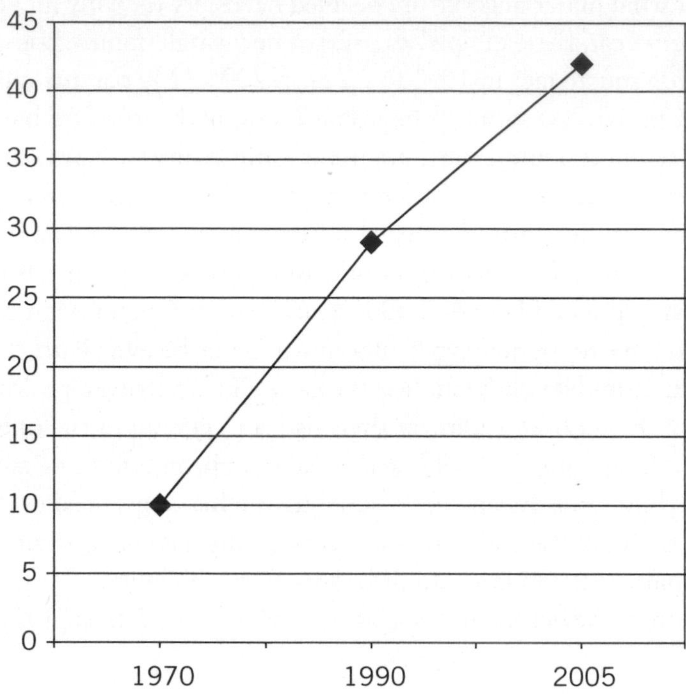

Source: National Association of Homebuilders, http://www.soflo.org/report/NAHBhousingfacts March2006.pdf (viewed online June 8, 2008).

the last 35 years, even as people were having smaller families, the size of homes increased 66%.

In addition, the number of large homes being built has increased dramatically. The number of homes exceeding 2,400 square feet has *quadrupled* since 1970. Today, nearly half of all new homes built are larger than 2,400 square feet.

Much of this trend is fueled by the desire to create more rooms for individual tasks for individual family members. The percentage of homes with only one bathroom has dropped from 52% in 1970 to under 5% today. In contrast, the number of homes with three or more bathrooms has gone from virtually none in 1970 to a little over 25% of homes today.

In the huge McMansions at the top end of the spectrum, children have individual playrooms or media rooms as well as bedrooms and private bathrooms. Some houses come equipped with theaters complete with tiered stadium seating; many others have master bedrooms that are actually suites. Keith went to a friend's new home recently and counted six rooms that made up the master bedroom suite (the bedroom itself, the bathroom, two walk-in closets, an office, and an exercise room).

There has been some backlash against the trend of building McMansions. Living in these enormous homes sounds great, but some people think that it promotes a sense of separation between family members and a distressing sense of soullessness. It also causes enormous environmental waste. In fall 2007, much of the southern United States experienced an extreme drought. Where Keith lives, in Athens, Georgia, there was a total outdoor water ban for several months. Yet in the midst of this crisis, one resident of the Atlanta suburbs used 400,000 gallons of water in one month, enough for 60 homes. The water was largely used to maintain the landscaping on a large estate.

The backlash against McMansions has resulted in some people wanting smaller homes, but not necessarily less expensive homes. This movement, described in the hugely popular architectural book *The Not So Big House*, describes how size can be exchanged for good architecture and very high-end finish work. In other words, it advocates living in a small home that is just as expensive as a big one. This approach to homebuilding is better for the environment, better for the neighbors, and probably for the soul, but not necessarily better for the debt picture.

If your quest for the monster home (or even a really sweet smaller home) was fueled by an interest-only mortgage, you will run into trouble when the payment hikes upward, you haven't paid a penny in principal on your house, you can't refinance because the value has dropped, and it gets increasingly difficult to afford food to set on those gloriously smooth countertops.

THE CASCADING CONSEQUENCES OF NARCISSISTIC SPENDING

The effects of easy credit for status seeking and luxurious living spills into society, affecting others beyond the narcissistic status seeker. Narcissism is a disease that causes others to suffer.

The government bailouts of 2008 are a prime example of this. Banks and homebuyers took narcissistic risks, and when the system imploded the American taxpayer was left holding the bag. Even people who pay off their credit cards every month, have an affordable mortgage, and take few financial risks will eventually end up paying their share of the billions, and possibly trillions, of tax dollars it will take to pay for the bailouts of firms like Bear Stearns, Fannie Mae, Freddie Mac, and AIG. Or, more likely, their children and grandchildren will.

We are not saying that narcissism is entirely responsible for the current financial crisis; poorly designed financial models and lack of oversight were culprits as well. However, the narcissism epidemic pushed people to spend beyond their means on depreciating assets and created a culture that accepted and even encouraged turning a fast buck selling risky, speculative financial products. Societal narcissism is the missing ingredient in understanding the financial meltdown.

In a recent *Newsweek* article, Eve Conant described how her grandfather, a World War II refugee, stored plastic bags of leftover bread crusts in his closet. "I also have plastic bags in my closet," writes Conant. "But they're filled with nice clothes I'm giving away because my wardrobe is too full." Conant, 36, admits, "My generation doesn't know how to be thrifty. How often do the words 'frugal' or 'thrifty' come up in conversation, especially as a compliment? The words have a distant ring of the 1930s to them." Saving is no longer cool.

Credit and other sleights of hand also make it seem like other people have much more money than you do, even if they're actually struggling just as much or more. In her book, *Green with Envy*, Shira Boss describes meeting her new neighbors: How could they possibly have afforded their condo? Wow—they hired someone to clean their house once a week. I wish *we* could afford that. It's common to get caught up in this kind of comparison today, Boss argues, because money is the Last Taboo. It's not polite to talk about it, although it's telegraphed through everything from your house to your clothes to your car to your vacations. But it's not polite to ask how much the mortgage is, or exactly how one can afford things. People hide their debt, but not their possessions. So it all looks easy—from the outside. Then the foreclosure sign goes up.

The exacerbated spending brought on by debt can also move beyond the quest for status and into the world of real sickness and pathology. Spending money on material goods provides a rush and can become an addiction. Psychologist Paul Rose found that narcissists are more likely to be compulsive shoppers, a behavior now recognized as an addiction. This shopping addiction was linked to materialism, an outcome of narcissism. Shopping addiction was also linked to impulsivity, a trait that, like narcissism, involves favoring short-term pleasures at the expense of long-term gains. In a recent MasterCard ad, a woman gets a pedicure, "has" to buy new shoes to show it off, and then "has" to get a red dress to match the shoes. The ad ends with the tagline of a narcissistic trap: "Living in the moment: priceless." The ad would have been more truthful had it said: "Paying 18% APR on a pedicure and new shoes for 20 years: Very, very expensive."

Like all addictions, shopping addictions spill over to harm other people, burning not just personal resources but also family resources. A spouse with an addiction to buying stylish clothes or flashy electronics can bankrupt an entire family. These addictions also lead to costs beyond the financial. The addict separates from others, because the pull of addiction is more important than having warm relationships. Trust breaks down as the addict tells lie upon lie about his or her spending behavior. It's estimated that 60 million Americans are addicted to shopping, and many families have been destroyed by compulsive spending.

Without easy credit, compulsive spending would be greatly reduced. The drunken sailor on shore leave can only spend until his money runs out, but the compulsive spender can spend until his credit runs out. In today's America, the well of credit is deep, and a compulsive spender will not be forced to stop until she is completely underwater.

UNCLE SAM DOES IT, TOO

As it turns out, the American consumer is just following the lead of the U.S. government, which is currently over $9 *trillion* in debt, which comes out to roughly $30,000 per citizen. And that number was calculated *before* the government started bailing out financial firms in 2008, which added somewhere around $2 trillion. Oops, make that around $37,000 per citizen.

Uncle Sam has opened a free lunch stand. Voters get free money in the form of artificially low taxes, Social Security benefits that pay more than they put into the system, and a troughful of pork projects, and, in turn, the people vote the politicians into office again and again. It amounts to a giant repeal of the reality principle, where we all get what we want. In theory, nobody has to pay for it. Outside of a brief reprieve at the end of Clinton's second term, the U.S. government has spent more money than it took in every year for decades. Almost 10% of the national debt is the interest payment on money that the government already owes.

About half of the money we spent to get into this heavy debt comes from our friends overseas. China and Japan, for example, were nice enough to lend the U.S. about $1 trillion combined. They got that money, in turn, partly from the sale of your new flat-screen TV, most likely made in China. You buy the flat-screen, the Chinese end up with some of the cash, and then lend it back to the U.S. government, which gives you a Social Security check or pays the interest on the money they borrowed last year. In 2008, when the government sunk further into debt by bailing out financial firms, the politicians got to look like heroes. Of course, it was a fantasy. These are the same politicians who got us into this mess (no, wait, it was the other party!) and all of the money was borrowed. The reality is that the United States is broke. But, hey, we all got sweet flat-screens and can still blame someone else for our problems.

The federal government has reached incredibly high levels of giving Americans something for nothing. And the citizens have no interest at all in dealing with this reality or taking any responsibility for it. They want their entitlements and pork and will kick out of office anyone who stands in their way. In the short run, everyone gets to feel good—they get their free money and can rave about what a wealthy and prosperous nation America is. In the longer term, however, the results are not likely to be pretty. In that sense, the federal debt is like drinking Bloody Marys to cure a hangover—it works in the short run, but not forever. The country is already seeing some of the consequences: Many economists say that the dollar has sunk in value partially because of our enormous national debt. In 2008, the U.S. dollar hit a record low against the euro, and, for the first time since 1977, was roughly equal to the Canadian dollar.

WHAT DID WEALTHY PEOPLE DO TO GET THAT WAY?

If a good chunk of the country—and the federal government—is living the fantasy of being wealthy big spenders, what do actual wealthy people do? Are they engaged in a debt binge as well? Not really. The secret to accumulating assets is building something of value such as a business or investment portfolio, or simply saving income. Multimillionaires didn't get that way by buying iPods and BMWs on credit. The most successful people substitute the immediate desire to look wealthy with the longer-term goal to actually accumulate wealth. In other words, they choose to follow the reality principle instead of the pleasure principle.

Thomas Stanley and William Danko, authors of *The Millionaire Next Door,* initially believed millionaires would have expensive tastes and habits. As they found out after some research, however, this wasn't true. At one meeting with people worth at least $10 million, the authors set up a table with the fancy food and wine they thought the millionaires would like. But when they offered a glass of high-end wine to one, he turned it down flat. "I drink two kinds of beer," he said. "Free and Budweiser!"

The millionaires Stanley and Danko studied were, in a word, frugal. Many drove used cars, spent very little, and saved large sums of money. Of the seven key factors Stanley and Danko identified in millionaires, at least two are directly at odds with narcissism. First, the authors found, millionaires live well below their means. Second, millionaires "believe that financial independence is more important than displaying high social status." So the wealthy people Stanley and Danko interviewed were not running after status, but instead wanted to achieve actual wealth and independence. Our current narcissistic culture asks, "Why be wealthy if you can't show it off?" Yet many millionaires said that having wealth gave them a sense of freedom, a feeling that far outweighed the fleeting pleasures of *looking* wealthy.

The findings presented in *The Millionaire Next Door* are counterintuitive. Americans see people with fancy cars and clothes and assume they must be rich. In reality, it is often safer to assume that they are in debt. The credit crunch that paralyzed the economy in the late 2000s is, at base, the conflict between the pleasure principle and the reality principle. Narcissism works on the pleasure principle—it looks great and gets what it wants, but it hurts other people and even the self in the long run. In contrast, the reality principle isn't flashy or self-promoting, but it does lead to actual wealth. At least until 2008, most Americans were living on the narcissistic pleasure principle. Easier and easier credit allowed them to live out grandiose, materialistic fantasies—until the bill came due.

Credit has now tightened, at least for mortgages, and this might lead to a slowing of the narcissism epidemic. But funky mortgages like interest-onlys make banks money most of the time, so they are probably here to stay. And it's still pretty easy to get a credit card—Keith's daughters (both under age six) get credit card offers all the time. When babies can drool on their first credit cards, it's time to worry.

SECTION 3

SYMPTOMS OF NARCISSISM

CHAPTER 9

Hell Yeah, I'm Hot!

Vanity

The woman in the commercial laughs, opening her mouth wide as she throws her head back in delight. A female voice exclaims, "Don't hold back! Express yourself by asking your doctor about BOTOX Cosmetic! It's all about freedom of expression." Botox injections were given 3.2 million times in 2006 alone, 49 times more often than in 1997. According to the Botox website, the procedure "reduces the activity of the muscles that cause those frown lines between the brows to form over time." In other words, you'll actually be expressing yourself a lot *less* after you get Botox. But that didn't stop the advertising campaign, which taps into the narcissism epidemic by promising both the individualistic value of personal expression and the physical vanity ideal of looking younger. You can't actually have both at the same time, but people want both, so it is promised.

Americans' growing obsession with appearance is a clear symptom of a narcissistic culture in love with its own reflection. True to the Greek myth, narcissists believe that they are more attractive than other people (even though, objectively, they're not). Narcissistic college students post sexier photos of themselves on Facebook than humbler students. It is possible to guess that someone might be a narcissist just by looking at them or seeing their photograph. A fascinating study by Simine Vazire and her colleagues found that narcissists are more likely to wear expensive, attention-getting clothing. Female narcissists wear more makeup and show more cleavage, and narcissists of both sexes are more likely to present a "put-together" look that requires a lot of preparation and time.

In other words, narcissists use their appearance as a way to seek status and attention from others.

In her famous song "You're So Vain," Carly Simon sings, "You had one eye on the mirror as you watched yourself." Narcissists like watching themselves on videotape, and report gaining self-confidence from gazing at their reflection in a mirror. The Narcissistic Personality Inventory contains items such as "I like to look at myself in the mirror," "I get upset when people don't notice how I look when I go out in public," and "I like to show off my body." Vanity seems harmless and often is, but vanity often occurs with self-centeredness, which causes so many of the negative behaviors associated with narcissism. College student Amanda Knox, accused of murdering her roommate, wrote in her jailhouse diary, "When I have an hour of outside time I sit with my face in the sun so I can get a tan. I have received letters from fellow inmates and admirers telling me that I am hot and they want to have sex with me."

We are not saying that everyone who has plastic surgery or Botox, wears expensive clothes, or shows cleavage is narcissistic. The narcissism epidemic has made these appearance enhancers not just more acceptable, but, in some neighborhoods, almost expected. As with other aspects of the epidemic, the trend was started by narcissistic people and then relentlessly pulled in the less self-centered. Put simply, standards have changed. A few decades ago a mother who had some belly flab was normal; looking matronly after you hit a certain age (back then, around 40, even 30) was par for the course. Now 40- and even 50-year-old women wear bikinis and belly shirts—at least the celebrities do, and in today's culture that means the rest of us aspire to it. But you have to have the stomach to pull it off, so under the knife you go. Or you forgo surgery, wear the belly shirt, and let it all hang out, displaying the other side of narcissism: complete obliviousness to how you actually appear to others ("I look really hot!").

Beauty has always been a virtue, but lately its pursuit has reached new levels. There is a new standard of vanity, where it's not enough to be beautiful; you have to be hot. Singer Avril Lavigne knows this very well—she appeared, apparently topless, on a magazine cover behind a yellow banner reading, "Hell, Yeah, I'm Hot!" There is even a popular website, hotornot.com, where people upload images of themselves to be rated by strangers. Ratings are made on a 10-point scale (10 is "hot," and 1 is "not"). According to the website, an amazing 12 *billion* votes have been cast to rate people's hotness.

Paris Hilton, one of the promoters of "hot" as the ultimate virtue, exemplifies the new vanity. When Paris's cell phone was stolen in 2004, it contained picture after picture of . . . herself. Above the sofa in her Hollywood home, Paris has hung a large picture of herself. And why not, given how much time and money she has spent on her appearance? Paris regularly applies self-tanner, uses hair extensions, whitens her teeth, and even wears blue contacts over her brown eyes, all recent innovations in the science of looking good. "One of my heroes is Barbie," Paris says. "She may not do anything, but she always looks great doing it."

IN PURSUIT OF HOTNESS

Many more people are doing many more things in the name of looking hot. Even for those who don't go under the knife (or the botulinum), appearance enhancement is on the rise. As recently as the 1990s, no one really cared if your teeth were a little yellow. Now that's a clear sign that you've let yourself go or can't afford teeth whitening at the dentist (or even Crest Whitestrips). In the '90s toothpaste buyers worried about tartar buildup and damage to the gums; in the 2000s we worry about whether our teeth are white enough.

Although your teeth should be white, your skin should not be. Tanning beds are popular, with parents worrying about teenagers using them too much. Self-tanners, virtually unknown ten years ago (partially because they once turned you orange), have skyrocketed in popularity, allowing you to get a natural-looking tan through sprayed-on pigment. And before you get your spray tan, be sure your body hair is perfect—particularly your eyebrows. Apparently this all began with Eliza Petrescu, who calls herself "the original arch artist." According to her website, Eliza "put brow styling on the beauty map, turning it into a grooming ritual that is not a trend, but a 'must-do' for both men and women." For a mere $120, Eliza will design the ideal look for your eyebrows. Just like teeth-whitening, eyebrow-shaping has spread: the celebrities do it, then your boss does it, your kids will want to do it, and then you will want to do it so you don't look like a Neanderthal. Next thing we know an "arch artist" will show up on Sesame Street, and we'll never recognize Bert again.

Twenty years ago, most Americans thought a spa was a big round tub with hot water and bubbles. Now it's common to take a "spa day" at a location where you can be pampered with pedicures, manicures, mud wraps, massages, yoga, and even cosmetic procedures like Botox. The number of spas has doubled since 1997, and the number of spa visits has tripled. More and more hotels and resorts offer spa treatments, and their array of services continues to expand.

Many of these tweakings of physical beauty were always fairly common in Hollywood and among actors, but standards once held only at Warner Bros. have trickled down to the rest of the population. A weight loss product promises, "Look like a Hollywood Star with the Wu-Yi System!" Many of our survey respondents mentioned how standards had changed since their parents' generation. "I feel more pressure than ever to do things to improve my physical appearance," said Jennifer, 35, from Tulsa, Oklahoma. "I color my hair and also wax my eyebrows. My mother NEVER did any of these things and was always very socially accepted and even admired. Coloring your hair and having hair removal are two practices that are now mainstream and 'required' to just live up to societal standards."

Some of these standards involve the continuing juvenalization of our culture. Not that long ago, looking older, particularly for men, was considered distinguished and respectable. Having gray hair was OK. Ditto for body hair. In the 1970s male body hair was considered attractive—think Burt Reynolds. It was a sign of masculinity: men have chest hair, boys do not. Not anymore, when everyone from 10-year-olds to 50-year-olds wants to look like a teenager or twenty-something. Young girls are aspiring to be teens much earlier; many third-graders now wear makeup, get professional pedicures, and have makeover sessions for their birthdays. Some twelve-year-olds get spray tans and eyebrow waxes. It's no coincidence that adolescence, the time of life that people of many ages now aspire to emulate, is also the peak of narcissism, and the peak time to concentrate on your appearance.

Perhaps because of the focus on youth, showing off the body has become much more common. As late as the mid-'90s, it was fashionable for women to wear big blousy shirts and generous, empire-waist dresses. Now it's more stylish to wear pants low enough to show off the obligatory thong, and a shirt low enough to show plenty of cleavage. High school prom dresses, once poofy, pastel tents, are now tight and strapless, and many have low-cut bodices or slits cut in the fabric to show the midriff. Jean was watching a 1988 episode of *Moonlighting* on DVD recently and was surprised to see that the vixen whom Bruce Willis's character picks up in a bar, although undeniably attractive, was wearing an outfit with a high neck that covered her entire body from her knees to her chin. Jean shouldn't have been that surprised; her own prom dress in 1989 resembled a mint-green tent.

There are now no excuses not to show skin. "It's not socially acceptable anymore to be able to say, 'I had a baby, so I gained ten pounds, so what?' " wrote Emily, 27, in our survey. "All of these celebrities have babies and look anorexic again two weeks later." Leaf through the pages of *People*, *Us Weekly*, or *Life & Style* and you'll see what Emily means. Nearly every magazine has a "Body after Baby" feature that highlights the genetically blessed (or personal trainer blessed), with the obvious implication that you, too, should be able to wear a bikini and look perfectly toned while holding your four-month-old. Women now aspire to be a MILF. (That stands for "mother I'd like to fuck." The modern age is nothing if not direct.) When Tori Spelling heard that there might be an update of *Beverly Hills, 90210*, she said, "They should give me a call. Every teen drama needs a MILF, right?" One blogger responded to her comment by writing, "It's called dignity, people. Derive some from something other than the fact that you remain, after childbirth, f*ckable in the eyes of horny TV-addicted guys who would probably f*ck anything anyways."

Displaying a tight stomach is now popular, all under the guise "If you've got it, flaunt it." Flaunt it is right. Students at San Diego State, where Jean teaches, participate in an "Undie Run" at the end of the fall semester every year (for charity . . . but nevertheless . . .). Pictures from the 2007 event, posted on a public website, show an expanse of well-toned undergraduate flesh posing for the camera, including three young women wearing briefs that say "Take My Photo" on the rear. In the picture, they stand with their buns to the camera, pointing at the slogan.

College students in their underwear are tame compared to what's now going on in high school. A 2008 survey found that a shocking 1 out of 4 teen girls has sent a nude or nearly nude picture of herself via the Internet or cell phone. These images, sometimes meant for one person, often end up circulating to hundreds of other teens.

One of the dark sides of the cultural emphasis on physical appearance is the increase in eating disorders. Many people with eating disorders suffer from the "vulnerable" subtype of narcissism, which is often accompanied by anxiety and depression. The combination of self-admiration with the social pressure to look physically attractive—both of which are present in the current cultural climate—are a recipe for creating eating disorders.

In some cases, vanity has taken on an even more narcissistic taste of competition, perhaps best exemplified by the popular hip-hop song that asks, "Don't cha wish your girlfriend was hot like me?" High school girls in some communities now "flirt" with guys they like by sending them nude pictures of themselves. In Columbus, Ohio, one girl sent such a picture and then called the guy and asked, "Am I better than your girlfriend?" As we'll see in Chapter 13, on relationships, these are not the behaviors likely to lead to a stable, emotionally close relationship (though it could certainly lead to a brief hookup). In most cases, the purpose of vanity isn't long-term relationships, but getting attention from as many people as possible.

Men are not immune to new high standards for appearance. It's now important for men to have a "cut" chest with "six-pack" abs. Times have changed: Ponch (the early '80s star of *CHiPs*) was considered a hunk even though he did *not* have ripped abs. But metrosexuals do, plus they know what moisturizer is. Even before the phenom of *Queer Eye for the Straight Guy*, grooming for men was becoming more important. Men's skin care is one of the fastest-growing segments in the multibillion-dollar grooming industry, with sales up almost 50% in 2005 alone. This is especially true for younger generations, who "get their bodies waxed, work out, style their hair, [and] go to tanning salons more than their predecessors," says Edina Sultanik-Silver, owner of a men's fashion public relations company. Why do they do this? "Because they were raised on MTV, the Internet and reality shows. Every minute of their lives is a photo-op, [so] they always want to look like they're ready for their 15 minutes of fame," she explains.

This is even more true of women. It's no coincidence that Abby, a 25-year-old who told her story in a Lifetime TV documentary, is more than $30,000 in debt partially because she "has" to have manicures, professional hair coloring, and the best clothes. When she went shopping with a friend, they described clothes as "a Jennifer Aniston type look" or "I saw these in a magazine with Jessica Alba wearing them." It's as if the paparazzi would be snapping their picture any moment. And when they do—even if the paparazzi are just your loved ones—it is important to look good. After Melissa, 31, had her first child, she sent her pregnant friends her "tips" for the hospital, which included having hairbrush and makeup ready so you can stop to primp before you push. The purpose? So you'll look more glamorous in the pictures of you and the baby after the birth.

UNDER THE KNIFE: PLASTIC SURGERY AS MUNDANE

If your stomach doesn't go back after those fabulous postbirth pictures are taken, just have surgery. The "mommy makeover"—breast lifts, tummy tucks, and breast augmentations done after having a few kids—is a growing trend, with 325,000 women ages 20 to 39 undergoing these surgeries in 2006. "Everyone I know says they are getting their boobs fixed after they have kids, and I don't know anyone in my mom's generation who did that!" says Katie, 27, from Denver.

Explaining plastic surgery to your kids is now such a common dilemma that plastic surgeon Michael Salzhauer published *My Beautiful Mommy* in 2008, telling kids what happens when mom gets a nose job, a breast augmentation, and a tummy tuck. The cover shows a thin but big-breasted young mother wearing a shirt that exposes her taut abdomen, surrounded by fairy dust, stars, and a butterfly. Her little girl stands on tiptoes next to her, arms spread wide in admiration as she holds her teddy bear in one tiny hand and smiles broadly at her mother with a delighted expression as if to say "I'm so proud of my mommy's flat tummy!" Inside the book, we see the mother visiting the doctor (all the girl hears of the details is "Blah, blah, blah") and then resting in bed with bandages on her nose and stomach. In the end, of course, the little girl is thrilled with her mother's "prettier" nose and how she "feels better." The text side-

Americans Undergoing Cosmetic Procedures (1997–2007)

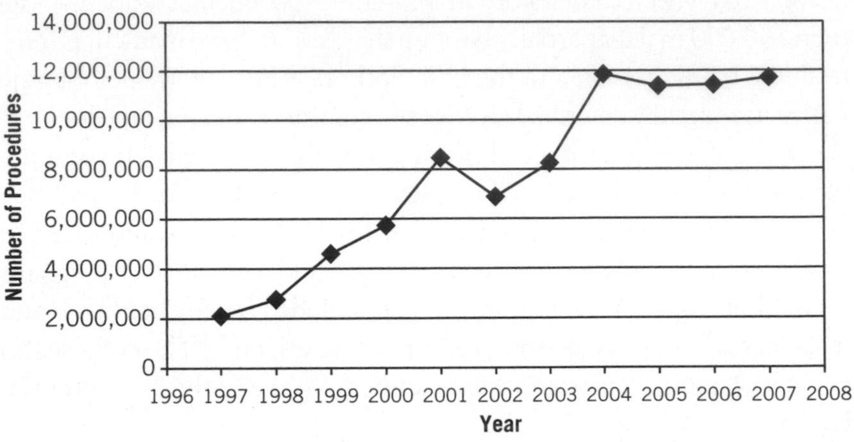

Source: American Society for Aesthetic Plastic Surgery, *Cosmetic Surgery National Data Bank Statistics, 1997–2007*, http://www.surgery.org/press/statistics-2007.php (viewed online September 18, 2008).

steps mention of the breast implants, but the "after" illustrations intentionally show Mom with fuller and higher breasts.

Plastic surgery, once relegated to women of a certain age living in Manhattan or Hollywood, has moved younger and more mainstream. The number of breast augmentation surgeries performed on American teens increased 55% in just the one year between 2006 and 2007. Overall, about 11.7 million people in the United States had cosmetic surgery and procedures in 2007, an 8% increase from 2006 and more than 5 times as many as in 1997. Botox was the most common procedure, accounting for much of the upswing (only 65,157 people got Botox in 1997, compared to 42 times more—2.8 million—in 2007). "I have had Botox. Everyone has!" claims actor David Hasselhoff.

Invasive surgeries are also increasingly popular. Four times as many women had breast augmentation surgery in 2007 (almost 400,000) than did in 1997, and more than twice as many had liposuction (almost half a million). Some of this increase can be attributed to the aging of the Baby Boom generation, but younger people seem to be catching the plastic surgery bug much earlier and are much more approving of the prac-

Rates of Specific Cosmetic Surgeries (1997–2007)

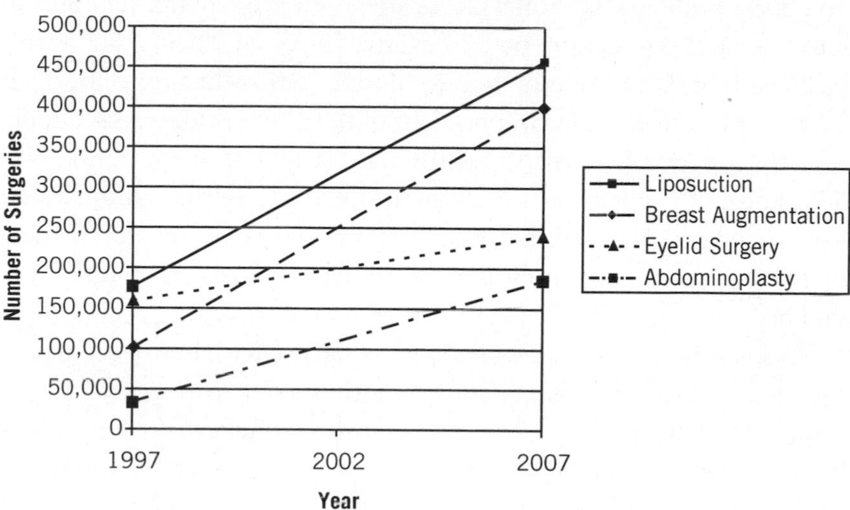

Source: American Society for Aesthetic Plastic Surgery, *Cosmetic Surgery National Data Bank Statistics, 1997–2007*, http://www.surgery.org/press/statistics-2007.php (viewed online September 18, 2008).

tice. A 2008 poll found that 69% of people 18 to 24 approved of cosmetic surgery. Among those over 65, in contrast, only 41% approved. Younger and younger Hollywood stars declare their comfort with plastic surgery as a way to lengthen their careers. "Oh, I definitely believe in plastic surgery. I don't want to be an old hag. There's no fun in that," said Scarlett Johansson. At the time, she was 21.

"It makes sense that young people are the most approving of plastic surgery," said Dr. Foad Nahai, president of the American Society for Aesthetic Plastic Surgery. "Twenty years ago people thought only movie stars and rich women had plastic surgery. Now people grow up knowing friends and family who openly talk about the plastic surgery procedures they have had or the ones they plan to have in the future." The reasons for surgery have also changed: not that long ago, plastic surgery was primarily used to help people with congenital malformations, burns, or facial injuries look like everyone else—not to help them look better than others or look younger.

As the *New York Times* explained in an article titled "It's Botox for You, Dear Bridesmaids," some brides are now asking their attendants to have cosmetic skin treatments. A Beverly Hills cosmetic surgeon says his business is up 40% since he began offering "Bridal Beauty Buffets" in 2006. William F. Heaton III, president of the Great Bridal Expo Group, says that in just five years, booths for plastic surgeons, dermatologists, and tooth whitening went from nearly zero to very common. Becky Lee's friend asked her and five other bridesmaids to have breast enhancement surgery—the surgeon was even willing to offer a "group rate." She said no.

In some circles, enhanced body parts have the cachet of an expensive luxury product. *Beauty Junkies* author Alex Kuczynski saw an acquaintance at the ballet one evening who promptly threw open her blouse to reveal, inside her lacy bra, the results of a surgery performed by Dr. David Hidalgo. "Darling," she said, "Just look at my Hidalgos! I got them two weeks ago!"

Lots of people who can't afford "Hidalgos" are also having appearance-enhancing surgery. The large majority of people interested in plastic surgery earn less than sixty thousand dollars a year. In June 2008, *People* magazine profiled a postal worker, a soldier, a dental assistant, and a police officer who had all gone under the knife, spending between $5,500 and $15,200 for breast implants and neck lifts. The postal worker put the $7,000 bill for her tummy tuck on her credit card at 9.9% interest.

Television shows have made plastic surgery cool. MTV's *I Want a Famous Face* features young people who get plastic surgery to resemble their favorite celebrity. The show's website explains, "*I Want a Famous Face* returns to follow the transformations of twelve young people who have chosen to use plastic surgery to look like their celebrity idols. Whether it's a Pamela Anderson wanna-be or a Janet Jackson hopeful, their goals are not just to look different, but to look exactly like their favorite stars." Twenty-year-old twins Matt and Mike, for example, wanted to look like Brad Pitt so they could become famous actors. (As is often the case, several symptoms of our narcissistic culture are entwined. Here, vanity meets the quest for fame and celebrity, with a dose of self-admiration thrown in: the online video clip from this episode is titled,

"The guys find confidence.") *Extreme Makeover* transformed people into good-looking shadows of their former selves through chin implants, tooth veneers, tummy tucks, and breast augmentations, as well as more conventional makeover staples such as new hairstyles, makeup, and better clothes. A similar show, *The Swan*, employed extensive plastic surgery to remake people into their ideal physical selves. And if you're still looking for your plastic surgery reality fix, there's always *Dr. 90210*.

These shows go beyond entertainment—they have apparently influenced many of the people who show up at plastic surgeons' offices. A research study published in the medical journal *Plastic and Reconstructive Surgery* found that an incredible 4 out of 5 plastic surgery patients reported that television shows influenced them to seek cosmetic surgery. Those who watched these shows on a regular basis felt more knowledgeable about cosmetic surgery and believed that these shows realistically portrayed what plastic surgery is like.

A 2008 poll found that 79% of Americans say they would not be embarrassed if other people knew they'd had plastic surgery. One out of 3 women said she would consider having cosmetic surgery, as would 1 out of 5 men. "There's no doubt that many Americans feel more pressure to look perfect," said one plastic surgeon. "There's certainly an emphasis on youth and . . . self-improvement. For some people that's a new suit or makeup. Plastic surgery is just an extension of that. It's one more option."

A recent ad in a mainstream magazine deadpans, "You know that feeling when you find the perfect pair. And we're not talking shoes." It goes on to detail "The Natrelle Breast Enhancement Collection," featuring both silicone and saline options "for you and your surgeon to consider." Another ad features three women and one man, all perfectly toned and clothed only in skimpy swimwear. Two of the women have dashed lines, arrows, and X's drawn on their skin in black, suggesting that they are about to have plastic surgery (including dashed lines around one woman's already overly firm, probably already surgically enhanced breasts). "Happily ever . . . what's your after?" asks the ad for Equinox—not a plastic surgery practice, but a fitness club. The ad takes it for granted that most people will recognize the dashed lines on the women's skin, and will conclude that a fitness club might be less expensive though require more effort to achieve the same results (well, except for the fake boobs).

Plastic surgery is increasingly common among ethnic minorities in the United States. More than three times as many Asian-Americans got plastic surgery in 2007 than in 2000, primarily eyelid surgery, nose jobs, and breast augmentations. Twice as many African-Americans got surgery, most commonly nose jobs, liposuction, and breast reduction. Surgeries nearly tripled among Hispanic-Americans, usually for breast augmentation, nose jobs, and liposuction. Although many of these procedures are common among whites as well, the numbers suggest that minorities are favoring a white ideal of beauty, with Asians wanting to change their eyelids and blacks their noses. The increase in plastic surgery rates between 2006 and 2007 was twice as steep among minorities as among whites.

More and more men are also going under the knife or the Botox injection. The number of cosmetic surgeries and procedures performed on men increased 17% in just one year between 2006 and 2007. Almost 10 times as many men underwent noninvasive procedures such as Botox in 2007 compared to 1997. "A lot of baby boomer men are at the age now when changes are more significant, and there's a greater acceptance of plastic surgery," says Dr. Michael McGuire, vice president of the American Society of Plastic Surgeons, who also noted that his patients are now 20% male, double the proportion of a few years ago. Now men don't feel the need to make excuses. "I can't deny that I'm a little vain," said Steven Goldgram, who got a facelift and a nose job. "I just wanted to look better."

It is now possible for pets to get cosmetic surgery. Pumpkin the dog got liposuction, and Bode had a facelift ("I've had my nips and tucks," explained her owner, pointing to her own face). Some dogs even have breast reductions. The most popular surgery is inserting false testicles (called "Neuticles") to the scrotum of a male dog who's been neutered. The dog doesn't really understand the difference, but the owners like the idea. As the reporter covering this story asked, "Are there any limits to the cosmetic surgery phenomenon, or have we all simply gone nuts?"

THE REASONS BEHIND THE NEW VANITY

Why the rise in the obsession with appearance? Much of today's desire for physical beauty springs from the fountain of self-admiration. For narcissistic people, good looks are just another way of gaining attention, status, and popularity. Having perfectly white teeth, great hair, a new sports car, or an attractive girlfriend all serve the same psychological function, making others think you are cool, special, popular or important. This desire to appear attractive is clear when you compare objective photos of narcissists with the photos they choose for public viewing—narcissists are more likely to choose a flattering photograph of themselves. We've all done this at some point. Keith once had a photo taken for his Web page that involved the strategic use of shadow to hide his double chin and pasty skin, a blue light shining from the side that made him look like he was on the Discovery Channel talking about alien ESP, and a bunch of images of brains on a computer screen to make him look smart—a smooth photo, but not really representative.

Many people have embraced narcissistic vanity in the quest for "self-esteem." Perhaps due to the desire to look tan, the skin cancer rate among women 15 to 34 has jumped 20% in the last decade. Yet ask young women why they still tan, and 18-year-old Jackie Harris's answer is typical: "It makes me feel better about myself. Right now, the idea of skin cancer doesn't concern me." Many people name "self-esteem" or some variant of self-admiration as why they had surgery (though much of what passes for self-esteem in our culture is actually narcissism). In this worldview, self-admiration is worth risking skin cancer or surgical complications. As Kuczynski writes, "The term self-esteem is a mantra that is repeated, yogalike" on plastic surgery reality TV shows. One man who had a neck lift and eyelid surgery explained, "I want to feel better about myself."

This reasoning is taught early. A website for teenagers considering plastic surgery advises, "Ask yourself if you're considering plastic surgery because you want it for yourself or whether it's to please someone else." The site implies that if you want it for yourself, it's OK. That's Ashlee Simpson's philosophy, too. After the singer got a nose job in 2006, she opined that plastic surgery "should be for yourself." An article titled "From drab to fab!" in *People* magazine peddled this philosophy as well, showing a picture of a haggard-looking woman with the caption "Your hair's lack of maintenance reflects your lack of love for yourself."

Extreme Makeover's website brought it all together. "Wearing the right clothes is . . . about owning something and turning it into something that's you. It's about attitude. Just look at celebrities on the red carpet. . . . It's their sheer confidence that you really want to grab on to, because that confidence transforms you into a star. . . . Stars don't put themselves on public display unless they're able to grab the attention of their audience, and that's the case even on their days off. At their frumpiest they are still starlike. The applause, the adulation, and their here-I-am attitude shape their style, their personalities, and how they carry themselves in their clothes."

Matt and Mike, the twins who went on MTV's *I Want a Famous Face* to resemble Brad Pitt, have also signed on to the self-admiration reasoning for plastic surgery. In a Q&A on the MTV website, the network asked, "What would you say to teens reading this who are thinking about getting elective plastic surgery?" Matt replied, "Why are you waiting? If any part of you drains all your self-esteem, then why live like that?" His brother Mike agreed: "Those who are down on themselves for a fault in their looks, if you know that surgery will make you happy, go for it."

With so many narcissistic individuals putting in the effort to look "hot"—and many others feeling compelled to improve their appearance in the interest of self-admiration—what happens to people who don't put all that much thought into looking good? Before long, everyone gets dragged into the "focus on looks" game. A sense develops that if you don't have the appropriate white teeth, cosmetic procedures, or abs, you should be embarrassed. There are even potential financial consequences to all of this. Some people now get surgical procedures such as chin implants or facelifts because they want to look young and energetic enough to get hired for a job. Some Hollywood actors and rappers (not to mention athletes) are reportedly taking human growth hormone and steroids in order to stay attractive and hip.

The emphasis on vanity appears in almost every realm of society: the media, the Internet, business, and even parenting. Only education has remained relatively immune to focusing on physical appearance, perhaps because of the stereotype that smart people are somewhat slovenly. When you think "nerd," you do not usually think "hot." Keith still takes pride in the times he has shown up to teach with two different shoes on. Even education is getting drawn in, however. On the popular website ratemyprofessor.com, professors whom students rated as "hot" receive a chili pepper icon. The site even lists the hottest professors in the country.

Television is one of the major forces pushing the importance of physical appearance in America and around the world. Every year since a youthful Jack Kennedy defeated a tired-looking Richard Nixon in a televised debate, American culture has become increasingly focused on appearance. Almost everyone on television is good-looking, placing more value on appearance and raising standards for looks. Even actors playing highly skilled brain surgeons have to be eye candy (ergo the smorgasbord of beauty that is *Grey's Anatomy*). Likewise, "reality" TV is far from real in terms of beauty. Shows like *Fear Factor* or *Survivor* that involve eating large insects or not showering for extended periods of time are still populated largely by great-looking people. And news reporters and anchors are certainly not a random selection of top journalism graduates. It's assumed that eye candy is necessary to get people to pay attention to the news. The classic example of this is Greta Van Susteren, who hosts a legal show on Fox News. By all accounts she is a very bright attorney and aggressive journalist, but as soon as she got her own show, she had extensive plastic surgery. This didn't seem so much an act of rampant individual narcissism on Van Susteren's part, but an outcome of cultural pressure to be attractive no matter how bright you are.

The same pressure for looks is also seen on the Internet. With the advent of digital photography and online dating, blind dates aren't so blind anymore (though they might be Photoshopped). Fifty years ago, people already knew everyone in their small town, so these things weren't an issue. There were only so many potential partners out there, you knew them all pretty well, and nobody was going to be able to make a radically new impression by getting a new haircut or outfit, much less plastic surgery. Now most people live in urban areas and meet new people almost every day; physical appearance is the first, and sometimes the only, thing they see. Finding a mate depends not on family contacts but on looks. This is even more true of hookups, the short-term sexual encounters now the norm among young people and that have all but replaced dating and boyfriend-girlfriend relationships. When you have to find a different sexual partner every time, appearance becomes paramount. "Only ugly people date," explains a TV character. So you better go buy that teeth whitener.

Some of the focus on appearance has been fueled by the trend toward the raunchy becoming conventional in other forms of media. As Ariel Levy documents in *Female Chauvinist Pigs*, ordinary college women now lift their shirts to reveal their breasts in *Girls Gone Wild* videos. Porn is now accepted as ordinary, with formerly risqué performers like Ron Jeremy and Jenna Jameson enjoying mainstream appeal. Jameson's book *How to Make Love Like a Porn Star*, for example, was a bestseller in 2004.

It is now not just acceptable but desirable to look like a porn star. For women, that means breast implants, continuous tans, and unnaturally groomed pubic hair. "Everyone I know waxes themselves these days—bikini waxes, eyebrow waxes, lip waxes, etc. are all just part of our regular 'beauty routines.' My mom says NO ONE got bikini waxes when she was my age, but people I know (including myself) just do it regularly now, as if it's unacceptable to have pubic hair or something!" wrote Katie, 27, in our online survey. As Alex Kuczynski writes, "Women who would never have even uttered the phrase bikini wax twenty years ago now have their nether regions shaped and trimmed and cleared of hair in the style of Brazilian bikini wearers (i.e., there's no hair left or, if there is any, it is just the tiniest symbolic strip to suggest adulthood)." Kuczynski notes that plastic surgeons are getting more and more requests for labiaplasty, presumably because most women's vaginas don't look as perfect as those of female porn stars. "I've spent so much money for the rest of me to look like Dolly Parton," says a woman Kuczynski interviewed. "So why should that," she says, glancing downward, "look like Willie Nelson?"

One would hope that parents were counteracting this trend. Most parents love their children no matter how beautiful or homely they are. And to a point, parents' unconditional love removes some of the pressure to seek beauty. However, parents are becoming more and more focused on enhancing their children's looks. More parents are paying for children's cosmetic surgery, with some parents giving breast augmentation surgery as a graduation gift. Many of these procedures are desired by the teens, but there are also cases where the parent pushes the teen toward getting the procedure. Sometimes this is done for the parents' own vanity (I don't want to be embarrassed by my unattractive kid), but it also comes out of concern for a child. Parents want their children to fit into today's image-obsessed culture.

TREATMENT FOR THE EPIDEMIC

In our media-saturated society, appearance is becoming more and more important. Americans need to take a step back from this mania and realize a few facts. First, this emphasis on appearance has not made us any healthier. Obesity is at epidemic levels at the same time that anorexic actresses dominate TV shows. Neither extreme is good. There is a growing movement toward focusing on healthy eating rather than thinness, and this should continue. However, it needs to be done in the right way. It's common for well-intentioned people to say things like "Until we wake up and say, 'I love myself,' we're going to continue to spiral out of control," as Camryn Manheim did in an article about the anorexic look of the new *90210* stars. However, one of the ultrathin stars, Shenae Grimes, reportedly refers to *90210* as "my show" and has a reputation as a diva—no problems with self-love there. Nor is teaching unconditional self-acceptance a good idea when more and more people are seriously overweight and need to accept themselves a little less. It's a tough balance to strike, but the emphasis should be on realism and health. Most people don't look like Shenae Grimes, and that's fine. There are avenues for achievement much more meaningful than looking stick-thin. Accepting that you don't look like a Hollywood star is a good type of self-acceptance; taken too far, however, loving yourself becomes narcissism, a risk factor for both eating disorders and the delusional thinking that leads some people to become obese ("I'm fine—I don't need to lose weight"). Finding the happy medium is the best approach here, emphasizing health rather than appearance, and forgoing the confusing self-admiration messages. *90210* actress AnnaLynne McCord said, "I could be as big as a barn—what's important is that I'm happy being who I am." More important than avoiding diabetes and heart disease?

The easiest way to combat the trend toward excessive vanity is to start with our children. The idea that girls should start looking sexy at five—or even earlier—has entered the mainstream. It needs to exit. You can now buy high heels for newborn babies. They come in a "runway bag" with a rhinestone clasp and are called "Heelarious," but a lot of people don't think that sexy footwear on a 10-pound baby is funny. The people who make slutty clothes for eight-year-old girls will stop making them as soon as parents refuse to give in. Frank discussions about bodies are also a necessity with girls, who might wonder why so few real women look like the media ideal of very thin with large breasts. Teen girls need to know that surgery produced these results. The shallow values inherent in plastic surgery are another good topic for discussion.

Talk frankly, too, about the reason often given for plastic surgery: "I wanted to feel better about myself." Isn't that better accomplished by achieving something, having a close friend, or helping others? Help teens realize that appearance is only one small part of attracting a mate. A stunning physical appearance helps you hook up with lots of people, but it only gets you in the door to most long-term close relationships. To have the steady partnership most women eventually want, looks are only part of the equation. This advice doesn't just apply to the parents of teenagers—it's important for adults to keep in mind as well. There are better ways to feel good about yourself, and to meet the right person, than going under the knife.

The parents of boys have an easier time, especially now that so many athletes are opening up about their steroid use. Boys no longer need to wonder how their baseball idols got so big so quickly when it took them months to develop a little muscle. They now know it was fake. Nevertheless, parents should be on the lookout for vanity among boys as well, with many appearance issues just now beginning to be prevalent among males as well as females. The gender barrier for appearance obsession is falling, and today's young boys may be the first generation to believe that pec implants are no big deal and eyebrow shaping is required.

As always, keeping a close eye on the type and amount of media that children and teens consume is important. The perfectly coiffed hair and surgically enhanced bodies so common on TV bear little resemblance to real life, even in a world where plastic surgery and cosmetic procedures have increased 450%. Too much media, and too much gazing at carefully chosen and even Photoshopped pictures on Facebook, gives young people a warped view of normal appearance. Even adults can be swayed by what they see. Jean's friends who became mothers were surprised their bodies didn't bounce back from pregnancy as easily as the celebrity flesh they saw in magazines. Overall, the world of magazines and TV can seduce us into a shallow worldview that undermines the invaluable, such as family, friends, and true learning. Slowly, real people are beginning to resemble what they see on the screens before them. "The media portrays a world of surface shine with nothing but emptiness beneath," wrote Chicago resident Susan, 57, in our survey. "Unfortunately, this is how people are becoming, maybe without being aware of it: Beautifully painted and clothed with an empty mind."

CHAPTER 10

The Spending Explosion and Its Impact on the Environment

Materialism

Abby, 25, looks perfectly put together during her appearance in a Lifetime TV documentary. But then again, she looks that way all the time, sporting a professional French manicure, frosted hair, and cool clothes, indulgences that she admits cost at least $600 a month. She just bought a beautiful new living room set for her suburban Kansas City apartment, part of her goal toward making it look like "a model apartment." She is fortunate not to have any college debt, since her parents paid for her education. But now, she says, "I'm completely on my own and have had to take out about $38,000 to support my everyday lifestyle."

Abby's choice of words is fascinating: she *had* to go $38,000 in debt to make her apartment perfect and spend $600 a month on her appearance. Materialism is one of the most obvious examples of America's narcissism epidemic. Narcissistic people want more things—but not just any old thing. Narcissism doesn't lead to collecting stamps or Pez dispensers or accumulating boxes of junk bought after late-night infomercial binges. Instead narcissism is all about buying and using products that confer status and importance—expensive cars, jewelry, clothing, a nice house, or anything else that displays status, power, and sophistication. A classic example is the opening scene of Donald Trump's show *The Apprentice*. A large plane with the Trump name on it lands in an airport, and a ridiculously expensive Mercedes comes roaring up the runway and screeches to a halt. Out steps The Donald. The message: I am a powerful and high-status man; tremble before me. (In case you didn't get the point, all of this is set to the soundtrack of the O'Jays song "For the Love of Money," which simply repeats over and over, "Money money money mon-ey!") "If you're not keeping up with everybody else, it's like you fall behind and it kind of can be looked down upon," says Abby.

Narcissists love to talk about their high-status stuff. In one study, for example, participants heard they were going to meet a stranger. When given the choice of topics to discuss, narcissists were more likely to talk about their material possessions, especially with people who were high in status and of the opposite sex. A feeling of entitlement, as we'll explore in Chapter 14, can also promote materialism. Mary, 63, wrote in our online survey, "My children think that if their neighbor is 'good enough' to have something, they are too—they deserve it just as much. So they go get it, too, even if they have to go into debt for it." The popular book *Affluenza: The All-Consuming Epidemic* detailed Americans' spending explosion over the last few decades, comparing our endless accumulation of stuff to a disease. We make a similar argument but suggest that one of the underlying causes of "affluenza" is narcissism.

The new materialism has dragged in plenty of people who are not otherwise narcissistic by nature. As Michael Silverstein and Neil Fiske argue in *Trading Up*, the growing emphasis on "living your best life" and rewarding yourself—in effect, cultural narcissism—has reduced the guilt Americans once felt for wanting luxury items. "It gradually became clear to consumers that they were being given permission to consume a little more aggressively than they had in the past," they write. "And, in a final act of helpfulness, influencers [like Martha Stewart] presented their audiences with lifestyles to emulate and endorsed products for them to buy." The luxury revolution sparked a new focus in business toward upscale products in everything from food (good-bye, Wonder Bread; hello, Panera) to appliances (Sears Kenmore is out; Viking professional ranges are in).

Advertising slogans shamelessly promote materialistic entitlement as a virtue. Many items on the entitlement scale—a measure that predicts behavior such as taking candy from children—are eerily similar to ads that tell people to buy things that, in reality, they don't need or are unhealthy. McDonald's tells Americans "You deserve a break today," just as entitled people agree that "people like me deserve an extra break now and then." L'Oréal hair color tells women to buy their product "because I'm worth it," similar to the entitlement item "I demand the best because I'm worth it." A quick Google search shows that the entitled statement "you deserve the best" has been used to sell massages, air tours of the Grand Canyon, home loans, cell phone service, guitar lessons, moving services, health club memberships, a weight-loss supplement called "SprayFlex," a DJ service, and even a "Life Strategist Coach" who insists that "you deserve the best life." An ad for a swimming pool company reads, "Do you really believe you deserve the best pool ever? Many people don't. Believe that you deserve the best, and you will get it." (As long as you have $80,000, of course.) One rap song is brutally honest about our materialistic values. "Money make me come," croons a woman in time with the beat. Money focus begins in childhood. A series of coin purses for kids make good use of materialistic clichés: One with a penguin says "Cold Hard Cash," and another with a dolphin proclaims, "Swimming in Cash." The shark has no qualms in admitting he is "Money Hungry." And so are Americans. We have become a nation of people who, like Veruca Salt in *Willy Wonka & the Chocolate Factory*, shouts, "I want it NOW!"

TRICKLE-DOWN NARCISSISM

It's not necessary for everyone, or even most people, to be narcissistic for materialism to increase in a society. Similar to the trends in vanity, narcissistic people begin materialistic trends that raise the standards for everyone else. They show off their possessions and make materialism cool through their charm and outgoing personalities. This has led to a growing focus on material things among American youth. In 1976, 16% of American high school seniors said that "having a lot of money" was "extremely important." This ballooned to 26% in 2006. High school students name "getting a good-paying job" as more important than "being ethical and honorable." When the Pew Center for Research recently asked 18- to 25-year-olds about the most important goals of their generation, 81% named becoming rich, more than twice as many as named helping people who need help, four times more than named becoming a leader in the community, and eight times as many as named becoming more spiritual ("becoming famous" came in second at 51%). In 1967, 45% of college freshmen said that "becoming well off financially" was important; by 2006, that number increased to 75%.

Before we are accused of railing too much against the young, it's important to note that college students have favored being "well-off" for a while now. The number who named financial comfort as an important goal has been over 70% since 1985, right around the time Madonna crooned, "We are living in a material world / And I am a material girl" and *Lifestyles of the Rich and Famous* became a runaway TV hit. Thus anyone born after about 1967 belongs to a generation raised in a highly materialistic culture. Even the Baby Boomers, the generation in college in the less materialistic 1960s, had a change of heart along the way. The hippie generation of the '60s became the yuppie generation of the '80s, discovering the joys of BMWs and Cuisinarts. As David Brooks hilariously points out in *Bobos in Paradise*, spending gobs of money is virtuous rather than sinful for Boomers—as long as they spend it on "high-end" stuff such as expensive cookware, slate shower stalls, and "professional grade" hiking equipment. Conspicuous consumption has reigned for a while now. In the late '90s Americans spent more on shoes, jewelry, and watches ($80 billion) than on higher education ($65 billion). An incredible 93% of teenage girls say that shopping is their favorite activity.

Obviously, money *is* important in many ways. The attraction of money is understandable in a time when the necessities of life cost so much more. Health care is staggeringly expensive, college tuition has far outpaced inflation, gas prices are up, and even small houses are now out of reach for the middle class in many areas of the country, even with the recent decline in prices. For many couples, it takes two incomes to achieve the financial stability that many of their parents achieved on one salary. What is less apparent is why this money is needed to buy material goods whose purpose is to tell the world—and even to prove to yourself—that you are important or successful.

IT'S NOT ENOUGH. I WANT MORE.

The largest change in materialism is the inexorable rise in standards. Ten years ago, only the rich had granite countertops in their kitchens. Just like superwhite teeth, granite countertops are now necessary to show that you're not poor, even though no one cared about these things back in the early '90s. Sarah, 40, is a single mom living in Alabama who responded to our online survey. Her eight-year-old daughter and her friends, she says, "are distressingly obsessed with money. I'm already hearing '*Everyone* gets to have such-and-such and has a huge house; I wish we were normal.' "

As economist Robert H. Frank points out in *Luxury Fever,* the spending of the rich has set a new standard that middle-class families are going into debt to reach. Frank tells the story of going shopping recently to replace the backyard grill he bought in the 1980s, which cost $90. One of his options, he found, was the seven-foot-long Viking-Frontgate Professional Grill for $5,000. The real significance of such expensive goods, he notes, is that "their presence makes buying a $1,000 unit seem almost frugal. As more people buy these up-market grills, the frame of reference that defines what the rest of us consider an acceptable outdoor grill will inevitably continue to shift."

Even in difficult economic times, having cool stuff is still in. *Us Weekly* used to call style-conscious celebrities "fashionistas." In 2008, it called those who found stylish looks for less "recessionistas." The emphasis is still on stuff—just on somewhat less expensive stuff, such as the bag that costs merely $500 instead of $5,000. Economists have found that the desire for conspicuous consumption is actually stronger in poor neighborhoods than in more affluent ones. People in South Carolina, for example, make about $10,000 less on average than those in California, but they spend 13% more on "visible goods," for example, cars, jewelry, clothes, and personal care, all status symbols designed to make someone look well-off even if they aren't. So even outside the affluent neighborhoods, material consumption is very important—thus the bling and flashy cars. The catchy slang term for this phenomenon is "ghetto fabulous." This research also suggests that the recent economic downturn will probably not mean the end to narcissistic consumption—if we are all poorer, more people will buy things to show that they're doing fine.

Of course, the better-hooved are not immune—they just show off with real estate instead of bling. Middle-class couples in areas like Dallas, Atlanta, and San Diego often begin their search for a home at the brand-new developments that have sprouted up in the suburbs, which often feature model homes furnished by professional decorators that include upgrades that can add tens of thousands of dollars to the price of the home. Jean and her husband visited one model home in San Diego with beautiful dark wood flooring in the entryway and living room. When Jean asked the sales agent how much this upgrade cost, the answer was $50,000—and that was for just two small rooms. (Context: Jean's grandparents' house in Willmar, Minnesota, sold for $50,000 a few years ago. The *whole house*.) The standard flooring for houses in the development, it turned out, was low-quality carpet available in three equally unattractive colors. So most people would end up spending a lot of extra money on flooring, even if they didn't spring for the yearly-salary-busting dark wood. Who's going to buy a nearly million-dollar home and cover the floors with bad carpet?

There is no end to the list of things you must spend wads of cash on, even if you're merely middle-class. Driving an old car is embarrassing (just ask Jean, who until recently drove her grandfather's 1993 Buick LeSabre, which elicited outright stares in San Diego). Designer clothing is also valued—like many narcissistic trends, this one really got going in the '80s. Before then, the name of the designer was not routinely displayed on your clothes, purse, or shoes. (When a 1980s Marty McFly tries to get *Back to the Future* in 1955, everyone assumes his name is Calvin Klein because it's printed on his underwear). Back in the '50s, a select few may have recognized your Chanel suit from its cut, even though the garment wasn't labeled as such, and that was enough. Now it's important to explicitly announce that you can afford the latest status symbol. When mothers and daughters shop for sunglasses, for example, "The mother wants a discreet logo at the temple, and her daughter wants the logo to be bigger than the lens," says Marshal Cohen, an analyst for the NPD Group.

Even when the brand isn't explicitly announced, the desire for luxury—or just for things that are a little bit better than everyone else's—has entered the fantasies of much of the middle class. Stores like Crate & Barrel, Williams-Sonoma, and Pottery Barn have raised the bar on home furnishing standards for the aspirational middle class. It's not OK to have plain old cookware or appliances anymore; it should be professional quality. In 2002 dollars, the average kitchen in 1955 cost $9,000. The average kitchen now costs over $57,000—even without a Viking range or high-end granite countertops. Patio furniture should be teak and have perfectly coordinated cushions. Open the Pottery Barn Kids catalog and you are transported into a perfect world where everything is cute and stylish, colors are perfectly coordinated, and children are always charmingly engrossed in a project they will clean up themselves. Jean spent hours poring over this catalog when she was pregnant, dreaming of the perfect nursery. It was so addictive it was like shopping for crack. In the end, she resisted the Baby Industrial Complex and simply bought a plain crib sheet. It came down to practicality: quilts are unsafe, bumpers might be, and diaper stackers are unnecessary, so most of the bedding set is useless. The fitted sheet, the one useful item, is just going to get spit up on, anyway. But, boy, was it tempting to spend $300 on crib bedding that should have cost $20—because it sure is beautiful, and it creates an emotional feeling that one has made it. And if you have, so has your newborn child.

THE RESIDENTS OF RICHISTAN

Gregg Easterbrook's *The Progress Paradox* opens by describing the landing strip next to an exclusive restaurant in a rural part of Oklahoma. Until recently, the book points out, few people could afford the private jets necessary to make this type of attraction possible. Now the restaurant is filled to capacity nearly every night. By 2007, nearly half a million U.S. households were worth more than $10 million. Over the last 10 years, the number of millionaires in the United States has doubled. This is still a very small minority of Americans, but as Robert Frank points out in *Richistan*, those worth more than $10 million could populate a small country—a country where people compete to have the longest yacht and owning a $50,000 car is embarrassing. Though some of this wealth began to deflate in 2008, there is still plenty of money to go around among the new rich, many of whom made their money by selling companies and are thus relatively unaffected by business cycles. The fat cats are still pretty fat.

For those with the cash, it's apparently not enough just to spend it—you have to spend it extravagantly, and in a unique way. "The challenge for today's rich is to set themselves apart from the merely affluent," says *Richistan* author Frank. "You want things no one else can afford or experience. The challenge is to always stay ahead." This is classic narcissistic thinking—what good is money if you can't use it to show that you are special, unique, and better than everyone else? For example, you might want a Patek Philippe watch, but they are rare and there's a long waiting list. So the new masters of the universe are buying them at auctions and paying thousands more than the list price. One sold recently for $1.2 million, "the additional $300,000 considered chump change for the joy of jumping the line," according to *Time*. Rolls-Royce enjoyed double-digit sales growth in 2007 (although much of that was, of course, outside the United States). Some Rolls-Royce models sell for $430,000. "People today are more comfortable standing apart," says Rolls-Royce spokesman Bob Austin. "Wealthy people have regained a certain confidence. Suddenly if you want to stand out, you need something special. This is a big-dog car."

Some of these trends are slowing down or reversing as the economy tightens, but many others continue. As Wall Street was melting down in September 2008, lines stretched far down the block in New York at a Hermès sample sale. These were not Salvation Army bargains; they included $900 boots, $2,000 jackets, and $200 toddler robes. Many of the women in line worked at investment firms and banks, but said they "just needed a break" from the bad news, or that "even if the economy's down, a sale is all the more reason to buy something nice." One woman didn't even consider the possibility of not buying something. "That wouldn't work," she said. Others said they bought the expensive merchandise to look good and thus feel good, seemingly oblivious to the possibility that they might soon not have a job to dress up for. "I'll only buy if it's something I really need," rationalized another. As a *New York Times* reporter pointed out, it's not as if Hermès sells lightbulbs and toilet paper.

Expensive tastes are filtering down to twentysomethings, the group least likely to be able to afford them. A recent issue of the *Time* magazine supplement *Style & Design* addressed "Luxury for the Next Generation." The table of contents featured a picture of a twenty-something model wearing a T-shirt featuring a picture of . . . herself. "You thought the Boomers were conspicuous consumers?" asks the headline. "Watch out," it says—Generation Me is even more over the top.

The article goes on to portray unadulterated narcissism as blandly normal, if not exciting. "One look at a college parking lot full of Audis,

Saabs, and BMWs demonstrates that this generation isn't waiting to 'earn' its luxury products and services; it already feels entitled to them," the article reports. "There's an expectation that they deserve luxury now—it's not something you wait for and earn," says James Chung, president of Reach Advisors. "I call them the prematurely affluent generation." Of "core luxury consumers," 93% agreed that "looking stylish is important to feeling good about myself." And of course that's because they deserve it: 92% said "I work hard, so I reward myself by splurging."

Among this group, 54% of those 18 to 27 years old said they were interested in owning a yacht, whereas only 31% of those 45 to 62 years old expressed this desire. Young people were also twice as likely to want to own a private jet or luxury sports equipment. Throughout the article, the crucial question goes completely unanswered: How, exactly, are people going to find the money to buy this fleet of yachts? And why do so many young people aspire to skippering their own boat? The answer to this second question is easy: for their entire lives, outsize materialism has been completely acceptable. The answer to how they will afford it is much less obvious. Their parents might have bought them an Audi to drive at college, but they are presumably going to draw the line at a yacht.

Advertising has driven the rise in standards. An ad for a Panasonic computer says, "It's not just a laptop. It's having your driver circle the building a few more times while you send a few more emails." Because, of course, we're all supposed to have chauffeurs now. An ad for MyJet announces, "In today's world, chartering a private jet has become a necessity." Just like food, clothing, and shelter, right?

THE QUAINTLY LOW MATERIAL STANDARDS OF THE AMERICAN PAST

So if a private jet is now a necessity, what were the material standards of previous generations? Getting rich was always attractive to a certain number of people. Even the phrase "New Gilded Age" hints at the original in the late 1800s—think Carnegie, Rockefeller, and Vanderbilt (although we shouldn't forget that each of those men used a part of their wealth to start a great university). Yet in this previous era most people simply accepted that they didn't have much money and never would.

To get a first-person perspective on this, Jean turned to a journal her grandmother used to record memories of her childhood. Alvina was born in 1911 and grew up on a farm in rural Minnesota. In the wintertime, she and her siblings ice-skated on a frozen pasture, but (in her words) "we didn't have no skates. We just skated with our shoes." There were too many children and too little money for the children to have birthday parties every year, though she did have one for her 10th birthday. The presents were not what today's children expect, however. "One little girl didn't have a gift," Alvina wrote, "so her mother wrapped a pair of salt and pepper shakers for me." Sometimes Alvina just wanted to run and hide, because, like all the children, she was required to do chores "like hoeing the garden, milking the cows, taking care of the younger children, washing dishes, doing the ironing, help with the cooking." Their house did not have indoor plumbing, and since her family could not afford vacations her first trip out of town consisted of riding the train to Minneapolis when she was 14 to visit her sister and her newborn baby. (Once there, she wrote, "I did housework for 3 days.") She shared a room with three of her siblings, two to a bed. On Christmas, each child got two presents and no more, often clothes or coloring books. Her school had one teacher for fifty children, all taught in the same room. Nevertheless, she loved school. She never "played hooky," she said, because if she did she'd just have to work on the farm. (Contrast this to today, when a child who stays home from school fills his day with entertainment such as video games and movies.)

Jean's grandmother's experience was not universal, of course. Some children at the time had much more—though others had even less. But even with some wealth, thrift was still maintained. Keith's grandmother was also a farm girl from the Midwest. She taught in a small school, married, and created several businesses with her husband. Eventually she ended up in large home in posh Brentwood, California, surrounded by celebrities. Even then, though, she still had chicken coops in her backyard and kept the blackout curtains on her windows needed during World War II when there was a threat of Japanese attack on Los Angeles. Long after the war was over, Keith's grandmother didn't see the need to spend the money to replace them.

It was a different world back then in many respects. Children were expected to work hard, and probably too hard, considering they often didn't finish school. They weren't told they were special and didn't get the idea they were better than others. Children had many siblings, and some of them died from diseases that are now treatable. And material standards were far below what they are now. Children then wanted a nice doll, not a $400 iPod. They were lucky if they got a birthday party at all, much less one with entertainment and lavish presents. Part of the difference then was the relative absence of advertising. There was no TV or radio when Alvina was young, so she was not constantly exposed to the idea that everyone deserves a birthday party with presents better than salt and pepper shakers. When Alvina's daughter, Jean's mother, was growing up in the 1950s, TV had arrived but usually featured middle-class families making middle-class purchases. By the time Jean was young in the '70s and '80s, the lives of the rich were regularly featured on TV. Jean's daughter Kate, born in 2006, will never know a world where TV is not filled with the trappings of riches—unless our culture makes a very abrupt U-turn. To Kate, her great-grandmother's life of hard work and few possessions will seem like another planet.

WHY WE WANT IT

Of course, salesmanship and advertising have existed as long as there have been things to sell, but we are now more vulnerable to it. To put it more bluntly, there are more suckers now. But why? As we explored in Chapter 8, easy credit has made materialistic dreams possible for more people, and this is certainly one of the engines driving this effect. But there are psychological reasons as well; if there weren't, people wouldn't make dumb decisions like getting up to their eyeballs in debt.

One reason is individual-level narcissism: more people are materialistic. Another is the increasingly narcissistic values of our culture. Americans throughout the country's history have aspired to be rich, but now wealth seems much more accessible. After all, anyone can get into Harvard if she's smart enough—a far cry from just a few decades ago, when the vast majority of Ivy League entrants were white men from the East Coast with the right connections. Previous eras certainly featured rags-to-riches stories as well, but there was more awareness and acceptance that these were unusual. Not that long ago, low-income teenagers aspired to middle-class dreams, for example, a three-bedroom house in the suburbs. These days, disadvantaged youth are more likely to say they want a mansion like the one they saw on MTV's *Cribs*.

With modern media, wealth is also much more visible than it once was. Back in the '70s, TV was filled with poor families like the Bunkers (who lived in a duplex in Queens) and Fred Sanford, who apparently furnished his house with finds from the junkyard he ran. Now TV features the adventures of rich people. Josh Schwartz, who created the show, *The O.C.*, about rich kids in California, next created *Gossip Girl* about rich kids in New York. *Gossip Girl*, he says, is "an entirely different show. Orange County is new money—the McMansions. You have to be born into [*Gossip Girl*'s] level of affluence." In other words, there are now so many shows about rich people on TV that it's necessary to distinguish what *type* of rich people it's about. Premiering the same night as *Gossip Girl* was a show with a title summing up the modern age: *Dirty Sexy Money*. The new *90210* kids are much wealthier than their 1990 counterparts; as the *New York Times* put it in a review of the show, "anyone who doesn't have a beach house and a butler might as well be on welfare." On these shows, boys don't impress girls by taking them for a ride in their sports car; they impress them by taking them for a ride in a private jet. The "poor" kids on *Gossip Girl*, Dan and Jenny, go to tony prep schools, and their dad is a rock star.

Reality shows also feature behind-the-scenes looks at the lives of rich and famous people. *Cribs* allows us to tour their extravagant homes, *My Super Sweet 16* to see their birthday parties, and *The Osbornes* and Hulk Hogan's show to see their family life. Outside of a few daytime screamfest talk shows, the only time poor people appear on TV now is during natural disasters like Hurricane Katrina. Viewers were shocked by the storm victims' poverty, even though there are many more poor people in America than people rich enough to be portrayed on *90210* or *Gossip Girl*. No one is shocked when rich people appear on TV.

Standards for once-simple celebrations like children's birthday parties have also reached new heights. Gone are the days when a few kids ran around the house with cake on their faces. Middle-class parents now debate the virtues of clowns versus elephants. Giant air-filled jumping cages are virtually mandatory despite their rental fees of several hundred dollars. Due to the changes in parenting discussed in chapter 5, children now have more say in their birthday parties, which often leads to requests for lavish parties like those featured on MTV's *My Super Sweet 16* complete with live concerts by famous rap artists, grand entrances with red carpets, and $50,000 luxury cars as gifts. The *Jewish Voice & Herald*, a newspaper serving a middle-class neighborhood of Providence, Rhode Island, advised parents that they should consider creative themes for their children's bar and bat mitzvah parties. How about your very own rain forest with a waterfall, tropical plants, and live fish? Or a Hollywood theme with "paparazzi" photographing all of the guests? And you can forget the rubber chicken or brisket: the hot (or in this case, cold) new food trend is the sushi bar (never mind that sushi ain't cheap). Fewer people will be able to afford such parties in a recession, but the desire to give your child the material best will not entirely fade.

The rich are also treated with an aspirational reverence—somewhat like the gods were to the Greeks, except that many people fervently hope they can soon join their ranks. A recent *Forbes* magazine cover promised details on "The Lives of the Very Rich," including sections titled "Masters of the Universe" and "Marrying Into Money." Of course, celebrity magazines basically feature this cover every week, with their peeks into the lives of the rich and famous, from their babies to their breakdowns.

Being rich is a narcissist's paradise. When our most cherished hopes are for ourselves, it is extremely easy to be drawn to the appeal of being rich. First, you can afford the best of everything (after all, you deserve it). And everyone is nice to you because you're footing the big bill, and money brings good service. Maybe you'll even leave a big tip or a nice inheritance to the people who kowtow the best. If you're wealthy enough, you can be your own boss and do whatever you want. Money also buys personal comfort. You can leave behind the shoe-removing, three-hour layover, starvation-experiment cattle car of modern air travel and fly on a private jet. At the very least you can fly first class and get more room and a hot meal. As Steve Rushin puts it in *Time*, "Airports resemble France before the revolution. First-class passengers enjoy 'elite' security lines and priority boarding, and disembark before the unwashed in coach—held at bay by a flight attendant—are allowed to foul the jetway."

Bigger houses mean no more waiting for the bathroom and no more yelling at Junior to turn down his music: he's got his own wing of the house. Last but not least, money helps you feel important and better than other people. You can buy your way out of lines everywhere, Rushin points out: "This summer I haplessly watched kids use a $52 Gold Flash Pass to jump the lines at Six Flags New England, [which] teaches children a valuable lesson: that the rich are more important than you."

Problems arise, however, because not everyone can be rich. As we saw in Chapter 8, easy credit has made the trappings of wealth more accessible to more people. But it has also bankrupted more people and caused more foreclosures on homes. Most of these financial challenges happen to people who just aspire to be middle-class, but a sizable minority involve people who overstretched to buy the huge house or the expensive car. And even with credit so much more accessible, it is not endless. The vast majority of Americans cannot, and never will be able to, afford much of what they see in magazines and on TV. Yet we still yearn for it, spending money on get-rich-quick schemes and wealth seminars like the one announcing, "It's *YOUR* Time to become a millionaire!" The U.S. government has gotten into the act. In 2008, "economic stimulus" checks went out to poor and middle-class adults with the hope that they would go out and spend it. This is a great message for our kids: let's go borrow billions of dollars from China, Japan and the Middle East and then give it to people to spend on stuff they don't need, ostensibly to help the economy. Our grandparents would weep.

WARMING THE EARTH, ONE OVERCONSUMPTION AT A TIME

It's popular to believe that people buying a lot of stuff keeps the economy going and doesn't hurt anyone. Unfortunately, materialism has real consequences. One of the largest consequences is the impact on the environment. People who want more and don't care about anyone else will be willing to do more environmental damage.

A prime example is the American love affair with cars. From 1969 to the late '90s, the number of vehicles grew by 144%, twice as fast as the number of drivers (72%). In 2003, the U.S. Department of Transportation reported that the number of cars per household was higher than the number of people. This wouldn't be so bad if cars had grown more energy-efficient over time. Since the '80s, however, sales of SUVs, pickups, and minivans have tripled. In 2001, more of these large vehicles were sold than passenger cars. SUVs, of course, burn considerably more gas than a regular car. The car commercials of the early '80s always ended with the gas mileage of the vehicle. By the '90s, those commercials had been replaced by ads showing SUVs climbing rugged terrain off-road—even though most SUVs were sold to suburbanites whose vehicles never left the pavement. Off-road meant parking on the dirt in front of one's under-construction, 5,000-square-foot home.

As we discussed in Chapter 8, homes in the United States have gotten much bigger, even though families have gotten smaller. Bigger houses consume more resources when they are being built and then use more energy over their lifetime. More and more people also own second homes than ever before.

The need for stuff has resulted in more places that sell stuff. The amount of retail space per person in the United States is a whopping 39.2 square feet, much larger than the figure for Australia (20.4 square feet), the United Kingdom (14 square feet), or Japan (10.8 square feet). Consumption even has its own holidays, such as "Black Friday," the day after Thanksgiving, when stores officially begin the Christmas shopping season. So after spending a day thanking the Lord for our family, health, and friends, we take the next day to get up at 4 A.M. and buy crap we don't need.

In the United States, we use more energy per person than any other nation, which represents a big increase in electricity use, but also a shift away from other sources of energy like gas and coal. Americans have even increased the amount of calories we eat to 3,770 calories per day, compared to 3,180 in 1979–81, an 18% increase. It takes a lot of energy and resources to grow, produce, transport, and sell all of that food.

Of course, the narcissism epidemic is not the sole cause of these changes in behavior. The shift to SUVs and minivans, for example, is in part an unintended consequence of laws mandating car safety seats for children. But plenty of people without a pack of kids buy these large vehicles, because driving one is also about ego: You are bigger than everyone else on the road, and they should get out of your way *now*. Or you will crush them like a bug (perhaps of the Volkswagen variety).

Americans also love to hold on to their stuff, sometimes for the sole reason that it is *theirs*. As a Chilean man once remarked to Keith with wonder (or disdain), "Americans are the only people on earth who actually rent apartments just to keep their things." He was referring, of course, to public storage units. Americans currently use 2.2 *billion* square feet of public storage space (think over eight thousand Superdomes of storage). We have stuff coming out of our ears.

The environmental picture isn't all bad, of course. By many measures, the U.S. environment has improved significantly since the 1960s. In 1969, the Cuyahoga River in Cleveland famously caught fire from all the pollutants in the water. When we authors lived in Cleveland in the early 2000s, things had improved dramatically across all of the Great Lakes. Jean swam in Lake Erie, and our advisor windsurfed there. Keith surfed Lake Michigan while at grad school in Wisconsin (it isn't Hawaii, but there are no crowds). The Great Lakes have gone from environmental disasters to success stories. In the '70s, it was common for school kids to miss recess in the beautiful weather of Southern California because the smog was too thick for children to safely play outside. Now bad air days are few and far between.

Littering and other environmentally destructive behaviors have dropped a great deal as well. It was common in the '60s, for example, for people to toss trash from their cars. They would toss their cigarette butts out the window and let their kids hurl their fast-food wrappers onto the highway. This practice, fortunately, has changed.

However, these changes and others did not result from the voluntary actions of individuals, but from stricter laws passed through collective group efforts. The Great Lakes and other bodies of water improved after the passage of the Clean Water Act, and air pollution improved after the Clean Air Act passed and emissions standards for cars were tightened. Fines for littering were increased and enforced. It's likely that similar collective or government action will be necessary to combat global warming. Although it has become cool to consider the environment in one's purchases, the growing narcissism in the culture has made it even cooler to get everything you want.

THE PERSONAL CONSEQUENCES OF MATERIALISM

Like many of the correlates of narcissism, materialism harms others and society, but it is also harmful to the individual in the long run. Psychologist Tim Kasser, author of *The High Price of Materialism*, has spent his career studying the consequences of valuing money and things. On average, materialistic people are less happy and more depressed. Even people who simply aspire to have more money suffer from poor mental health; they also report more physical health problems such as sore throats, backaches, and headaches and were more likely to drink too much alcohol and use illegal drugs. Striving for financial success, apparently, makes people miserable.

Part of the reason is that it is very hard to get ahead for more than a short while in the materialism game. Fashion and style change so rapidly that only the very wealthy—or those willing to carry enormous amounts of debt—can keep up. Beyond the brief feeling of excitement you get when buying a hot new product and showing it to your friends, the pleasures of materialism are fleeting. Lots of things are fun to buy, but not so many are fun to own. The boost to narcissism that you get from beating the Joneses lasts only until they get their own new BMW or home cinema.

Materialism is also a real stumbling block in narcissists' relationships. Narcissists' partners, for example, often say that the narcissists' interest in material goods interferes with the relationship. She's more interested in stainless-steel appliances, fancy handbags, and Manolo Blahnik shoes than our relationship, guys will say. (Simply insert "a huge flat-screen TV, Rolex watches, and expensive suits" to switch the sexes.) The partners might have a point: If you can get social status from either an expensive watch or a trophy partner, what does that say? Narcissists also sort their friends according to material standards. Karen, 34, bragged to a group of friends that she had bought not one but three Coach diaper bags, adding that she waited to share this news until after the departure of friends who were not fashion-forward enough to appreciate her taste. Her advice for those yet to deliver their babies was to bring gift bags to bribe the nursing staff.

TREATMENT FOR THE EPIDEMIC

We should enact policies that limit the ability of narcissistic materialism to get out of hand. Tightening the regulations on mortgage lending is clearly necessary to rein in the dangerous overconfidence of both banks and homebuyers. The only way to prevent narcissistic risk taking in mortgages is to outlaw it.

More control of credit cards would also help rein in spending. Credit is not a bad thing in and of itself; wealth creation almost invariably involves credit (just look at the balance sheet of any company). However, most consumer debt does not generate higher returns for the borrower and thus is often a mistake. Banks need to stop extending credit to people who can't afford to pay. It sounds simple, but those regulations are currently not in place.

Many goods that generate status, such as cars and clothes, quickly depreciate in value. One simple (but not easy) way to discourage the trade of status for debt is to change the social norms that make it socially acceptable to use credit. Only a few generations ago people were ashamed to be in debt.

There should also be more of an incentive to save. Through a media campaign or other means, saving needs to be cool again. This is tough to do, because Americans are happy to brag about how much money they have spent, but find it impolite to talk about how much they have saved. If this could be changed so that people could get status by saving money rather than spending money, it would counteract some narcissistic materialism. How about giving Warren Buffett a TV show?

Similarly, Americans could try to align lower levels of materialism and proenvironmental behavior with narcissism and self-admiration. This bit of psychological judo would be difficult, but not impossible. It would mean turning the phrase "less is more" into a self-admiration statement. The difficulty is that it is easy to show off stuff, like a new iPhone or handbag. It is harder to show off not having stuff. One way to do that would be to brand the "nonmaterialist lifestyle" with a symbol of some sort. You need to say to the world, "I have a ton of money and status, but I am so above material goods that I do not need to show them off." There could also be a social movement that, like all social movements, consists of a certain style of dress and choice of products—in this case, less expensive things. The key is to make this choice seem cool.

Parents can also play a big role in raising less materialistic children. Of course, parents want to make their children happy, and children want stuff. Thus parents buy them stuff. And children are happy, but only for a short period of time. Then they want even more stuff. If, in your mind, every time we thought about buying your child stuff, you substituted the word *crack*, it would make the reasoning much easier: I want my daughter to be happy. Crack makes my daughter happy. Therefore I will buy her crack. This will make her happy for a short time and then she will want more crack. Buying your kid more toys doesn't sound so good when put in those terms. We're not saying that stuff is as bad as crack, of course, and every child needs some things of her own, but it's clear that kids in America have way too much stuff. It's got to end somewhere.

For birthdays or holidays, a good approach is giving children just one toy but several gifts that have personal meaning, such as cards or homemade gifts. Children can also be encouraged to give personally created gifts as well. A child's drawing with the words "Mommy, I love you" is worth much more than anything he could buy. But it has to go both ways—otherwise the child gets the idea that it's OK to give things that don't cost money, but he wouldn't want those gifts himself.

Education could help as well. Students are rarely taught about saving versus spending, especially the power of compound interest in either direction. Society would be far better if schools taught basic economic principles to students. With the increase in life expectancies, and decrease in pensions, our children are going to have to start saving for retirement very, very early. Education could also tackle how easily credit card debt can spin out of control and why taking out a mortgage that costs 80% of your income is not a good idea.

Although Keith usually hates arguing for more government regulation, we both agree that this might be one of the few ways to reduce consumption enough to improve the environment. As economists have pointed out for years, people's behavior is determined by incentives. If there is little incentive to conserve water (that is, water costs very little) few people will save water. In fall 2007, for example, Georgia experienced an extreme drought. Although there were rules put in place for outdoor water use, indoor water use was not regulated at all. Even at the height of the drought, Keith could take 20-minute showers and pay only pennies. The state came within weeks of running out of water when winter rains finally arrived. Next time, Georgians might not be so lucky. Using more water than your share is going to have to cost more money if the binge is going to stop.

Another crucial direction for change is improved technology. If Americans are going to keep consuming no matter what, it would be useful to develop technologies to make our material addiction inflict less environmental damage. So-called green technologies are starting to catch on. Incentives are again the key. Jean probably wouldn't have spent thousands on a solar heating system for her pool if gas heat had been inexpensive, as it was ten years ago. But it was more than worth it now that heating a pool with gas can cost upwards of $1,000 a month. After the initial cost, solar heat costs nothing and is an environmentally friendly, sustainable resource.

Fortunately, environmentalism is well on its way to being cool. Social norms are changing, with businesses exploring "green" options and celebrities buying Priuses left and right. But we still have a long way to go, as those same celebrities own many houses and fly private jets—and so many people read about this lifestyle in gossip magazines or see it on TV. It doesn't help much to have a Prius when it's parked in front of your sixth house and its bumper sticker reads "He who dies with the most toys wins."

CHAPTER 11

Seven Billion Kinds of Special

Uniqueness

Of all the responsibilities a parent has, naming a child is one of the most intimidating. This is the label your child will carry his or her entire life—unless you really screw up, and then he might change it. The biggest trend in baby names recently isn't a particular name; it's that fewer children receive common names. In a classic example of the "alternative" or "maverick" viewpoint becoming more popular than the mainstream it was meant to critique, unique names are all the rage. The Social Security Administration has compiled a database of the names given to every American child born since 1879, providing ample data to test this hypothesis. (You might want to check it out yourself at www.ssa.gov/OACT/babynames/)

In 1946, more than 5% of baby boys were named James and more than 4% of baby girls were named Mary. So just two generations ago, about 1 in 20 babies were given the most popular name that year. One out of 3 boys received a name that ranked in the top 10 for popularity, as did 1 out of 4 girls. Half of the boys born in 1946 received one of the top 23 names. Back then, naming a child was about belongingness and fitting in instead of uniqueness and standing out. Many families had multiple relatives who went by the same name. For example, Keith shares his first name, William, with his father, uncle, and grandfathers. This tradition stretches as far back as his family can trace.

But over the last few decades, parents tired of common names, wanting something unique for their children. At first it was a slow progression: as late as 1987, 3% of boys were named Michael and 3% of girls were named Jessica, with 1 out of 5 boys and 1 out of 6 girls receiving one of the ten most popular names. Then, during the 1990s, unique names caught fire and fewer and fewer children were given common names. By 2007, only 1% of children received the most popular name for their sex (Emily or Jacob), and only 1 out of 12 girls and 1 out of 11 boys went by a name in the top 10. Imagine a first-grade class at recess, with 30 children running around the playground. In 1952, you'd find at least one boy named Jimmy in the average first-grade class. In 1993, every two classes would have at least one Michael. When the 2007 babies reach first grade in 2013, you'll need six classrooms of kids on the playground to find even one Jacob, even though it is the most popular boys' name. The trend can't be explained by changes in ethnic composition such as the increasing number of Hispanic-Americans—the same trend toward unique names appears in the six U.S. states with the smallest percentage of Hispanics in their populations.

The name you receive from your parents is just the first act in a lifetime of trying to stand out, be unique, and be different—one of the central goals of Americans, and one that has developed only recently. It used to be a good thing to have a common, popular name, partially because

Percent of American Babies Given Common Names, 1945–2007

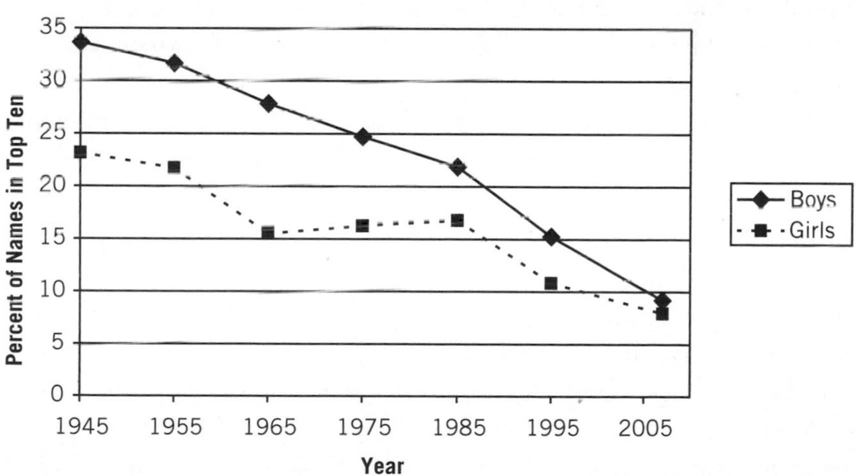

Source: Twenge, J. M., Abebe, E. M., and Campbell, W. K. (2008). Fitting in or standing out: Trends in American parents' choices for children's names, 1880–2007. Manuscript under review.

having a weird name would get you beaten up. Now it's considered better to stand out as an individual and be "unique." (In fact, 223 babies born in the 1990s in California were named Unique, with some parents putting teeth into it with names like Uneek, Uneque, or Uneqqee.) Parents will now say, "I've never heard of anyone named Kumquat," and proceed to name their child that. (This trend was in place well before websites like the Social Security Administration's made it easy to determine which names were unique and which were common.) Unique spellings are also trendy—why name a child Michael or Kevin when they can be Mychal or Kevyn? There are at least 10 ways to spell the popular girls' name Jasmine (also including Jazmine, Jazmyne, Jazzmin, Jazzmine, Jasmina, Jazmyn, Jasmin, and Jasmyn). "Today, there's this perception that naming a child is almost like naming a product—there's this huge national drive now to not be like anyone else," says *The Baby Name Wizard* author Laura Wattenberg.

Discussions about names are common on message boards for expectant parents such as babycenter.com. One expectant mother was considering naming her son after his father, to which a poster responded, "I wouldn't do it. Everyone deserves their own name and their own identity." Another set of parents were debating between Isabella and Sophia, two names in the top 10. "I didn't vote today. Isabella and Sophia are too popular for my taste! I see or hear about another Isabella every day!" wrote one woman, who described herself as "mommy to princesses, Blair & Haley." Then there are the parents who wanted to name their son Ocean. One poster said she loved this idea, writing, "I like it because it's not too popular." Another wrote, "I LOVE this idea! Shows you have some imagination, and don't just want to follow the crowd." Other posters disagreed. "If you name your child Ocean, he will get the snot beat out of him every day," wrote one. "Parents are becoming too obsessed with naming their child something different. While that is OK, don't name your child something that will haunt them." Even this poster felt that a unique name was fine, as long as it wasn't *too* unique.

Once again, we have celebrities to thank for this trend. No matter what you think of names like Apple, Suri, Shiloh, Phinnaeas, or Kal-el, there's no arguing that they are unique (if you don't read *Us Weekly* as regularly as Jean does, these are the offspring of Gwyneth Paltrow, Tom

Cruise, Brad Pitt, Julia Roberts, and Nicolas Cage, respectively). There is an element of narcissism to the idea that your child's name should stand out. *The Baby Name Bible* author Linda Rosenkrantz explains, "Celebrities crave being the center of attention and want their offspring to share in this uniqueness." Contrast recent celebrity offspring names with Elvis, the possessor of an unusual name himself, who named his daughter Lisa Marie, and Elizabeth Taylor, whose two sons are named Michael and Christopher.

The desire to give a child a unique name has been both facilitated and dictated by technology. Some expectant parents now Google names before choosing one—a good idea, because then you can avoid unwittingly naming your child after a serial killer or a bad musician. Fans of the movie *Office Space* might remember the character named Michael Bolton who wasn't *that* Michael Bolton; people kept asking him "Are you related to that singer guy?" "No, it's just a coincidence," he would say tiredly. When people suggested he go by Mike, he'd say, "Why should I change? He's the one who sucks." Many parents, however, don't want their child to be named after anyone, bad *or* good, and thus try to choose a name that doesn't appear on the Web at all. If your name is unique enough, people will easily be able to Google you. Jean's name falls into this category, mostly because of her unpronounceable Anglicized Norwegian last name (it's pronounced "Twangy"), but type Keith's name into Google without the W. and the first site you'll get is a guy who calls himself a "Hair Architect." And no, this is not Keith's second job. You will also find the scientist Keith Campbell, who helped clone Dolly the Sheep, which Keith knows because he has gotten the other Keith's hate mail.

Unique names aren't necessarily bad, and we don't mean to pass judgment on them. Keith's older daughter McKinley has one, for example—it's a family surname, and thus fairly uncommon. But the individualistic focus on children being unique and different fits squarely into the narcissism epidemic. Scales of narcissism reliably correlate with standard assessments of the need for uniqueness, because narcissists like the idea of standing out and being different from other people.

There are some advantages to more unique names: schools will no longer have the confusion of many children with the same name in one classroom (Jessica R., meet Jessica K.). As the trend toward unique names continues, however, teachers are going to find it difficult to remember all of their students' unusual first names, especially the "interesting" spellings.

Advantages and disadvantages aside, the trend toward more unique names says a lot about our culture. Naming rituals are central to cultures around the world and always have been. The names we choose for our children reveal our deepest wishes and desires. We now wish so fervently that our children will stand out from the crowd that we equip them with unique labels from birth.

I TOO AM NOT LIKE YOU

A diaper commercial opens with a thirty-something guy doing John Travolta moves to '70s-sounding music next to his toddler-age daughter. "This is your dad," says an amused female voice. "Fortunately, you don't move like him. You develop your own unique way of moving as a baby. . . . Pampers Cruisers, for the freedom to find your own moves."

From the first products we use, American advertising appeals to our desire to be unique and different. It begins when we are in diapers, but grows ever stronger when we are teenagers and adults. Imagine ordering a decaffeinated cappuccino with nonfat milk at a café. In the United States, no one would question this order, and you would feel good about getting the product exactly the way you wanted it. If you placed the same order at a café in Korea, however, the server might be annoyed that you were ordering something so different, and you would feel ashamed that you asked for something so out of the ordinary. The same might have been true in the United States not that long ago; imagine trying to order a decaffeinated cappuccino with nonfat milk in 1975—you'd probably end up with a cup of regular coffee with nondairy creamer. Since the '90s, however, Starbucks has offered so many different combinations of choices that there are more than 19,000 possible coffee orders, allowing at least 19,000 of us to be unique in our coffee orders. Triple grande soy iced decaf five-pump no-whip Mocha, anyone?

The emphasis on uniqueness is rampant in advertising. Bank of

America invites you to "make your credit card as unique as you are by adding a custom feature." Capital One advertises its "Card Lab" where you can customize every aspect of your credit card, including choosing any picture you want for the card's background. Cars can be customized with combinations of hundreds of options. In 2006, Wendy's sold uniqueness at the bargain price of $1.99 and threw in a hamburger as a bonus: "Paul does the Paul burger, not a generic, John Doe burger. Don't compromise. Personalize. . . . Do a hamburger made just for you." A Mazda ad enthuses, "someone has finally built a vehicle that adjusts to you, not the other way around." After decades of selling standard sizes, clothing companies like Lands End are now offering custom-made shirts. The children's CD *Sing Along with Elmo and Friends* now comes in more than 100 versions, each for a different name, so children can hear Elmo say their name and sing just for them. You can now buy customized T-shirts, M&M's, fortune cookies, playing cards, and calendars.

It's tempting to conclude that products are personalized because it makes them sell. But that kind of advertising works best in the United States. When Heejung Kim and Hazel Markus looked at American and Korean magazine advertisements in 1999, they found that Korean ads relied on conformity and tradition to sell products. ("Our company is working toward building a harmonious society"; "Our ginseng drink is produced according to the methods of 500-year-old tradition"). American ads instead trumpeted uniqueness. ("Ditch the Joneses," "The Internet isn't for everybody. But then again, you are not everybody.") Advertisements are not mere entertainment—they are part of a system that transmits cultural values to individuals. As Kim and Markus write, "The messages in American advertisements convince Americans that being unique is the right way to be, and the messages in Korean advertisements convince Koreans that being like others is the right way to be, and thus perpetuate these cultural values." The same paper reports an intriguing experiment: when given the choice of several pens, four of which were the same color and one of which was different, Koreans were more likely to choose one of the pens with the common color, and Americans to choose the one that was different.

American ads didn't always emphasize uniqueness so much. At one time, themes of group harmony and strength in numbers were more common than they are now. Although Coca-Cola urged consumers in 1925 to "refresh yourself," they also emphasized that "six million a day" drank their product, "the sociable drink." By 1956 it was proclaimed the "friendliest drink on earth." In 1963, Coke's slogan was "Things Go Better With Coke," with one ad promising "girl, team, fun, friends." Pepsi's slogan from 1953 to 1961 was "Be Sociable." A 1964 ad for Lucky Strike cigarettes says, "Here's where a cigarette wins friends . . . or loses them. It all comes down to taste . . . Millions of Lucky smokers seem to think so."

Today, everything is supposed to be unique, including our weddings. As an article on usabride.com notes, "By putting their own personal touches into their wedding ceremony, couples can ensure that their personalities are fully incorporated into their wedding day." That includes writing wedding vows just for you, as "couples often find that their own words can be more meaningful than traditional vows." We're not saying this is bad; it's just another display of the emphasis on uniqueness so common now. Before the '70s, it was unheard of to write your own wedding vows.

Celebrity superspreaders also love to dispense individualistic advice. Brittany Murphy recommended, "Cultivate individuality. Don't ever try to look how somebody else wants you to look. Go and dye your hair pink if it makes you happy." Suuure, you'll get lots of dates/jobs/acting roles with pink hair. If Murphy actually took her own advice it would go something like this: "Stay as fat as you were in *Clueless* if it makes you happy. Don't try to lose weight just because someone else (e.g., all of Hollywood) wants you to." *People* describes Drew Barrymore's style tips as "Follow Your Heart" and "Break the Rules." Barrymore's advice: "Just keep taking risks and going for it, and don't play it safe . . . don't dress for what you think someone else will like." This was in *People*'s Best and Worst Dressed issue, where the derided stars in the "worst dressed" section of the magazine took plenty of risks, clearly didn't dress for what someone else would like, and apparently followed the wrong heart.

The value of uniqueness is taught very early in American culture. A preschool in Manhattan designated September as "All About Me Month," with the first week titled "Focus on the Individual." The lesson plan for the classroom of two-year-olds: "Today we will each 'study' ourselves in a mirror." The goal was for each student to notice his or her individual attributes. ("My name is Fred. I have red hair.") The link between uniqueness and preferences for products was also actively taught; the lesson noted that "students will be encouraged to consider the individual preferences they possess," including deciding on a favorite animal, color, and food.

Many parents even want to give their child a unique education, one of the many reasons behind the movement toward homeschooling. "Schools are conformity models, training kids instead to do what they are told when they are told to do it. Curiosity and independent thought are squelched. A one-size-fits-all approach to education is not best for kids," wrote a parent from North Carolina, commenting on an msnbc.com story. There's a smaller movement that takes personalized education even further. In "unschooling," children decide what they want to learn—if anything—on a given day. There are fifty times more unschooled children now than 20 years ago—as of 2006, between 100,000 and 200,000. Education experts say that number is growing by 10% to 15% each year. The central tenet of unschooling is that children should do what they want. As an unschooling website explains, it involves children "creating structure to suit his or her own purpose," and "the focus is upon the choices made by each individual learner." It is the ultimate in individualized instruction, with no set schedule and no lesson plans. Even as a child, you are your own boss and can do whatever you want. As one critic put it, "What happens when the child gets a job and 'doesn't feel like' working?"

The American obsession with uniqueness is often contradictory. Advertising seems to say that everyone should buy a product because it will make you feel unique . . . but of course anything that's popular won't be unique anymore. The emphasis is also on being different without being *too* different. It's certainly unique for a woman to choose not to shave her legs, but advertising isn't promoting that particular expression of individuality—or anything else that doesn't fit the current narrowly defined vision of "hot." In today's vain culture, the unique choice might be to pay very little attention to one's appearance, but that's not the kind of uniqueness that sells products.

It's also somewhat odd that the obsession with uniqueness is occurring at the same time that there are more and more people. The world is more crowded than it used to be, with more traffic jams, longer lines, larger classes at universities, and less personal service for the average person. It now costs extra to talk to a real person to make an airline reservation. Even though each of us is unique, we receive impersonal treatment in a consumer culture that makes us a number: a customer number, a patient number, a Social Security number, a reservation number.

MYSPACE AND IPOD: THE USE OF THE FIRST PERSON IS NOT A COINCIDENCE

Television, the biggest media influence until very recently, is not very democratic. A small group of people decides what will be on television and puts it there. This group became a little bigger with the advent of cable and infomercials in the 1980s and '90s, but it was safe to say that not everyone could have their own TV show.

With YouTube, now you can. With the advent of MySpace and Facebook, everyone can have their own Web page. On Second Life, you can have your own virtual reality. As we explored in Chapter 7, the self-branding of Internet uniqueness has created new ways to stand out as an individual in our increasingly narcissistic culture. Cell phones allow everyone in the family to have his or her own phone. Teenage siblings no longer have to fight over the phone line or nervously ask their crush's father, "Is Jacob there?" You can also customize your phone with rhinestone bling, a unique ringtone, and the screen wallpaper of your choice.

Technology also allows us to customize our media experiences. My Yahoo! allows you to choose your news sources, stock portfolio updates, sports team scores, and horoscope. Your iPod probably has only a few—or no—songs in common with mine. You can use TiVo or a DVR to watch shows when you want to. The upside is that you don't have to sit through stuff you don't like. The downside is that media is no longer a collective experience but rather an individual experience. There will never again be a summer like 1967, when everyone under 40 was talking about *Sgt. Pepper's Lonely Hearts Club Band* and everyone listened to the album with the songs in the same order. Water cooler conversations about what happened on *Grey's Anatomy* on Thursday night can't always take place on Friday morning, as many people save the show to watch over the weekend.

The biggest exceptions to this are reality competition shows like *American Idol,* which most people watch live—perhaps one of the reasons they have stayed so popular. There's another more narcissistic reason for its popularity, however: everyone who watches the show has the opportunity to shape it by voting for contestants. The "judges" on *Idol* just give their opinions; individual Americans decide who stays and who wins (which explains oddities like Sanjaya from 2007). One 2007 reality show asked viewers to vote on which contestant's "lifelong dream" would be fulfilled. In 2003, the show *Married by America* asked viewers to vote for male and female contestants with the plan that two would marry on air. Fortunately for everyone, no wedding took place. But the message had been received: television is now democratic, and everyone has a say.

There will soon be a way to avoid bad TV like this and watch only what you want to—and without programming your TiVo. A program called Joost, designed by the same guys who invented Skype, will bring 50 TV channels to the Internet. Eventually there will be thousands of channels, all playing at the discretion of the individual. "Today TV is 500 channels but we're not far from a 5,000-channel world," says the CEO of a firm specializing in Internet TV. "And in 10 years, we could easily be at 50,000 channels from all over the world." And then the atomization of entertainment will be complete.

I AM SPECIAL. LOOK AT ME!

One of the items on the Narcissistic Personality Inventory (NPI) is "I think I am a special person" (the non-narcissistic choice is "I am no better and no worse than most people"). Feeling special is one of the central traits of narcissism, helping justify the narcissist's belief that it's OK to cut in line, get something for nothing, and treat others as inferior. Less narcissistic people like to say, "Yes, I'm special, but so is everyone else." But *can* everyone be special? The *American Heritage Dictionary* defines *special* as "surpassing what is common or usual; exceptional: [e.g.,] a special occasion." Thus it is logically impossible for everyone to be special. Even young children can figure this out. In a column in the *Minneapolis Star Tribune*, Katherine Kersten described her then-seven-year-old daughter's reaction to a school day when every kid wore a badge that said "[Blank] is special" with their name filled in. She commented, "Mom, if everyone is special, then no one is special."

So what about the idea that "everyone is special in their own way," as a song in *High School Musical* puts it? Maybe, but with almost 7 billion people in the world, that's a lot of different kinds of special. It also sounds more like being unique rather than special, two different words many people use interchangeably. Being unique emphasizes difference but not necessarily superiority, whereas being special means being a star and getting special treatment—not just different, but better than what everyone else gets. Uniqueness is often emphasized to children with phrases like "There is no one in the world quite like you." A Sunday school song for preschoolers points out: "My hair's a special color. My eyes and skin are too. God did not make me to be like you." In secular schools, children learn the same lesson when they are told that "everyone is a unique snowflake." (Or, as www.despair.com parodies it, "Individuality: Always remember that you are unique. Just like everybody else.")

Special is uniqueness with the extra added twist of being great—someone who is special is not just unique and different, but *better* (unless someone is referring to "special needs," or, as one of our Web survey respondents somewhat cruelly put it, "short bus special"). When discussing uniqueness with people, we often hear the argument that everyone really is unique, because he has his own unique fingerprint, or DNA, or he is the only person who has had his exact life experience, or she is the only one who occupies her own location in space and time. This is true. We are all unique in these ways, so it is a mundane uniqueness. None of this makes us special, however.

The Associated Press story on our study of the rise in narcissism mentioned the "I think I am a special person" item from the NPI. The story ended with a quote from University of Vermont student Kari Dalane: "It would be more depressing if people answered, 'No, I'm not special.' " Kari was not alone; we got an avalanche of questions on this issue. "Everyone likes to hear they're special and wouldn't it be just creepy if 7-year-olds walked around saying, 'I'm not special?' " asked the *Daily Kent Stater* in Ohio. When Jean did radio interviews on this topic, many callers were shocked when she suggested that feeling special isn't a good thing. Newspaper columnists, such as Joe Vulopas in the *Lancaster* (Pennsylvania) *New Era*, responded to this suggestion with "Puuuleeeeeaaase . . . Are these researchers upset because their mommies and daddies didn't say they were special?" (Yes, that's exactly why we went into psychology.) Vulopas noted that he regularly greets his daughter with "You're the most beautiful little princess in the whole world!" and insisted he would continue to say "She is special . . . EVERY CHANCE I GET." The *Reading* (Pennsylvania) *Eagle* argued that if parents "stop telling their children they're special in an effort to keep them from becoming narcissistic, parents could run the risk of damaging their children's self-confidence." In our online survey, we asked, "Is it important to tell kids they are special?" Nicole, 29, gave a version of the most popular response: "Definitely. It builds self-esteem and confidence, and I believe it also helps them to respect others."

In some ways, these responses make our argument for us. We are a nation fixated on the idea of being the exception to the rule, standing out, and being better than others—in other words, on being special and narcissistic—and we're so surrounded by this ethos that we find it shocking that anyone would question it. Fish don't realize they're in water.

But feeling special is narcissism—not self-esteem, not self-confidence, and not something we should be building in our children. There's a difference between narcissism and self-confidence. You can tell your child she is good at math, or that she *will* be good at math if she works hard, without telling her she is "special." Feeling special may give people a grandiosity-tinged sense of comfort, but in a real world of collaborating with others, waiting in lines, and getting cut off on the freeway, it just leads to frustration. And it is unlikely to lead to respect for others, as Nicole theorized; people who believe they are special often want to be the exception to the rule, which is usually unfair to everyone else. And, no, we are not saying that you should kick your five-year-old's butt in basketball to give him an accurate assessment of his abilities, or tell your daughter that she is awful at spelling when she is just learning. We are arguing that it is better not to focus on "specialness" at all, and instead concentrate on the love of learning and on rewarding effort.

Even though everyone cannot be special, everyone is unique. But why should we emphasize our differences rather than our similarities? We might all be unique, but we also share many common experiences, challenges, and traits. Even those with less common challenges—for example, a physical disability, a genetic disease, or an addiction like alcoholism—can find tremendous comfort in support groups, knowing there are others like them.

An overemphasis on uniqueness has negative consequences for individuals as well. Studies have found that teenagers who have a "personal fable" of uniqueness believe that no one understands them. Teens with these beliefs are significantly more likely to be depressed and to think about suicide. These problems got worse as the teens got older and still believed that no one understood them—because they were unique.

We will offer one exception: children are of course very special *to* their parents. As Kevin, 38, put it in our online survey, "I am special to some people. I'm special to my parents, my family, my friends, my romantic partner, my colleagues, my students. Everyone is special to someone, but specialness is relative, not absolute. No one is inherently special." This is a crucial difference. For example, Jean's daughter Kate is very special *to her*, but that doesn't mean that the rest of the world should treat Kate as special. As nice as that sounds, it wouldn't be fair to the other kids at Kate's preschool if the teacher treated her as special. Frankly, it wouldn't be fair to Kate, either. Even if she did think she was truly special, Kate would eventually encounter a situation where she was treated—oh, the horror—just like everyone else. Michelle, 30, remembers going to a church that taught "God Made Me Special" in Sunday school. "The disappointments came later, because we realized that life itself did not treat us 'special,' " she wrote. And if you're thinking that the world *should* treat everyone as special, it's time to realize that that's just not possible.

Loving your children, and telling them so, is *not* the same as telling them that they are special. Love creates a secure base for a child and a connection that they can count on. In contrast, telling a child she is special sets her apart and creates disconnection—a recipe for narcissism. Loving your children provides a secure base from which they can explore the world and has no real downsides.

Consider this: What if your child really is special? If he has a disability (and has "special needs"), your hope is probably that he will be able to do as many typical, nonspecial things as possible. And if your child has special talents—a genius IQ, perfect musical pitch, or stunning sports ability—you probably have the same wish, that he will still learn how to live with others and enjoy a normal life. As a parent of a gifted child, you'll probably focus much more on teaching humility and consideration than telling your kid how special she is. You will want others to treat her "just like any other kid." No one likes an arrogant jerk, and even gifted kids don't want to be seen as fundamentally different from everyone else, so most parents don't tell the kid who truly is special just how special he is.

TREATMENT FOR THE EPIDEMIC

The American emphasis on uniqueness is not entirely bad or good. It is a cultural construct that most of us take for granted, one that has increased its pull over time. With advertisements continually urging us to stand out by buying more stuff and two-year-olds encouraged to notice how they are different, the seduction of uniqueness has passed over into narcissism. As a culture, Americans should set aside this overemphasis on uniqueness.

It's time to get real. You cannot be a unique rebel and fit in at the same time. We all have to follow certain rules to get by in society, and we all have to do some things to fit in. There is nothing wrong with that. There is also nothing wrong with doing your own thing (within reason), but that doesn't mean you should be lauded for it (and then copied, ultimately defeating the purpose). Names are a good example of this. It is not a bad thing to give your child a common name. Scores of people in previous generations survived this just fine, and, as a bonus, everyone can spell their name. Having a unique name does not lead to success, Elvis and Madonna notwithstanding. A name that other people also have is a good thing, connecting your child to others, and it might save them a few fights in grade school. And if your child does actually decide to be an entertainer, he or she can change her name at that point, as Bob Dylan, Elvis Costello, Sting, and Bono did.

As a parent, question school lessons that highlight uniqueness and tell kids they are special. Instead of children studying themselves in the mirror to see how they are different, a better lesson might be to notice the ways we are all alike. Instead of asking each child to choose a favorite food, each could ask another child why he or she likes or dislikes something. The child might be surprised to encounter a perspective different from his or her own; this is also a more cognitively challenging task. It teaches empathy and perspective taking, a valuable skill.

Don't tell your kids that they are special. Tell them that you love them. This is a double guard against raising a spoiled, narcissistic child: you have emphasized emotionally close relationships instead of entitled expectations of special treatment. The role of parents and the society should be to help children understand that the world doesn't revolve around them. As parents ourselves, we know what it is like to be besotted with a child, and we want our daughters to know that we love them with abandon. That's exactly why we don't want to teach them to be narcissistic.

CHAPTER 12

The Quest for Infamy and the Rise of Incivility

Antisocial Behavior

In a vicious attack, six girls took turns pummeling another girl in the face, slamming her into walls, and slapping her as they screamed at her. At one point she was knocked unconscious. Two boys stood outside as lookouts to make sure the victim couldn't run away. The beating went on for 30 minutes, leaving the victim with a concussion, two black eyes, and damage to her left ear. Incarcerated in Polk County, Florida, one of the alleged perpetrators wanted to know, "Am I going to be released in time to go to cheerleading practice tomorrow?"

The beating, which was aired on television for weeks afterward in 2008, was supposedly retaliation for the victim insulting her attackers on her MySpace page. The case had another Internet-age twist: like an increasing number of adolescent fights, it was videotaped so it could be posted on YouTube.

Of course, high school age teens have been fighting even before there were high schools. What's new, and potentially related to narcissism, is the trend toward seeking fame by hurting—or even killing—someone else. Internet sites and 24-hour cable news have made it increasingly possible to become famous, and many people don't care if what they get instead is infamy. A search for fights on YouTube locates hundreds of videos, despite the site's recommendation not to post videos of people getting attacked. Often they are simply flagged as "inappropriate for some users," but they remain on the site. A cursory search turned up many fight videos that weren't even flagged. "The more they can do that's outrageous the more people are going to visit their site," said Parry Aftab, a lawyer specializing in Internet privacy. "It makes them famous—it gets them attention and it makes an impact."

Even apart from the search for fame, narcissism is a significant risk factor for aggressive and violent behavior. In our culture of self-admiration, it seems paradoxical that a narcissist—who, after all, admires himself quite a bit—would hurt someone else. Americans subscribe to the idea that if you like yourself, you will like other people and thus won't be aggressive. However, narcissists are aggressive exactly because they love themselves so much and believe that their needs take precedence. They lack empathy for other people's pain and often lash out when they feel they aren't getting the respect they deserve—and they feel they deserve a lot, because they are, of course, better than everyone else. Consider the mass murderers of history, such as Hitler, Pol Pot, Saddam Hussein, or Stalin. Do they strike you as people with low self-esteem? No, they were so confident in themselves and their beliefs that they killed millions of people. Their narcissism allowed them to disregard the most basic rights of others.

Narcissists are not necessarily aggressive all the time—unprovoked, they act just like everyone else. But they do lash out when someone else takes them down a notch. In a series of experiments conducted by Brad Bushman and Roy Baumeister, college students wrote essays and received rigged feedback, ostensibly given by another student, that said, "This is one of the worst essays I've read!" Eighty percent of those high in narcissism were more aggressive than non-narcissists after receiving this insult. Narcissists weren't aggressive toward someone who praised them, but an insult set them off. As in the Florida teen attack, the narcissistic reaction is often out of proportion to the provocation. "There is nothing our victim could have said on the Internet that would have caused that kind of beating," said Polk County sheriff Grady Judd.

Narcissists are also aggressive when someone tries to restrict their freedom: "Who are you to tell me what I can or can't do?" An aggressive response to freedom restriction was painfully demonstrated in 2007 when several Philadelphia schoolteachers were allegedly attacked by students, one when he asked a student to turn down her music, and another when he ordered a student to stop making prank phone calls on a classroom phone. Four teachers were seriously injured in separate incidents, and three of the student attackers ended up in jail for assault.

The ABC News show *20/20* filmed several participants going through Bushman and Baumeister's experiment. One young man—let's call him Nick the Narcissist—scored in the 98th percentile on narcissism and laughed as he administered strong noise blasts. Afterward he was shown the video of himself and told he could choose whether it was aired. Nick said, sure, air it. Brad Bushman took him aside and explained that he might not want to look like a highly aggressive narcissist on national television. Nick said he thought he looked great, and wanted to be on TV. Perhaps the TV producers could at least digitize his face, Bushman suggested. No way, Nick said incredulously. And, he added, it was too bad they couldn't show his name and phone number, too. This is one of the keys to understanding narcissists: they don't really care if they look like jerks; they just want to be famous.

Bushman and Baumeister recently updated their study to more closely examine the role of self-esteem in aggressive behavior, wondering if perhaps narcissism led to aggression, but only for those with low self-esteem. A study by some other researchers had found a connection between low self-esteem in boys in New Zealand and their aggressive behavior as reported by parents and teachers, but that study was correlational, meaning that the link could be caused by other factors. The study controlled for some of these factors, such as family income, but not others such as family and peer relationships. In a controlled experiment (which, unlike a correlational study, cannot be explained by extraneous factors), Bushman and Baumeister found that people high in both self-esteem and narcissism were the most aggressive—more than those high in narcissism but low in self-esteem, or those low in narcissism but high in self-esteem, or those low in both. Far from discouraging aggression, self-admiration causes aggression when it crosses over into narcissism.

In another study, preteen children with high self-esteem justified their aggression toward others by rationalizing it away. "By belittling and blaming others," the authors wrote of aggressive children with high self-esteem, "they can feel better about themselves and can continue their antisocial ways undeterred by anticipated negative self-sanctions." Much more than aggressive kids with low self-esteem, those who felt great

Source: Bushman, B. J., Baumeister, R. F., Thomaes, S., Ryu, E., Begeer, S., and West, S. G. (in press). Looking again, and harder, for a link between low self-esteem and aggression. *Journal of Personality.*

about themselves were able to preserve their self-admiration by convincing themselves that other kids deserved to get beaten up. So why not put it on YouTube?

"ISN'T IT FUN TO GET THE RESPECT THAT WE'RE GOING TO DESERVE?"

Just as overall crime rates were beginning to sink in the mid-1990s, a specific type of violent crime was becoming more and more common: school shootings. Virtually unheard of before 1996, school shootings began occurring more and more frequently, from Pearl, Mississippi, to Paducah, Kentucky, to Columbine High School in Littleton, Colorado. The shootings abated for a few years after the nation's collective experience on September 11, 2001. At the time, Keith predicted that, after 9/11, mass killings would no longer be seen as cool by the perpetrators. However, Keith was wrong. School shootings started up again in 2005 when a student killed seven people in Red Lake, Minnesota. Since then, the shootings have grown even more gruesome.

On April 16, 2007, Seung-Hui Cho shot and killed 32 students and faculty at Virginia Tech University before turning his Glock pistol on himself. Police puzzled over why Cho killed two victims at 7:15 in the morning and then waited until 9:30 to begin killing again. Their question was answered the next day when NBC News employees received a package from Cho containing papers, photographs, and videos postmarked the day of the shootings. In his "media package," Cho angrily rants against others and proclaims that he will die a martyr. "You have vandalized my heart, raped my soul and torched my conscience. Thanks to you, I die like Jesus Christ to inspire generations of the weak and the defenseless people." Apparently, Cho took a break during his killing spree to inform the media—and thus the whole world—why people owed him something.

Robert Hawkins, who killed nine people at a mall in Omaha, Nebraska, in December 2007, seemed to have similar motives. "Just think tho I'm gonna be fucking famous," he wrote in his suicide note.

In videotapes made before the April 1999 massacre at Columbine High School, shooters Eric Harris and Dylan Klebold debated which famous director would film their story (Spielberg or Tarantino?). Harris makes several statements that are shockingly similar to items on the Narcissistic Personality Inventory (NPI). "Isn't it fun to get the respect we're going to deserve?" he asks while picking up a gun and making a shooting noise, similar to the NPI item "I insist upon getting the respect that is due me." He also said, "I could convince them that I'm going to climb Mount Everest, or I have a twin brother growing out of my back. I can make you believe anything." This is similar to the NPI item "I can make anyone believe anything I want them to."

These young men clearly had problems that went beyond narcissism. For one thing, all were socially rejected by others, or at least felt as if they had been rejected. We authors wondered if narcissism and social rejection were two risk factors that worked together to cause aggressive behavior. We set up a lab study that measured narcissism, manipulated social rejection, and then assessed aggression. Participants first met a group of their fellow students and talked with them for 15 minutes before being separated in individual rooms. We then informed them that no one had chosen them as a partner for the next part of the study—in other words, their new friends had rejected them. Participants who were both narcissistic and socially rejected by others were highly aggressive toward someone else—similar to the pattern that appears in many mass shootings. As David Von Drehle put it in *Time* magazine after the Virginia Tech slayings, "It's not about guns or culture. It's narcissism. Only a narcissist could decide that his alienation should be underlined in the blood of strangers."

Given the upswing in the narcissistic values of American culture since the '90s, it may be no coincidence that mass shootings became a national plague around the same time. However, if the rise in narcissism were the only explanation, school shootings would have started earlier—perhaps in the late 1970s and '80s when the narcissism epidemic was just getting going. However, these types of social behaviors need to get attention before most people think about perpetrating them. Before school shootings received extensive media attention in the late '90s, people didn't think of shooting a group of their fellow students as a way to get fame. Columbine and the other late '90s shootings provided a script for how to commit a mass killing at a school, and demonstrated that these shootings could be linked to fame. If you ask students today, "How do you commit a mass killing at a school?" they know what to do. Before Columbine, few students would have thought about it. As American culture has grown more focused on self-admiration and more enamored with celebrity and fame, and now that mass killing in schools is seen as a direct avenue to fame and attention, the frequency of mass killings has increased dramatically. Fistfights that got wide exposure have shown a similar pattern. After the Florida beating, a younger group of girls in North Carolina carried out what appeared to be a copycat assault on another girl.

The personality traits linked to crime more generally are low self-control and two personality "cousins" of narcissism, antisocial personality disorder and psychopathy. Many crimes are committed by impulsive people doing destructive things for short-term, selfish benefits. Narcissism is linked to violent crime in certain contexts: when there is the possibility of gaining fame, and when there is an ego threat or rejection. However, narcissism does not account for most crime. Demographics play a large role: young people commit the most crimes, so as the number of young people in a society increases, so does criminal activity. Another large influence is the economy: when the economy worsens, crime rises. Many crimes are linked to buying or otherwise acquiring and selling drugs, or committing criminal acts after using drugs. Much of the drop in crime since the early '90s is attributable to demographics, improved economic conditions, and the winding down of the crack epidemic. In contrast, narcissism plays a role in crimes linked to fame, attention seeking, and threats to the ego. Getting in a fistfight is one thing; posting it online to get attention is another thing entirely.

STFU

Of course, narcissistic aggression doesn't have to be directly physical. Allison, the *My Super Sweet 16* reality star, was displaying a form of aggression when she declared that her party was more important than the people who wouldn't get to the emergency room when she blocked off the street for her grand entrance.

Verbal aggression—people being cruel to one another with words—also seems to be on the upswing in the United States. Seventy percent of Americans say that people are ruder now than they were 20 years ago. One professor at a college in Ohio groused in our online survey, "I've experienced extreme rudeness from students recently. They get extremely upset and aggressive if I ask them to turn off their cell phones. And God forbid I ask them to stop text messaging during class—this results in an outright confrontation that has come close to requiring the presence of security." In April 2007, *Allure* magazine ran an article titled "Life's a Bitch," in which they pointed out that blogs are now "venomous," reality TV is "snide," and Hollywood stars are "vicious." "Grown-up mean girls are everywhere," they concluded.

Incivility has become shamelessly common, nowhere more than on the Internet. The comments on many Internet sites reach high levels of intellectual and grammatical sophistication such as "Your a dickhead." During one week in 2007, for example, a video of a six-year-old girl singing about her Iraq War soldier brother mostly attracted comments such as "awh! so cute" (though several posters left backhanded compliments like "im suree she will be a good singer when she grows up"). Others found the need to say things like "shes homosexual," or "wow . . . she sucks." That prompted a lofty level of discourse in return, such as "you retarded twat, you're the pathetic one, that kid is hella cute" and "NOO one cares about ur opinion u stupid prick." Even children with no connection to war or politics sometimes get attacked. One Escondido, California, man posted a video of his seven- and nine-year-old sons' excited reaction to receiving a new video game system on YouTube. After a few days of the obligatory "they're so cute" comments, several posters called the kids fat and ugly. It only got worse from there, and the father pulled the video off the site.

Much of this is driven by the anonymity of the Internet, yet these vitriolic comments display an unmistakable narcissism. There is the anger and verbal aggression against someone who dares to disagree. There is the assumption that "my opinion matters," yet, at the same time, the stubborn insistence that other people's opinions are wrong or irrelevant. ("No one cares about your opinion"—with various grammatical mistakes and/or texting shorthand—is a common posting on these sites.) And finally, there is the utter disregard for grammar and spelling, as if to say, "I'm too busy and important to bother with writing well—why follow all of those arbitrary rules just so it's easier for other people to read it?"

As we explored in Chapter 7, there's plenty of antisocial language on Web pages even when people aren't anonymous. Many people post their aggressive attitudes right on their own MySpace pages, telling people to go away if they disagree. Levi Johnston, who earned his 15 minutes of fame for being the father of former vice presidential candidate Sarah Palin's grandchild, noted on his MySpace page, "Ya fuck with me I'll kick yr ass." This sounds unusually aggressive, but many teenage boys make similar threats on their MySpace pages.

Of course, this pales in comparison to "cyber-bullying," in which teens use e-mail, texting, or MySpace messages to insult and attack someone else. Bullying and teasing have always been common among adolescents, but cyber-bullying often means that victims cannot escape the reach of their tormentors, even in their bedroom at home. Their cell phones and MySpace pages are their connections to the world, but that is where they are also most vulnerable to attack. "Fuck you bitch. Before I leave yo gay azz page lemme tell you dis . . . ima get you!!! I no where you skinny ass lives," read one message received by a teen. Even adults have gotten into the game; in 2008, a Missouri woman was indicted for pretending to be a boy interested in her teen neighbor, and then cruelly dumping her. The teen committed suicide. Although most cyber-bullying incidents involve relatively minor insults, a 2006 study found that 12% of adolescents were physically threatened, and 5% feared for their safety.

A website called juicycampus.com encourages college students to post nasty gossip about their classmates, whether it is true or not. "One of the categories [on the website] was ugliest girl," said a student from Boston University. "Another was girls who have hooked up with a lot of guys. Most of the topics are mean things." One Duke University student visited the site only to see that someone had posted all kinds of cruel untruths about her—that she is ugly, that she once attempted suicide. Of course, the poster was allowed to remain completely anonymous. A Baylor University student was able to identify who had defamed her online—and it turned out to be one of her closest friends. "That hurt me 10 times more," she said. "The site can do that—ruin friendships and reputations."

Verbal abuse at the hands of narcissists is widespread in the real world as well, even in professional workplaces. In *The No Asshole Rule*, Robert Sutton describes office "assholes" as arrogant, angry, and inconsiderate—all prominent traits of narcissists. One mean boss went through 250 assistants in five years. Some of the assistants quit because he yelled and swore at them, but others were fired for offenses such as bringing the wrong breakfast muffin. Another narcissistic boss repeatedly nagged his secretary to pay the dry-cleaning bill when she accidentally spilled some ketchup on his pants. Other bosses manage to demean employees without yelling. During conversations with his boss, an office administrator noticed that the manager rarely looked at him when they were talking; instead, she gazed in the mirror behind him, alternately admiring her reflection and fluffing her hair.

Abusive workplace behavior is shockingly widespread. In one survey, 90% of nurses said doctors had verbally abused them. More than a third of employees at the U.S. Department of Veterans Affairs reported "persistent hostility" from coworkers. Consistent with the research showing that narcissism does not lead to success, businesses found that their profits went up after these jerks were fired, even if the narcissists were high producers. It's tough to make a business profitable when no one wants to work there.

Antisocial attitudes show up surprisingly early among children these days. In the early 2000s, elementary schools around the country reported an alarming rise in the number of kindergartners who swore at or physically fought with teachers. Even children's T-shirts seem to encourage rudeness. Shirts for six-year-olds include one showing a monkey with its hands over its ears, saying "I'm not listening," clearly mimicking a disobedient child tuning out a parent or teacher. Another announces, "I'm talented. I can play video games and ignore you at the same time." One boys' T-shirt has "The perfect sister" printed over a crude drawing of a girl with her mouth X'd out. Another shirt for one-year-olds proclaims, "I'm this many" over a drawing of a child's hand giving the finger.

EVERYBODY CHEATS

As the CEO of WorldCom, Bernie Ebbers was worth $1.4 billion, owned Canada's largest ranch, and was one of *Time* magazine's Digital 50 in 1999. Not long afterward, though, WorldCom realized things were starting to fall apart—but if this were disclosed, the stock price and the personal wealth of the executives would suffer. In June 2002, the company admitted to $3.85 billion in accounting misstatements, and the company imploded. After a series of trials for fraud, Ebbers was convicted in 2005 and sentenced to 25 years in prison. He drove himself to jail in his Mercedes.

Ebbers is far from alone in his embrace of cheating to get ahead. The energy giant Enron went belly-up under similar circumstances, after a corporate culture that encouraged competition turned out to encourage cooking the books as well. Tyco CEO Dennis Kozlowski and two other employees took white-collar crime to another level when they used millions of dollars from the company to buy things for themselves and their families, including a $6,000 shower curtain in Kozlowski's New York residence. Kozlowski also threw a birthday party for his wife that cost $2 million and featured an ice sculpture of Michelangelo's David tinkling vodka from its penis. Corporate fraud was so rampant in the early 2000s that Congress took action by passing the Sarbanes-Oxley law, requiring that company CEOs certify the accuracy of their revenue reporting.

It isn't just the bigwigs who are cheating to get ahead. In 2007, a six-year-old submitted an essay to a contest that began, "My daddy died this year in Iraq." The girl won four tickets to a Hannah Montana concert and a free makeover. The only problem was her father had never served in Iraq, much less died there. The girl's mother was matter-of-fact about the deception. "We did the essay and that's what we did to win," she said. "We did whatever we could do to win."

Recent scandals have also exposed cheating in sports. After years of baseball fans noticing that players sure were a lot bigger than they used to be, the massive amount of steroid use obvious to fans was finally exposed. Most of the great moments in baseball of the 1990s and 2000s, it turned out, were accomplished through cheating. Sammy Sosa and Mark McGwire, fan darlings during the home run race in 1998, were likely both on steroids and/or androstenedione. Barry Bonds's eclipsing of Hank Aaron's lifetime home run record of 755 in 2007 was tainted by the accusation that Bonds shot the juice. Marc Ecko, who bought the historic 756th home run ball, polled Americans on what should be done with the ball. Ten million people voted in the poll, and 47% voted to brand the ball with an asterisk before it was donated to the Baseball Hall of Fame, a shameful symbol of a tainted record. Almost 20% felt even more strongly, voting to banish the ball from the earth by blasting it into space.

Other sports have fallen victim to cheats as well. Marion Jones admitted to using performance-enhancing drugs before winning five medals in track events at the 2000 Olympics. Before the scandal broke, she was on the cover of *Vogue* and had become a millionaire several times over. Afterward, she was sentenced to six months in prison. Bicyclist Floyd Landis was stripped of his 2006 Tour de France title after testing positive for injected testosterone. A year later, five different competitors on the tour were found to be doping. Cheating in sports has reached all levels: in 2001, Little League pitcher Danny Almonte was disqualified from the Little League World Series because his father had doctored his birth certificate. Little League players must be 12 or under; Danny was actually 14.

Journalism has been overtaken by cheating scandals in the last two decades. Stephen Glass fabricated dozens of stories when he wrote for the *New Republic* and was finally caught in 1998. Jayson Blair plagiarized material for several stories from other reporters' articles and was fired from the *New York Times*. *USA Today* correspondent Jack Kelley fabricated several stories for the newspaper.

Our own profession is not immune. Karen Ruggiero, a social psychologist who was a professor at Harvard and then the University of Texas, published research containing unrealistically clean results that others found difficult to replicate. In 2001 she resigned her professorship and admitted to falsifying data in several studies. Disclaimers withdrawing her articles appear in databases of psychology research such as PsycINFO.

Cheating is also rampant, and growing, among students. In 2002, 74% of high school students admitted to cheating, up from 61% in 1992. In 1969, only 34% of high school students admitted to cheating, less than half of the 2002 number. A large 2008 survey of teens found that two-thirds admitted to cheating and nearly one-third had stolen something from a store. Nevertheless, 93% said they were satisfied with their personal ethics—a classically narcissistic disconnect between reality and self-concept. The cheating continues into college; a 2002 survey found that 80% of students at Texas A&M University admitted to cheating; a 2007 poll of students at 12 different colleges found that 67% admitted to cheating. Although competition for grades may have fueled the increase, attitudes have shifted along with the behavior. A 2004 study of 25,000 high school students found that 67% of boys and 52% of girls agreed that "in the real world, successful people do what they have to do to win, even if others consider it cheating."

Technology has facilitated this dishonesty, with students passing exam answers through camera cell phones and downloading papers on the Internet. A website called affordabletermpapers.com charges $9.95 a page for a custom-written essay. The antiplagiarism site turnitin.com, designed to help teachers catch cheaters, gets one hundred thousand submissions a day.

Narcissists often see nothing wrong with cheating. It's all about them, so who cares if a few rules are broken? Unfortunately, this is an illusion: Forget the rationalization that cheating "doesn't hurt anyone," because it does. For every person who cheats on his income taxes, other Americans face cuts to government-funded services. Cheating students shortchange those who actually do the work, and shortchange themselves of learning in the long run. Shareholders lose their life savings when companies report imaginary earnings. Baseball players who play clean can't keep up with those doped up on steroids, who go on to break records and make millions, resulting in broken bodies for the cheaters and broken careers for those who followed the rules. Of course, narcissists don't think about this, because they don't consider the effects of their actions on others. A study of German white-collar criminals found that they scored significantly higher in narcissism than a comparison group of noncheating managers.

Why are so many people cheating these days? Our hypercompetitive, individualistic, self-admiring culture is at least partially to blame. As David Callahan argues in *The Cheating Culture*, the current "winner-take-all" mentality, fueled by increased competition, encourages people to break the rules to get ahead. And when a few people start doing it (often the more narcissistic), it cascades until more and more people feel that if they don't cheat there is no way they will ever win. "People not otherwise prone to cheating come to do so because they don't want to put themselves at a disadvantage. Arguments that 'everybody does it' serve as a key rationalization for cheating," Callahan notes. Like other types of narcissistic behavior, cheating raises the bar for everyone and draws more and more people into the vortex begun by just a few super-spreaders.

TREATMENT FOR THE EPIDEMIC

The first step toward severing the link between narcissism and antisocial behaviors is to make socially inappropriate behavior go unnoticed and unrewarded. If the goal of a violent crime is attention seeking or fame, eliminating that possibility would reduce the number of crimes. Take the Florida beating case as an example: although the girls were caught before they could post the video of the fight on YouTube, it was shown numerous times on network television, and was *then* posted on YouTube.

Stopping video from getting posted on the Web is practically impossible. However, stopping video from being shown on news channels is not. The news media, for example, stopped showing one of the most horrific videos of our time, the plane crashes of 9/11. The news media should institute a policy that they will not show criminal video made in the interest of seeking fame and/or humiliating a victim. In fact, one could argue that the large Internet sites are ahead of the news media in this regard. According to YouTube's official policy, "Graphic or gratuitous violence is not allowed. If your video shows someone getting hurt, attacked, or humiliated, don't post it." Enforcement is of course more difficult, but apparently the mainstream news networks don't even have this policy in principle. Likewise, MySpace forbids material that "is patently offensive and promotes racism, bigotry, hatred or physical harm of any kind against any group or individual; harasses or advocates harassment of another person; exploits people in a sexual or violent manner; or contains nudity, excessive violence, or offensive subject matter or contains a link to an adult website." Again, easier said than done. Nevertheless, this would be a useful policy for the news media. Stories could still be reported, but without the video—usually the crucial piece in the attackers' attention-seeking revenge strategy. If teens are doing stupid, violent things to seek attention, adults need to act responsibly, use some discretion, and not broadcast those images. Such rules are debated by journalists partially because they are caught in a trap: if they take the high road but their competitor doesn't, they will lose revenue and maybe their jobs. Thus, to be effective, these policies have to be shared across media networks.

The consumers of these media messages are also guilty. Many people respond to videos of beatings by labeling the perpetrators as evil, notorious, or infamous, which, to younger viewers, often translates into "cool." A better response would be to call these acts what they are—in most cases, immature people doing stupid things because they have been taught that it is a path to all-important fame. In truth, it is sad, pathetic behavior. If we treated it that way, the "cool" factor would diminish and no one would want to do it anymore. Being pathetic and sad is not considered cool by anyone.

More generally, punishment works as a strategy for minimizing bad behavior. In the case of white-collar crime, the threat of prison is a very powerful inducement for proper behavior; for violence, criminal prosecution can have a similar effect. Teens (and others) need to know that you can go to jail for having a fistfight, particularly if you are overconfident enough to film it. Punishment also has an impact on cheating. Unfortunately, especially at the corporate level, it is very hard to get people to report cheating and similar criminal behavior.

Many whistle-blowers say it took extraordinary measures for them to come forward. Companies are just now instituting systems to deal with reports of cheating. Education lags even further behind. Much plagiarism is not caught. When students are caught, many campuses give what amounts to a slap on the wrist, giving the student a "second chance." Because careful records are often not kept, that second chance can turn into a third, a fourth, and so on. Other campuses have harsh penalties, but few students are caught. We have both heard of cases of students plagiarizing papers verbatim but not getting punished at all, sometimes because a parent intervened. In other instances, punishment is applied too harshly for minor and possibly unintentional acts of cheating. In short, many students report cheating in anonymous surveys, very few get caught, and punishments vary dramatically. Behavioral psychology suggests that this is not a structure that will reduce cheating. The key to effective punishment is consistency and reliability. If people knew they would get caught—even if the punishment was not dramatic—the rate of cheating would drop dramatically.

Another solution is suppressing narcissism with a culture that encourages and even celebrates honor and integrity. Some colleges have a strong tradition of an honor code. Research by Donald McCabe shows that honor codes reduce cheating as long as the school has a strong social norm enforcing it. At Vanderbilt University, every first-year student signs an agreement affirming his or her commitment to the honor code, and these signatures are posted on a large banner that hangs in the student center.

Some elementary schools are instituting programs called "character education," which teach about honesty, following rules, responsibility, and fairness. Most programs focus on these types of commonly held values that transcend any particular culture or religion. YMCA camps and classes have taught these values for years, concentrating on the four core values of honesty, responsibility, respect, and caring. In some elementary schools, children write rules at the beginning of the year (edited, of course, by an adult). They usually come up with rules against lying, cheating, and stealing, and are more likely to follow them because they have had a part in writing them.

Unfortunately, many of these character education programs also teach self-esteem, and self-esteem programs usually end up teaching a form of narcissism such as "I am special." These programs are based on the mistaken premise that children who feel good about themselves will be more likely to follow the rules and not cheat or lie. However, special people don't need to follow the rules, and narcissistic people are *more* likely to cheat, not less, just as they are more likely to be aggressive.

Sometimes, however, a narcissist doesn't have to cheat or be aggressive to do damage. Sometimes all you have to do is date him.

CHAPTER 13

The Chocolate Cake Trap

Relationship Troubles

Kim, 32, lived her dream last year when she met a charming and good-looking man at a restaurant in Boston. He was everything that she ever dreamed of: outgoing, confident, successful, and attentive—but not too attentive. Kim felt special and beautiful when she was around him. Whenever they went out, she felt that the eyes of everyone at the bar or club were on her. Kim was swept off her feet. Within a month the new couple was traveling to the Cayman Islands on a scuba-diving trip. It was the most exciting time in Kim's life.

Amanda, 37, lived her worst nightmare a few years ago when she was diagnosed with cancer, enduring six weeks of radiation and ten months of chemotherapy. Married with a baby daughter, she was at first happy she didn't have to go through the ordeal alone. That was until her husband started to complain that her medical appointments inconvenienced him because he had to shift his work schedule by half an hour. He also commented that her cancer-induced weakness embarrassed him in public. And then, Amanda says, "While I was at home undergoing chemo, raising his daughter (my stepdaughter) and our baby girl, he was off on 'business trips,' cheating on me with a female co-worker."

While these stories seem to be diametrically opposed, they are both about relationships with narcissists. These relationships can be very good in the beginning, as Kim's story illustrates, but then they often turn very bad, as Amanda discovered. Many relationships with narcissists feature a big start and a disastrous finish. Relationships with narcissists can become particularly bad if you get too committed to them, too attached, or give them too much power. This is what happened to Amanda; she was married to a narcissist and had two children to raise. When her needs were not aligned with her narcissistic husband's wants, the wheels came off the relationship.

Narcissists are both exciting relationship partners and awful ones. Their relationships are all about feeding the ego—definitely their egos and sometimes even your ego. Narcissists' relationship partners primarily serve to make narcissists look and feel powerful, special, admired, attractive, and important. Love, caring, commitment, loyalty and all those other things at the core of healthy relationships matter less to narcissists, who move on when they can't get the needed ego gratification. Kim had a great time with a narcissist, because, like many new relationships, it was all about being exciting, fun, and novel—which was also appealing to the narcissist. That's also why Amanda had such a terrible relationship experience—her husband was embarrassed to have a wife who had had cancer surgery, which he apparently thought hurt his image.

Narcissists can sometimes be surprisingly honest about their lack of relationship skills. In her song "The world should revolve around me," Little Jackie sings, "I've had a lot of failed relationships . . . I don't need you around I know I rock!"

Narcissists act in ego-driven ways in other types of social relationships as well: on Internet social networking sites, in friendships, as parents, and in the workplace. But narcissism in romantic relationships is especially easy to see because people are willing to put up with a lot from someone they love, and because the "rules" for how to behave in romantic relationships are not as clear as they are in, for example, the workplace. Narcissism is especially damaging in romantic relationships. Keith wrote a book on the topic, *When You Love a Man Who Loves Himself*, in part because of all the tragic e-mails he received from women (but also a few men) who had suffered in relationships with narcissists. Since then, he has heard from many people going through divorces from narcissists, from women who have considered suicide and hospitalization as a result of these relationships, and from people who just want to share amusing stories about their past relationships with narcissists (these stories, of course, are only funny in retrospect—at the time they were incredibly painful). There was the narcissist who constantly compared himself to

Jesus, because he was Jewish and born in late December; the husband who went out shopping for school clothes for the children and came back with a set of golf clubs for himself; the man who bought *himself* a diamond earring for his wife's Christmas gift; and the boyfriend who took pictures of himself in the mirror every night—he was so enraptured with his good looks that he had to record them or he couldn't sleep.

THE NARCISSISTIC APPROACH TO RELATIONSHIPS

Marriages and other committed romantic partnerships usually have two important factors. One is love, the emotional component that initiates the relationship and adds much of the depth. Love typically involves feelings of warmth, caring, and passion. At the early stages, love is often experienced as passion, and as the marriage progresses it is based more on caring. The other factor is commitment to the spouse and the marriage. This can involve financially supporting each other, taking turns making dinner, and dividing up responsibilities for child care and household chores.

This same basic model of relationships, but without the element of sexual passion, works in other relationships as well. Parents and children feel love and commitment and have responsibilities to one another. Likewise, in friendship there is love and commitment, but with an emphasis on loyalty and trust. Because friendships are voluntary and relatively easy to end (unlike family relationships), just enjoying being around a friend is crucial. Relationships founded on love, commitment, and loyalty are also good for the broader community: stable relationships mean stable individuals who are better citizens, coworkers, students, and leaders.

To understand narcissists' approach to relationships, take every one of these ideas and throw them away. In place of love for another person, put love for the self; in place of caring, put exploitation; and to commitment, add "as long as it benefits me." Narcissists' approach to relationships is simple: it's all about them. They want to look and feel good, and if the relationship is a way to do this, great; if not, it's time to find another one. People often use the term "feeding the ego" to describe narcissists' approach to relationships. If the relationship proves to be sufficient food, it works, and if not, it doesn't.

Relationships can successfully sustain a narcissist's ego in scores of ways. He can marry someone who looks good and serves his needs—a so-called trophy wife. Or he can have lots of friends ("I have 3,000 friends on MySpace"), milk others for esteem ("my child is the smartest kid at Middlebrooke High School"), gather a posse of admirers and sycophants (this is a popular approach for celebrities, as detailed in HBO's *Entourage*), or simply bludgeon people with verbal abuse. He can let his eyes glaze over when he talks to others to keep an air of dominance, or can jump into whatever spotlight is available. In each of these cases, the "relationship" is really about the needs of the self. Don McLean's classic song "Everybody Loves Me, Baby" captures this aspect of narcissism: "The ocean parts when I walk through," he sings. "Everybody loves me, baby, what's the matter with you?"

Not only are relationships about the narcissist's ego, but, for the narcissist, relationships are interchangeable. Economists have a great term for this: *fungible*. Gasoline is fungible: you can buy gas from one gas station or another and it doesn't make a difference. For narcissists, relationships are fungible: one trophy spouse can be exchanged for another, and as long as the narcissist's ego is being fed the same amount of admiration, that's fine. For narcissists, relationships and material goods are almost interchangeable. Imagine trading your relationship with your husband for a beautiful new home, or your relationship with your girlfriend for a Porsche. If what you really need from the relationship is status, esteem, and attention, why not? You might get more of it from the Porsche than the girlfriend.

Take Scott, 25, featured in an MTV documentary. Scott has a "friends with benefits" relationship with Rachel, meaning they see each other regularly and sleep together, but aren't committed in any way. When Rachel confessed she was beginning to feel attached to Scott, he casually stretched his hands behind his head (a classic dominance pose) and said, "I don't think I'm attached at all." In a "real" friends with benefits situation, he said, "none of this conversation would even exist. You're not supposed to get too mixed up in whatever the other is feeling or anything—just kind of go with the flow." When Rachel gets upset, Scott says, "I just don't let myself get attached. I need to start lying to you more. Maybe that would just make everything better. What you don't know won't hurt you." After Rachel leaves the apartment, Scott admits to the interviewer, "Rachel isn't everything I'm looking for in a girl. This is something to keep me occupied for the time being. I'd rather be kind of with her than just be alone."

This mix of ego feeding and fungibility leads to all sorts of nasty relationship behaviors. Much of narcissists' behavior in relationships is "game playing." They are deceptive and dishonest; they will signal commitment at one time and then pull away the next; they will play people off against one another; and they will avoid real commitment. Game playing has some real benefits for the narcissistic spouse, boyfriend, or employee; it can give them power over others due to "the principle of least interest," which dictates that the person with the least interest in the relationship has the most power. Game playing also has the benefit of allowing freedom by "keeping your options open." If you resume finding potential "hookups" or competing companies that might hire you, you can switch relationships or jobs quickly.

This game-playing strategy works pretty well for narcissists, but it doesn't work so well for their current partners. These short-term relationships with narcissists aren't always as enjoyable or as exciting as they sound (or look on TV). Narcissists tend to end relationships that don't live up to the promise of a status or self-esteem boost—or the relationship partner, whether it's a spouse or employee, finally gets fed up and dumps the narcissist. For example, by the end of the MTV documentary, Rachel and Scott had ended their "friends with benefits" arrangement, mostly because Rachel got tired of being with someone who clearly didn't care for her. As the figure on page 216 shows, relationships with narcissists start off great, but relationship satisfaction quickly craters as time goes on and the narcissist's downside becomes evident.

A narcissist thinks of a relationship partner as fuel. Narcissists use others to power their status and esteem, and when the other person no longer provides that, they are dumped in the trash bin. The classic example is the man who has a series of trophy wives. The relationship lasts only as long as the trophy is doing her job and making the narcissist look powerful and important. When the trophy is no longer as attractive (or a more attractive trophy is found), she is replaced. Some narcissists will marry young woman after young woman, each kept until she is no longer attractive or desirable. We have heard many times from people who end relationships with narcissists and report being "used up," "sucked dry," or

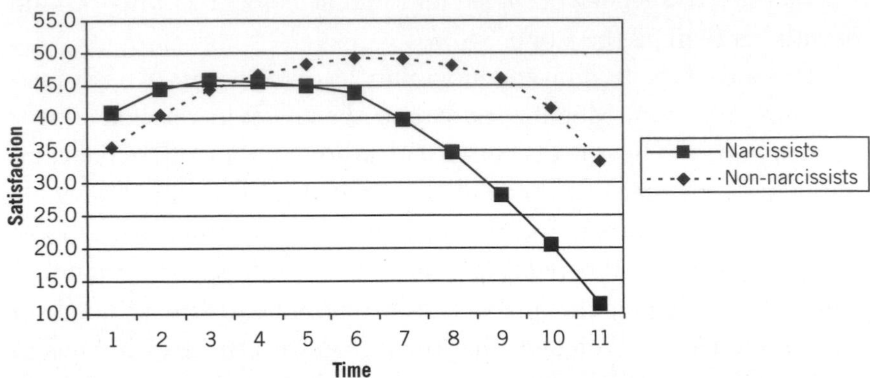

Source: Campbell, W. K. (January 2006). "Narcissism and romantic relationships." Paper presented at Relationships Preconference at the annual meeting of the Society for Personality and Social Psychology, Palm Springs, California.

simply "burned." It is an absolutely awful feeling to love someone and then come to realize—sometimes after years—that the person never really cared about you at all.

It is not surprising that narcissists' partners feel so damaged. What's worse is that they often cannot safely express those feelings to their partner, who responds to criticism with denial, abuse, and even violence. Any criticism of the narcissist can provoke a hostile reaction. Those living with and working with narcissists quickly learn to keep their opinions to themselves. Or they will coat them in more sugar than a child consumes on Halloween, sweetly suggesting that it might be better to tone down the arrogance—not because it's unjustified, but because other people are, naturally, jealous of the narcissist's greatness. Social rejection also provokes strong reactions from narcissists, not because they care that much about their partners, but because they feel a sense of pride and ownership. Many cases of spousal violence occur when a narcissist feels rejected or abandoned. Narcissists also get angry and aggressive when they feel their freedom is restricted—in other words, when they can't do what they want. Brad Bushman and his colleagues have found that this reaction occurs in some rapes, where the narcissist is told "no" and this activates his aggression. These three triggers of aggression—ego threat, rejection, and saying no—make a relationship with a narcissist feel like tiptoeing though a minefield. The excitement at the beginning is not worth the stress, anxiety and sometimes fear that come later.

IF NARCISSISM IS SO BAD, HOW DOES IT SPREAD ACROSS RELATIONSHIPS?

One of the key features of epidemics is that they spread. Yet once people figure out how something is spread, they can quarantine themselves. In the flu epidemic of 1918, for example, Americans stayed in their homes. After AIDS began to spread, more people used condoms. So why don't we avoid relationships with narcissists the same way we avoid kissing someone with a bad cold? It should be relatively easy. In a perfect world, you would select someone to have a relationship with—as a spouse, friend, employee, or employer—who was committed, loyal, trustworthy, and enjoyable. Because our emotions would line up with our best interests, the selection of a caring, committed spouse would be accompanied by feelings of attraction. We would be repulsed by folks who are vain, narcissistic, self-absorbed, and cocky.

Unfortunately, with relationships—especially romantic relationships, but also in friendships and even in picking CEOs—people have a major problem with selection. We really want two things from relationships: the sizzle, the fun, exciting, confident, charismatic outgoing and "magic" part, and the substance, the commitment, caring, and teamwork part. Narcissists' secret to success in relationships is that they deliver the sizzle up front, but then fail to deliver the substance. Instead, you end up with a bevy of relationship problems like those described above.

One great example is the character Dr. Mark Sloan on *Grey's Anatomy*. Known as "Dr. McSteamy," Mark delivers all the sizzle: he is handsome, confident, socially dominant, and oozes sex appeal. At the same time, he is a disaster for relationships. He slept with his best friend's spouse and ruined their marriage; then he followed his friend to Seattle and hit on his new girlfriend. All the while, he was purportedly trying to rebuild the friendship with his former best friend. Clearly, McSteamy is bad news, yet he manages to have short-term relationships with several women and is fantasized about by the rest (and probably a huge number of Americans).

The love for McSteamy is a classic example of what Keith likes to call the Chocolate Cake Trap. Imagine sitting at the table with two plates of food. On one is a beautiful chocolate cake, covered in a delicious chocolate fudge frosting; on the other is a plate of steamed broccoli. Your job is to pick one plate to eat. If you are like us authors, you pick the chocolate cake. Chocolate cake is awesome. It tastes great, gives you a rush of sugary goodness, and can almost make you feel loved. There is nothing better than chocolate cake . . . for the ten minutes you're eating it. After that, especially if you're trying to eat healthily, the chocolate cake that you loved so much turns on you. You feel depressed as the sugar leaves your system. Crawling under your desk and taking a nap sounds nice. You realize that you and chocolate cake have no long-term future together because the cake will increase your weight and give you cavities. The cake might even cheat on you by getting eaten by someone else. You feel vaguely guilty and confused about why you still want chocolate cake even though you know it's bad for you.

On the other hand, had you eaten the broccoli, it would have been a much different story. You wouldn't have gotten the big rush at the beginning, but it would have been OK—broccoli isn't that bad. Twenty minutes later you would have felt good, healthy, positive about your eating choices, and there would have been no sugar crash. You would sit at your desk and work rather than wanting to crawl under it and listen to an old Pink Floyd album. The bottom line is that broccoli is the better choice . . . and the next time you are given the choice you will still eat the chocolate cake.

This same pattern holds in many relationships with narcissists. There is a rush of excitement in starting a relationship with an exciting and charismatic figure. You feel flattered that the narcissist is paying attention to you and bringing you into his or her life. You feel pretty special, too, because the narcissist shines brightly in social situations. Psychologist Del Paulhus did a terrific study on narcissism in a small group of strangers who met several times over a semester. During the first meeting, the narcissists were seen as exciting and outgoing and were liked more than the others. After several meetings, however, the narcissists became less liked and quickly wore out their welcome. This same pattern seems to hold with leadership. In small groups, narcissists are perceived as leaders even after very brief discussions, which is fine with the narcissists because they want to be leaders. Over repeated meetings, however, the others grow tired of narcissists' leadership strivings.

In a recent FedEx commercial, a group of business types are sitting around a table discussing ways to save money. A midlevel corporate type suggests using FedEx. No one else at the table pays attention. Then the well-dressed boss at the head of the table says the exact same thing, but uses his hands in a decisive chopping gesture. Everyone around the table then pipes up in agreement. When the employee who originally made the suggestion points out that he said it first, he is told he lacked the confident hand gesture. This commercial is funny because it matches reality sadly well. In the corporate world, sizzle often wins over substance, at least in the short term.

Narcissists save the bad stuff for later in the relationships. Your fiancé tells you that your best friend can't be in the wedding because she is too fat and will ruin the pictures. Your wife racks up an enormous credit card bill paying for her plastic surgery, and then runs away with the plastic surgeon. The seemingly "fun and cool boss" steals your ideas and gets you transferred. A coworker starts sabotaging your performance and you're fired.

In a *Tango* magazine article, Isabel Rose wrote about getting in bed with her husband the night of her birthday. "Did you forget something?" she asked. He said, "What do you mean?" She said, "A card? A present? I don't know. Something. It's my birthday." After a pause he replied, "I'm your present." A few weeks later, he ignored her when she asked him several questions. "Are you going deaf, or are you just ignoring me?" He replied, "I don't like to answer dumb questions." Needless to say, he is now her ex-husband.

Because Keith has written a book and many articles on narcissism and relationships, he often gets calls from people who have experiences like this and have nowhere else to turn. These people are hurting so much that they pick up the phone, call a complete stranger, and burst into tears. One woman was concerned about her daughter, who was married to a dishonest, self-absorbed man. The daughter left repeatedly, but was constantly conned into taking the husband back. This is an absolutely heartbreaking situation for parents to watch. It is easy to see narcissism at work as an outside observer, but someone in a committed relationship has a more difficult time gaining perspective.

Scott Peterson, convicted of murdering his wife, Laci, is a study in how narcissism can lead to disaster. Peterson was a charming, good-looking, and seemingly likable guy. He had a problem, however: his wife was having a baby and he wanted to enjoy life with his new mistress. His solution was simply to toss his wife into San Francisco Bay. He could have gotten a divorce (not a great gesture, but it happens), but the divorce would have been expensive and made him look bad. He decided murder was a better solution for him.

But the story doesn't end there. In an amazing tribute to the seductive powers of narcissism, Peterson, while sitting in jail for murdering his wife and unborn child, received numerous marriage proposals. Although he was able to win the hearts of dozens of complete strangers, the other prisoners felt exactly the opposite; Peterson had to be isolated because men who kill women and children don't fare well in the prison population. Apparently, killing women and children is frowned upon by even hardened criminals, but not by would-be lovers.

Narcissists may seem like a tasty treat when you first meet them, but they are not. Narcissism is *absolutely corrosive to social relationships*. People who have been deeply involved with narcissists can tell you this. These relationships destroy trust in others. You learn not to trust anyone after being mistreated by someone so charming and likable. You also lose trust in yourself. If you couldn't see this coming, what does that tell you about your judgment? And then, to dip the wound in salt, relationships with narcissists are remembered and ruminated about for a long time. People ponder what went wrong; they ruminate about the warning signs they should have seen; and they waste a lot of time trying to figure out what made the narcissist into a narcissist.

THE NARCISSISTIC CULTURE AND ITS IMPACT ON RELATIONSHIPS

Although most people are not going to turn into Scott Peterson anytime soon, a range of relationship behaviors, from troubling to humorous to just plain bizarre, has accompanied the narcissism epidemic. These behaviors, which would have been considered immature, odd, or even shocking in the past—if they had been thought of at all—are now relatively normal and getting more so.

One pattern of relationship behaviors is the "fear of settling" or "fear of missing out on the magic." In the old days this would have been considered simple immaturity. You would have been told to "take the good with the bad" or "relationships are not all about you." Today there is a different cultural message. In May 2007, a Chicago law firm advertised its services with a large billboard saying "Life's short. Get a divorce" flanked by a picture of a large-breasted woman in a black bra on one side and a bare-chested man with great abs on the other. The sign drew hordes of negative media coverage and was taken down within a week, but it had done its job, because the divorce attorneys got lots of calls—probably from people who wanted to move on to the next and newer model.

Our individualistic culture narcissistically teaches people not to compromise. "Whether we're talking about an eight-year marriage or an eight-week fling, you should never stick with someone you aren't 100 percent sure about just because you're afraid you won't do any better," writes former ABC TV Bachelorette Jen Schefft in her 2007 advice book, *Better Single Than Sorry: A No-Regrets Guide to Loving Yourself and Never Settling*. "If you're a self-assured woman with a lot to offer, there's no excuse for it. Low self-esteem is . . . one of the forces of evil that drives women to settle." In other words, you shouldn't put up with any flaws in your partner—you're too good for that. While some partners do have truly major flaws, anyone who's been in a relationship for more than a few months can tell you that there are *always* going to be times when "you aren't 100 percent sure" about your partner. No one is flawless, and if you expect perfection from a partner you are either delusional or narcissistic. Yet Schefft's statements are squarely in the cultural mainstream, with TV, movies, and magazines promoting very similar messages. "Many GenXers feel entitled to a relationship that is always fun and easy," notes Jillian Straus in her cultural analysis *Unhooked Generation*. "Many [of them] wanted to 'do their own thing' and expected love and relationships to be on their schedule, on their terms, and to come without too much personal sacrifice. . . . [There is] a 'What have you done for me lately?' attitude in relationships." And if the answer is "not enough," it's on to the next partner—after all, goes our narcissistic cultural patter, you deserve better.

It's difficult to focus on someone else when you've been taught your whole life to focus on yourself. Jean recently overheard a conversation between two college students, one of whom had been dating her boyfriend for six months, her longest relationship ever. "Does it feel weird?" asked her friend. "It feels really weird," she replied. "I'm used to having time to myself. I'm used to being able to work on myself, instead of taking care of someone else." Of course, people have always had to make adjustments when they enter committed relationships. Not that long ago, however, the concept of "working on myself" would not have been so important or so relevant.

Many people believe that self-admiration is good for relationships as long as it doesn't balloon into narcissism—in other words, you have to love yourself to be able to love someone else. This is a pervasive belief in our culture; in our online survey, people mentioned this over and over as the main benefit of self-admiration. "If you don't love yourself, how can you expect others to want to love you?" wrote Bryson, 22. "If you didn't love yourself, you wouldn't know how to love anyone else," wrote Lisa, 39. This idea is often mentioned in the popular media as well. Megachurch pastor and *Become a Better You* author Joel Osteen told *People* magazine that he advises people to "Love God, love yourself, love others—in that order. . . . I don't think you can show compassion, be respectful and kind, if you can't love yourself."

This sounds good, but there's little evidence it's true. People low in self-love or self-esteem are somewhat clingy, seek reassurance of their partner's love, and can get hung up on their insecurities, but they choose partners just as well as everyone else and genuinely care about their partners. The protagonist in Curtis Sittenfeld's bestselling novel *Prep* is a good example: she clearly has low self-esteem, but loves with a poignancy the more popular girls could never reach. Unless he's very depressed, chances are that a low self-esteem person will truly love you and will be a decent relationship partner—much better than a narcissist, who really loves himself but won't care about you much at all. Which would you rather have: someone who wants reassurance of your love or someone who doesn't truly love you? For most people, that's a pretty simple choice, and shows that loving yourself isn't all that important for loving others.

A related idea is that if you don't like yourself, other people won't like you, either (or "If you don't love yourself, how can you expect someone else to?"). This has a grain of truth to it, because if you're really depressed and down on yourself, you won't be much fun to be around, and will drive away other people. (Even this isn't caused by too little self-admiration, however: depressed people are no fun mostly because they keep turning the conversation back to themselves and their problems.) Certainly, a very outgoing, larger-than-life personality, as narcissists often are, can be a pleasure to be around at a party; however, they're usually not a great friend or partner in the long term. Self-admiration can make loving others and treating them well almost impossible, because too much self-admiration encourages people to put themselves before others. We need a new cultural belief: *if you love yourself too much, you won't have enough love left for anyone else.*

Self-esteem isn't always an asset for making friends. In one experiment, after high self-esteem people learned they did poorly on a test, they became defensive, arrogant, and rude. The person they just met didn't like them very much. They put so much effort into maintaining their self-esteem that they acted like jerks. Narcissists are even worse, often lashing out with aggression when they are challenged. Their self-admiration helps them treat others badly, as they think they are better than everyone else. People with low self-esteem, however, were restrained and subdued when talking to a new person during the study, and came across as likable and friendly.

Humble, self-deprecating people aren't unlikable—in fact, they can be very endearing. When he worked as a bellman in the 1980s, Keith met the great musician Ray Charles during a rehearsal. Ray had worked hard to improve his performance, but was still uncertain about it. "Was that any good?" he asked Keith, who had no business giving Ray Charles feedback. Keith, however, told him the truth—it was terrific. If self-admiration were required to be liked by others, Keith should have disliked Ray. But did he? Of course not. He thought Ray was an amazing musician and a class act. If Ray had instead broadcast his self-admiration and said, "That was awesome! I'm the best musician who ever lived!" *then* Keith would have disliked him. Self-admiration isn't necessary to be liked.

HOOKING UP AND CHECKING OUT EMOTIONALLY

Another cultural-level manifestation of the narcissism epidemic in relationships is the trend toward "hookups," "friends with benefits," and other commitment-free relationships. These types of sexual encounters are perfect for a narcissist, who can get what he wants but then easily move on to the next partner, no strings attached. Hooking up has become the norm in many high schools, on most college campuses, and among twenty-somethings. In an early 2000s survey, 80% of twenty-somethings agreed it was common for their peers to have sex just for fun with no commitment. And 46% of women age 18 to 35 said they had a "booty call" partner they could ring for a quick hookup. Among high school students, hookups often take the form of oral sex. Although fewer high school students now engage in sexual intercourse than did ten years ago, 35% of "virgins" now have experience with oral sex. There have been more and more reports of middle school students having oral sex, usually hookup style outside of a relationship.

Hookups are not only uncommitted but devoid of emotional connection. Some people who hook up don't even talk to the other person. "Hooking up is also very selfish," says a George Washington University student. "It's all about what you want, not what the other person wants." As Laura Sessions Stepp documents in *Unhooked*, her in-depth study of sex and dating among young people, loving has become uncool. "Dating couples rarely said 'I love you,' " she notes. "They might be engaging in oral sex but wouldn't think of holding hands as they walked across campus." Many of her young interviewees felt it was better to retain control by hooking up; some made it sound like a narcissistic game of dominance. Tonya, a Duke sophomore, liked to jump out of bed right after sex with a guy, which "makes men feel feeble. It gives me such a rush." Her friend Alicia nodded and said, "Sometimes you just want to screw them before they screw you." Not exactly a caring approach.

Popular music in recent years has encouraged this manipulative, emotion-free attitude toward sex. According to a study by public health researchers, two-thirds of the popular songs in 2005 that mentioned sexual intercourse described sex that was degrading to the other partner, usually a woman. ("Ay bitch! Wait 'til you see my dick. Imma beat that pussy up.") The average teen now spends a full half hour a day listening to songs that describe degrading sex.

Hookups move the focus of sexual relationships away from the whole person and toward physical attractiveness. The trend has spawned a new array of products designed to help women look sexy at all times, from Victoria's Secret bras to the idea—unheard of just 15 years ago—that women should wear thong underwear to work. Overall, it is striking just how many symptoms of narcissism appear in the trend toward hookups, including lack of emotion in relationships, physical vanity, and antisocial attitudes and behavior. Like so many cultural shifts related to narcissism, non-narcissists are unwittingly pulled into the vortex of the now-acceptable narcissistic behavior. With hookups, that often plays out with broken hearts when one partner wants the hookup or "friends with benefits" arrangement to evolve into a real relationship, and the other doesn't.

Some parents have unintentionally taught their children a narcissistic attitude toward relationships, advising that achievement must always come first and "love can wait." Of course, telling teens not to have romantic relationships is not, at least in today's culture, going to stop them from having sex. So they have sex anyway, disconnected from relationships and often devoid of close emotional connection. The focus is on physical gratification, with messy emotions like love left out of the picture—or at least putting on the front that one is not that vulnerable. Novelist Jodi Picoult spent many hours talking to high school girls while researching her recent books about teen issues, *The Tenth Circle* and *Nineteen Minutes*. These girls told her that hookups were the norm, and that although they sometimes wanted an actual relationship, it wasn't cool to say so. After these conversations, Picoult concluded, "It was clear to me that we're turning out a generation of kids who don't know how to have a relationship with someone."

TREATMENT FOR THE EPIDEMIC

The personal and cultural pull of narcissism on relationships is not an easy problem to solve. The simplest solution, avoidance, is in many ways the hardest, but it works: avoid relationships with narcissistic individuals as much as you can—when dating, choosing friends, or selecting bosses or employees. A big part of the difficulty in avoiding narcissists is identifying them, so keep your radar active: if someone seems highly charismatic, charming, or confident, take some time before entering a relationship with him or her. If this person is truly narcissistic, he or she has left a trail of heartbreak, deception, or unmet expectations. At the very least, they may give clues to their attitudes through the things they say. One guy Jean dated said, "Look, you should know I'm a selfish person." She didn't really believe him and thought he could change, but he couldn't. Another date liked to point out how he would do things better than other people, even when he had no expertise in the area (echoing the test item "If I ruled the world, it would be a much better place"). Another was convinced he would be famous. These guys are the reason that Jean gave her future husband the Narcissistic Personality Inventory on their fourth date. (He scored low, and, even more remarkably, didn't dash for the door when she whipped out the test.)

Even when you can identify narcissists, you are often stuck with them, especially in the workplace, where you have little control over a new manager or coworker. The key in this case is to protect yourself. Put up reasonable boundaries. Be friendly but not friends. Do not put yourself in a situation where you have to rely on a narcissist's trustworthiness or integrity. Also, keep records of your interactions. If things go bad, these might be useful.

You can also try to use the manipulation strategies that work on narcissists. A woman with a narcissistic husband once told Keith that her relationship worked because, as she put it, "I manipulate the hell out of the son-of-a-bitch." This is best accomplished by giving narcissists what they want: flattery, admiration, and attention. If you do this well, they will respond accordingly. One former madam noted that in the world of call girls, narcissistic men were often described as "marks" because they are so easily manipulated.

It is one thing to try to avoid or manipulate narcissists, and quite another to try to change them. Narcissists rarely change, especially in relationships. Occasionally, though, trying to change someone might be an option. You could have an employee who is a terrific salesman, but awful team player, or a spouse who is a good provider of material goods, but not of warmth and affection. We don't recommend challenging the narcissists' inflated self-image ("you really aren't all that attractive"; "you really have only a somewhat better-than-average intellect"), which will be met with defensiveness and hostility. Instead, try to encourage feelings of morality, caring, and kindness in the narcissist, which will not be seen as threatening and has the potential to change the narcissist's behavior in a positive way.

One possibility is to set up a situation where acts of caring and kindness are aligned with admiration and success. In other words, show narcissists that they can get their narcissistic needs met by acting like decent, caring people. Even our narcissistic culture does this in some ways. Society praises fathers who care about their children and take care of their families, admires corporate tycoons who make donations to charity, and assigns hero status to soldiers, policemen, and firemen who risk their lives to save others. You can get a lot of ego gratification from being a decent person. Encourage that belief in others.

In one recent study, psychologist Eli Finkel and colleagues (including Keith) wanted to see if they could make narcissists report being more committed in their dating relationships simply by activating communal, caring thoughts outside their awareness. You might have heard rumors about movie theaters showing subliminal images of popcorn or soft drinks during films, which supposedly made moviegoers spend more money on snacks. While movie theaters probably never actually used this technique, such subliminal message exposure can lead to behavioral changes in certain situations. Psychologist John Bargh found that college students subliminally shown words related to the elderly subsequently walked down the hall more slowly, just as an older person would.

In Finkel's study, college students in dating relationships saw three photographs of smiling, caring people; others saw neutral images, such as pictures of trees. The catch was that these images were shown on a computer very quickly—35 milliseconds, to be exact. The students then saw a list of words: if a word described them, they pushed a button for "me"; if it didn't, they hit a button for "not me." Buried in this list of words were five words related to commitment. Sure enough, the narcissistic people reported greater levels of commitment after they were subliminally shown the pictures of the caring people. In fact, the narcissists embraced just as many commitment words as non-narcissists. It's not possible to show every narcissist in the country subliminal images of kind, caring people every day. However, this study demonstrates that kind, caring thoughts can influence the self-concepts of narcissistic people.

In another study, researchers studied whether kind, caring thoughts could help narcissists be more committed marriage partners. They asked each person whether their partner made them feel generous, caring, and compassionate. These couples were then followed over several months to see how their commitment levels changed. Encouragingly, narcissists who felt their partners elicited caring and kind thoughts reported becoming more committed to the marriage. We still don't suggest that you marry a narcissistic individual, but this study gives us another bit of evidence that somehow activating feelings of kindness and emotional closeness can be an antidote to narcissism.

Another possibility is to educate people on the many benefits of stable, caring, and committed relationships. Relationships often lead to better lives for everyone involved. Marriage, for example, is especially beneficial to men. Yes, it is hard to work 60-hour weeks with a working spouse and young children, but at the same time, family can keep you in line. Married men binge drink less, don't stay out as late, and in general do fewer really stupid things. For all its difficulties, marriage is a good thing.

At the cultural level, our society should value stable, caring, committed relationships. And we certainly do, but there is also an amazing amount of attention paid to exactly the opposite—self-centered, short-term, and egocentric relationships. Even the way American culture glorifies weddings and getting married seems to ignore the self-sacrificing, committed relationships these celebrations should be showcasing. Instead, they end up celebrating narcissism. As Rebecca Mead points out in *One Perfect Day: The Selling of the American Wedding*, "the bridal magazines promote . . . the idea that a bride deserves to be the center of attention for the entire period of her engagement. . . . For sixteen months, it is her privilege, her right—indeed, her obligation—to become preoccupied with herself, her appearance, her tastes, and her ability to showcase them to their best advantage." The self-obsession of some brides has inspired a new word: *Bridezilla* (complete with its own reality TV show, of course). As Wikipedia put it in 2008, the term describes "a difficult, unpleasant, perfectionist bride who leaves aggravated family, friends and bridal vendors in her wake. A bridezilla is obsessed with her wedding as her perfect day and will disregard the feelings of the family, bridesmaids, and even her groom in her quest for the perfect wedding." Slate.com's Emily Yoffe asks, "When did getting married become an exercise in acquired situational narcissism?" One photographer told Mead that "the prevailing goal of all wedding photography" was "that the bride must be made to look as much like an image from a celebrity magazine as possible." Weddings have become more lavish, with ordinary Americans aspiring to mimic the details of the over-the-top, million-dollar soirées of celebrities. The average wedding cost more than $27,000 in 2006, 18% more than in 1990 even when adjusted for inflation. As the still-high American divorce rate shows, these attention-getting, expensive celebrations do not necessarily lead to more stable unions.

Our culture often sends the message that shallow relationships are good models. For example, TV and movie writers seem to be obsessed with the search for "magic" in relationships. Everyone wants a magic relationship that feels different and special. Ordinary relationships, apparently, are for undesirable people and previous eras. Unfortunately, in the real world these magic relationships are about as stable as some atomic particles, disappearing faster than they can be measured. We understand that it is much more interesting to watch a television show about selfish individuals in shallow relationships (this really hasn't changed since Shakespeare), but there has to be some balance. The family sitcoms of the 1980s and 90s, like *Family Ties*, *The Cosby Show*, and *Home Improvement*, have given way to shows about single people in New York; rich, bed-hopping teens; narcissistic doctors; and reality TV with celebrities trying to find love with other TV celebrities. The closest TV has gotten to a top-ten-rated family show in the last few years is *Desperate Housewives*—not exactly a showcase of caring.

In short, our culture needs to focus on the substance rather than the sizzle. We need fewer stories of Bridezillas, hot celebrities, exhibitionistic reality show contestants, and selfish CEOs, and more models of warm, committed, and respectful relationships.

CHAPTER 14

All Play and No Work

Entitlement

Keith recently got a call from a relative eager to relay a scene he was witnessing: an SUV parked in a no-parking zone, facing in the wrong direction, and blocking a stop sign. The SUV had a bumper sticker that said, "I ❤ ME."

Many people in the United States today are simply oblivious to others' needs, or, worse, think that others' needs are just not as important as their own needs. This state of mind is called entitlement, the pervasive belief that one deserves special treatment, success, and more material things. Entitlement is one of the key components of narcissism, and one of the most damaging to others. When narcissists feel entitled to special treatment, someone else invariably gets the shaft. Entitlement may work for some individuals—sometimes demanding students get their grades changed even when they don't deserve it—but it has terrible consequences when everyone in a society feels a sense of entitlement. This is the trap of entitlement: it can be great to think that you are number one, but it is not so great living with or working with others who also think they are number one. Unlike some of the other symptoms of narcissism, such as materialism or vanity, entitlement is like a ghost, difficult to see in solid form, but increasingly wafting its cold, cloudy fingers into everything.

Entitlement is fun while it lasts. You live in a fantasy in which the world owes you more than you contribute. You can feel entitled to a flat-screen TV without earning the money to pay for it. You can park in the handicapped space because you are in a rush. You can graduate from college and expect to get a fulfilling job with a six-figure salary right away.

Or you can literally take candy from children. Keith's lab actually studied this. College students filled out a questionnaire measuring their feelings of entitlement (for example, "If I were on the *Titanic*, I would deserve to be on the *first* lifeboat!" and "I honestly feel I'm just more deserving than others"). Then a confederate passed around a bucket of candy labeled "Child Development Lab" and said casually, "You can take as much candy as you think you deserve." The students who scored the highest on entitlement took the most candy, not really caring that this would leave less for the children.

Historically, entitlement meant having a social position or a claim to ownership granted by some legitimate authority. Having a title (or being entitled) meant having a clear claim to a social rank or piece of property, such as being a lord or duke in British society. As a facet of narcissism, entitlement means acting as if you have a title—or a right—to something even when you don't. There's some overlap with the historical definition: an entitled person acts like he's royalty and isn't like everyone else. A student might demand a high grade as if it is his by right rather than something to be earned. A woman might purchase an expensive car on credit even though she can't afford it because she thinks she deserves to drive a Mercedes.

ENTITLEMENT ON CAMPUS

College professors often comment that today's students feel they deserve special treatment. In 2007, a Harvard professor noted that, 20 years ago, "When a few students were sick and missed an exam . . . they used to be apologetic and just grateful that I would even offer a makeup. These days I have kids who think it's no big deal to miss a test if they have any conflict and then they think *they* should decide when I give the makeup." Some students say, "I *need* an A in this course," as if an A were an entitlement rather than something to be earned. Others expect to get good grades just for paying tuition, even telling faculty members, "You work for me." The most entitled have decided that they get good grades by arguing, saying things like "I'm not leaving your office until you change my grade to an A."

A survey of college students published in 2008 confirmed these perceptions. Two-thirds of students believed their professor should give them special consideration if they explained they were trying hard (apparently missing the point that grades are given for performance, not just for trying). One-third believed they deserved at least a B just for attending class. And—perhaps most incredible—one-third thought they should be able to reschedule their final exam if it interfered with their vacation plans.

One faculty member in North Dakota who responded to our online survey received an e-mail from an angry parent that said, "I am a high school English teacher, and I know that my daughter is an A writer and you have no reason to give her a C." The professor wanted to—but didn't—reply with the truth: "Yes, mom, I do. Your daughter failed to attend class and to turn in all of her work and then enlisted you in the fight for a better grade. P.S. She was an average writer." We authors have both received e-mails from students who seemed to think they could get a better grade just for complaining. Others ask to do extra credit—*after* the class is over. Jean's favorite was a student who asked for an extra-credit assignment two weeks after the end of the semester—his e-mail address was "famousstars" and he used the subject line "Please Read ASAP!!"

For the past 15 years, Joan has worked as a financial aid counselor at a satellite campus of the University of North Carolina; she told us her story in our online survey. Students often tell her, "I don't want loans; I want financial aid," and she has to explain that financial aid consists of more than outright gifts of money. One student came into the office and announced, "I was just at the Cashier's Office to pick up my refund check, and they said I didn't have one. I want to know who the slacker is around here." When Joan looked at the file, she found that the student had not even filed a financial aid application. When confronted with the truth that *she* appeared to be the "slacker," the student said, "My parents are so stupid—they were supposed to do that for me."

Of course, professors themselves are not immune from feelings of entitlement. The job itself probably builds narcissism; after all, several times a week, people take notes when we talk.

HOW ENTITLEMENT CORRODES RELATIONSHIPS ON AND OFF THE JOB

Entitlement causes real problems in relationships. First, entitlement leads to conflict. Everyone at some point does or says something nasty in a relationship, and how you respond to your partner determines whether the nastiness will be a passing squall or turn into a full-blown storm. Ideally, you'll respond in a constructive or positive way when your partner does or says something mean or stupid.

Imagine that your partner comes home and immediately says, "What did you make me for dinner?" You could be accommodating and say something like "Oh, you must have had a tough day at work—would you like to tell me about it?" Or you could just ignore the rude question and say, "Hi, honey, it's great to see you." If you're less accommodating, though, you could say nothing and withdraw for the rest of the evening, giving him the "cold shoulder." Or you could get creative and shoot back, "I made go-to-hell pasta with a side of you're-sleeping-on-the-couch."

Clever, yes, but not the best response—because it invites your partner to verbally hit you back. "Sounds good," he might parry. "Is it better than the usual I-suck-at-cooking-pasta that you usually make?" Incensed, you throw the food against the wall and say, "Actually, we're having my-fat-husband-should-skip-a-meal pasta." Next thing you know, your husband has said he always hated your cooking, his mom was right about you, and he takes off in a huff. As he drives away, you are yelling at him that maybe a mama's boy like him should move back with his mama. A squall has turned into a hurricane.

Being just a little bit more accommodating can lead to much less conflict in relationships. That's the problem with entitlement: you're special, so how dare anyone not show you respect? Your spouse's nasty comments or behavior are seen as fundamental challenges to your special stature in life, and thus you can't just let them slide. The result is spiraling relationship conflict. The same is true in work relationships. Let's say that Brandon is an entitled employee. If Brandon's boss criticizes his work, he'll think, How dare she criticize me? and might protest "But I worked hard on that!" Entitled people often confuse working hard with actually producing something good. Brandon is also likely to have trouble getting along with his coworkers. If one of them asks him to do something differently, or says something Brandon construes as mean, the conflict is likely to escalate.

Entitled people are also unwilling to see the world through another person's eyes and find it difficult to empathize with another's misfortunes. When you are entitled, all your focus is directed toward your own experience, your own outcomes, and your own needs. This is an obvious recipe for disaster in a romantic relationship, but it doesn't bode well for work relationships, either. Entitlement is also linked to a fundamental lack of respect for other people. The entitled person considers his needs paramount, and others' needs minor.

Entitlement is also expressed in the odd perpetual adolescence of many American adults. Adolescence is the most narcissistic time of life, and adolescence is being extended beyond all previous limits. First there's the well-known phenomenon of twenty-somethings taking longer to settle into careers and marriages, with more and more living in with their parents. But it goes way beyond that. An article in *New York* magazine in 2006 called "Up with Grups" (the term means grown-ups who can't grow up) asked, "When did it become normal for your average 35-year-old New Yorker to . . . walk around with an iPod plugged into his ears at all times, listening to the latest from Bloc Party, . . . decide the Sufjan Stevens is the perfect music to play for her 2-year-old, because, let's face it, 2-year-olds have lousy taste in music, and *we will not listen to the Wiggles in this house;* . . . quit the office job because—you know what?—screw the office and screw jockeying for that promotion to VP, because isn't promotion just another word for 'slavery'? . . . and besides, now that she's a freelancer, working on her own projects, on her own terms, it's that much easier to kick off in the middle of the week for a quick snowboarding trip to Sugarbush, because she's got to have some balance, right?"

Not that long ago, 40-year-olds wore suits, and 20-year-olds wore T-shirts and jeans. Now both wear T-shirts and jeans. The whole phenomenon is laced with the idea that one should be able to attain individualistic nirvana by keeping the good parts of adolescence (comfortable clothes, self-centeredness, a laissez-faire attitude toward work) while jettisoning the bad parts (not having any money, other people telling you what to do). Only a select few can achieve this fantasy; for the rest, snowboarding in the middle of the week is going to eventually mean no snowboarding at all because they will have run out of the money they need to go snowboarding.

THE EMPLOYEE PROBLEM

In business, entitlement often boils down to an equation: less work for more pay. Plenty of workers today want that, but they also want more flexibility, balance, meaning, and praise for their work. "If you just expect them to stand behind a register and smile, they're not going to do that unless you tell them why that's important and then recognize them for it," says John Spano, a human resources director at a theater chain. Bob runs a business that staffs industrial and clerical jobs in Minneapolis and answered our survey. "It's not uncommon for an employee to call my office before I arrive for the day to inform me, their employer, that they are too tired to go to work and they must get more sleep. They really see nothing wrong with staying home from work to sleep." One employee who did this three times in one week was fired, only to call a few months later wanting another job.

Managers in white-collar businesses have noticed this as well, complaining that workers want to know what the company will do for them (an on-site gym, lots of time off), rather than what they will do for the company. High expectations are also a new norm; stories abound of employees expecting to change established business practices during their first week at work, or believing that they will be running the company within five years. The new employee mantra might be "I want a job that is fulfilling, flexible, and pays six figures." If they don't get it all, and quickly, many workers simply quit, fueling a trend toward job-hopping that has frustrated many managers. In a 2007 survey of 2,500 hiring managers, 87% agreed that younger workers "feel more entitled in terms of compensation, benefits, and career advancement than older generations."

When Jean has surveyed her undergraduate students at San Diego State—admittedly not a nationally representative sample, but still interesting—they have consistently chosen "lazy" when asked to describe the negative characteristics of their generation (materialistic, self-centered, and disrespectful round out the top four). At first Jean was skeptical about this, wondering if her students were simply parroting an accusation they heard from their grumpy elders. No, they said—they'd just noticed many of their peers were lazy.

Unfortunately, many managers and observers are beginning to agree. In a U.S. Labor Department survey of corporate executives, many said that they outsourced jobs to other countries because foreign workers had a better attitude toward work. "American employees . . . need anger-management and conflict-resolution skills," said U.S. labor secretary Elaine Chao. "Too many young people bristle when a supervisor asks them to do something."

BALANCE IS BUNK

Or take the new business buzzword *work-life balance*. This trend began with the awareness that many people wanted to stop getting home from the office after their kids were already asleep. This is a great goal, and one we're personally glad we both get to achieve most of the time because of the potential flexibility in our professorships. We can cram work into early mornings or late evenings, type at home while a baby bats toys in a bouncy chair, and have cell phone meetings while driving around town. This, however, is far from "work-life balance"—it is more like work-life collision. We still feel lucky to have it, but it's not exactly relaxing.

The real conflict in society that spawned interest in work-life balance—that is, the highly important and often competing goals of caring for children and of working—quickly expanded to include more self-centered goals, such as having plenty of time to travel, pursue your hobbies, and hang out with your friends. The group that talks about work-life balance the most are twenty-somethings, most of whom are childless and want a flexible schedule so they can drop everything to go kayaking with their friend who's in town or take a "mental health day." Even if an employee wants "balance" so she can take time off to volunteer to help others—usually the opposite of entitlement—it's still problematic because the employee feels entitled to do less work for the company while still getting paid the same. If someone who applied for a faculty job on either of our campuses said he wanted to do less teaching and research so he could volunteer in the community, he would not be hired. This may sound harsh until you consider that faculty salaries at public universities are partially funded by tax dollars, and taxpayers expect that money to fund great research and teaching, and not the volunteer organization of the faculty member's choice. Volunteering is a great thing, but when you do it on the back of the tuition payers or taxpayers, it isn't so great.

There's hard evidence of the desire to work less in Monitoring the Future, an ongoing study that has surveyed a representative sample of American high school seniors every year since the 1970s. Between 1976 and 2006, more and more students agreed that "work is just making a living" and favored jobs with more vacation time. More said that if they got enough money to live comfortably, they wouldn't want to work. Fewer said they were willing to work overtime to do a good job. At the same time, they were more likely to want a job that pays a lot of money and is viewed by other people with respect. Unfortunately, wanting more money for doing less work is a fairly succinct definition of entitlement. As we noted in Chapter 5, young people have been conditioned to expect this: younger generations have gotten better grades in high school even though they do fewer hours of homework.

There is a growing trend to work part-time even in the most prestigious professions. The number of doctors working part-time jumped 46% from 2005 to 2007. Some of the increase comes from women wanting flexible schedules to raise families, but almost a third of male doctors who moved to a part-time schedule said they wanted more time for "unrelated professional or personal pursuits." (Golf?)

As Keith Hammonds notes in a *Fast Company* article titled "Balance is Bunk," work life balance is now seen as a right rather than a privilege: "In the last generation, balance has won huge cultural resonance. No longer mere cocktail conversation fodder, it has become something like a new inalienable right, creeping into the American ethos if not the Constitution: life, liberty, and the pursuit of balance. Self-actualization and quality time for all!" It's as if people are saying, "I want to be a top performer in my career, but also have a wide-ranging life outside my work." Sure, no problem. You can join the nonexistent ranks of really successful people who give a full 58% to their careers. We have no problem with people who dedicate themselves to their careers and become top performers. We similarly have no problem with people who dedicate themselves to their families but not careers. We even have no problem with people who don't dedicate themselves to their careers or families, but have an active and fun social life. And we empathize with people who want to dedicate themselves to both their careers and families, something we're both struggling to do ourselves. But the narcissism epidemic is clearly spreading into the culture when you have legions of people who don't want to dedicate themselves to their careers and also think they deserve to be top performers.

In a *Wall Street Journal* article in 2007, a partner at a prestigious law firm noted that the young associates demanded praise for their work; some even cried when they got critical feedback. The older partners at the firm were confused: when they were young associates, they remembered, not getting yelled at was considered praise. The partners had to bring in outside assistance to learn how to cope with the new workers. Some companies are hiring "praise consultants" who advise that bosses should not criticize an employee who is late to work; instead they should praise the employee when he or she gets in on time. One praise consultant throws several pounds of confetti a week. In a previous era, the reward one got for coming to work on time was called "not getting fired," and many argue that expecting praise for showing up is the definition of entitlement.

SCREW YOU AND THE HORSE YOU RODE IN ON: ENTITLEMENT AND CONFLICT

The willingness to get ahead by harming coworkers is another highly corrosive aspect of entitlement in the workplace. Narcissists often take advantage of their teammates in their attempts to succeed at all costs. These are the "glory hogs," "suck-ups," or "backstabbers"—people who get ahead at the expense of others and jeopardize the success of the organization. When narcissists work with others on a group task, they take credit for the successes of the group and blame their coworkers for their failures, even if they have a close, friendly relationship. This self-serving approach might make the narcissist look good to her boss, but it destroys the narcissist's relationship with her coworkers. In the end, it backfires when no one wants to work with the narcissist again.

Entitlement also has a more far-reaching and corrosive effect on society, destroying practices of reciprocity and obligation. The basic principle of reciprocity is that if someone does something for me, I need to do something for them in return. For example, if you receive a Christmas card from someone, you feel compelled to send them a card as well. If you fail to do this, you feel guilty.

Reciprocity really pays off when the stakes are higher. Let's say a friend helps you when your computer goes down. According to the rules of exchange, you owe her. The next month, your computer-savvy friend calls because she needs to move some furniture into her house and can't do it alone. You are in pretty good shape, so you swing by and help her out. So, both of you helped the other at minimal cost—it wasn't hard for your friend to fix your computer and it wasn't hard for you to move the couch—but both of you gained a great deal. These informal exchanges happen all the time in society and play a huge role in making the world work. The key is that people reciprocate the help at some point.

What happens if you are dealing with someone with a large sense of entitlement? He might ask you for a favor and you comply. You are a helpful person and are happy to do so. You don't get a thank-you, but you let that slide. Then the person asks for a favor again, and again you comply. The next week, however, you ask the person for a little favor in return and he flat out refuses. Maybe he even looks surprised that you would ask him for a favor. You get a little miffed, and the next time he asks for a favor, you decline. You are now a little less helpful in general, and less inclined to trust other people again. This is a major problem with entitlement: entitled people don't see reciprocity as a two-way street, they see favors as a one-way on-ramp that leads to them. The result is that the whole concept of reciprocity gets diminished and life gets a little harder and more isolated for everyone. Reciprocity is the glue that binds society together, and entitlement dissolves that glue.

A WARMER AND DEPLETED EARTH, COURTESY OF ENTITLEMENT

Entitled people feel it is their right to take more "stuff" from the world, whether it's fish or fuel. If more people feel this way, the resources will run out, leaving nothing for future generations. In one study, Keith and his colleagues asked students to play the role of the CEO of a forestry company, one of four harvesting timber from a forest. Because forests are renewable resources (like fish, cattle, and crops), the forest will grow back and can be harvested in perpetuity if the companies take only a limited amount at a time. However, if they take too much at one time, the forest will be destroyed. Narcissistic participants cut down more trees, thus "winning" in the short term, making it appear that being selfish and shortsighted is a winning strategy. However, the more narcissists were playing the game, the more quickly the forest disappeared. Four narcissists cutting trees destroyed the forest far more quickly than four less narcissistic people. Maximizing profit while still preserving resources required more cooperative, less narcissistic individuals. More people won in the long run when the participants were less entitled. Nonrenewable resources such as fuel suffer even more when entitled people take more. The more Hummers clog the roads, the faster oil will run out for the entire planet.

TREATMENT FOR THE EPIDEMIC

One of the best ways to combat entitlement is to be grateful for what you already have. In one fascinating study, people were asked to list all the things they were grateful for once a week for ten weeks. Compared to a group of people who did not do this task, those who thought about everything they were thankful for reported a greater sense of well-being, enjoyed better health, and exercised more. They were also more emotionally supportive to others. Gratitude is the opposite of entitlement: you think about what you already have, instead of what you deserve to have but don't.

Everyone can practice gratitude on his or her own, and can also encourage it in families and children. When we authors were kids, this was the "children are starving in China" argument, which seems to have fallen out of favor, and not just because there's more food in China. When they watch TV, children see all the things they don't have, and rarely—on TV or in real life—see the lives of less fortunate young people. Now more than ever, it is important for children to learn that there are many kids who are worse off. Jean likes to joke that the best response to anything bad is the midwestern standby "It could be worse." Most of the time, that's actually true.

In addition, thoughts of gratitude can be shared with the family at mealtimes and holidays. This is common practice at Thanksgiving, but not so much the rest of the year. Other small practices can encourage gratitude as well. Thank-you cards, for example, are a great way to express your gratitude to other people. They do not just have to be for gifts; thanking people for helping you in some way or just being a good friend, mentor, or parent benefits both people. Of course, one of the best ways to get your kids to express gratitude is to express it yourself. Ideally, the expressions of gratitude will whittle away at those feelings of entitlement. Another holiday tradition is also worth adopting—the Jewish practice, at Yom Kippur, of asking the important people in your life for forgiveness. No matter what your religion, relationships are smoothed by apology and forgiveness. To apologize for anything you've done to wrong someone is to discard entitlement and move toward a true connection with someone else.

In the workplace, one of the best ways to combat entitlement is to have workers experience a job that gives them some humility. Summer jobs and career training (so-called paying your dues) teaches people they were not born on home plate and imparts useful skills. Paying your dues has fallen out of favor lately; one book by a twenty-something for twenty-somethings is called *Grindhopping: Build a Rewarding Career Without Paying Your Dues*. Although it's true that it would be great to found your own company and be the CEO instantly as the book advises, very few people can go this route. And even when you own your own company, there is plenty of grind involved. Ask anyone who owns a small business—they'll tell you about the long hours and all the times they had to work the counter.

Here's the unfortunate truth: virtually every job requires some grind, especially at the beginning. We both love our jobs as professors and researchers, but we started out as graduate students like everyone else. We ran seemingly endless studies in windowless labs, entered data for hours from stacks of papers several feet tall, and photocopied article after article on the library copier. It wasn't working in the salt mines or cleaning hotel rooms, but it wasn't a glamorous intellectual exercise or constant fun, either. Even now, for all the fun times we have, such as writing this book or working with our students on research ideas, we also slog through unreadable student papers, grade exams, go to committee meetings that reliably spark thoughts of self-immolation, and still sometimes enter data. We're not complaining—just the opposite—but we also wouldn't expect to have jobs that were enjoyable all the time. Heck, even recreational pursuits like fishing, golf, or bowling require you to pay your dues.

In general, Americans have lost the idea that there is value in an honest day's work for an honest day's pay, even if the work isn't fulfilling. This issue has come up recently in the heated discussion around illegal immigration. Some on the pro-illegal-immigration side argue that "illegal immigrants do jobs that Americans are unwilling to do." There is something really disturbing about this statement; it implies that certain jobs are beneath Americans, that Americans don't want to get their hands dirty or their backs sore doing the work that keeps the country running, so they have to import people whom they consider beneath them to do it. This is one of the twists of logic of the narcissism epidemic: apparently, being lazy and unwilling to work makes Americans better than the people who are willing to work.

If this is true, it bodes very poorly for our future as a nation. Traditionally, everyone does lousy jobs when he or she is young. This was seen as an opportunity to learn humility and character. One of Keith's great experiences of humility came when he was working the graveyard shift taking inventory in a store in downtown Oakland. The job was very simple: he read numbers on merchandise and wrote them down on a clipboard. Keith was working next to a woman who was likely schizophrenic—while she was working she was having a heated conversation with someone who wasn't there. The manager came by, looked at the schizophrenic woman's work, and said, "good job." He then looked at Keith's sheet and pointed out that Keith was not following directions—he had put hash marks through the middle of his 7s in the European fashion. There were samples to show the employees how to write numbers correctly, which Keith didn't bother to read because he was so smart. Humiliation experienced and humility learned.

Young people, especially from wealthy families, should be encouraged to do some difficult work in order to learn humility, compassion, the link between work and pay, and the value of the dollar. Such work would teach young people a sense of connection to those who make careers of these jobs, rather than a vague sense of superiority over them. We also think it is crucial to treat people who do low-wage work with dignity and respect. It's easier to sit at a desk all day than it is to wait tables at a diner or pound nails into a roof during the Georgia summer; yet somehow many middle- and upper-class Americans feel they are superior to people who do this kind of work. That has to change. Instead of glorifying people who strike it rich with little effort—including many celebrities—the new American hero needs to be the old American hero: the guy or gal who gets up in the morning, works for a living, and doesn't bitch about it all day.

CHAPTER 15

God Didn't Create You to Be Average

Religion and Volunteering

Mary, the last of eight children from a Roman Catholic family, went to Mass with her family every Sunday, learning the religion's traditional values, such as charity, modesty, peace, and promoting the common good. In the late 1960s, she moved away from her hometown, returning five years later to get married in the 100-year-old church, just as her parents and all of her sisters had. Mary and her husband soon moved away to a bigger city, but they joined a Catholic church there and sent all three of their children to Catholic school. Mary's faith has been a constant in her life, from her baptism to her wedding to her youngest child's graduation from high school.

Stories like Mary's are becoming less and less common. Not that long ago, the vast majority of Americans were born into a religion and stayed in that faith all their lives. But when the Pew Forum on Religion & Public Life surveyed 35,000 American adults in 2007, they found that 44% of respondents had left the faith of their childhood for another denomination, another religion, or no religion at all. "The American religious economy is like a marketplace—very dynamic, very competitive," said Pew Forum director Luis Lugo. The Catholic Church has lost more members than any other faith tradition: 1 in 3 Americans was raised Catholic, but under 1 in 4 said they are Catholic today. Mainline Protestant denominations are losing members as well. In an annual survey of American college freshmen, 17.4% of 2006 students reported no religious preference, more than twice the number who espoused no preference in 1978 (8.3%). The Pew survey found that 1 in 4 people age 18 to 29 in 2007 had no religious affiliation.

Religion and volunteering to help others should, in theory, counteract the narcissism epidemic. But even these aspects of social life have been changed by the epidemic. The religions and volunteer organizations that have aligned themselves with individualistic values have thrived, while those that have not have often withered. Neither has played a major role in causing the narcissism epidemic; in fact, most of the time both mitigate it. At the same time, both have adapted to a new culture that favors a focus on the self. The religious and volunteer organizations that have succeeded have given the people what they want, which is often self-admiration. Once groups have drawn people in with promises of self, however, religion and volunteering often go on to counteract the excesses of modern culture. It's a bit of narcissistic jujitsu; the promise of having their narcissistic needs met brings people into an organization, but their individual narcissism is ultimately reduced by the organization.

The bad news is that traditional religious organizations—those that have little to offer the individual up front—are withering in the United States and Europe. This is worrisome, because religion has traditionally put the brakes on narcissistic behaviors. Many religious beliefs directly promote the reduction of narcissism (or related concepts like pride and selfishness), teaching the belief in something larger than the self, the idea that one should live according to certain rules that apply to everyone, and the value of a community of fellow believers. The individualistic, even narcissistic, motto of "Do what's right for you" doesn't fit very well with the same-for-everyone rules and beliefs of most religions. The Christian gospels are full of verses praising the humble and meek and chastising the proud. A verse in Proverbs reads, "The Lord will destroy the house of the proud." The Sermon on the Mount notes that the meek "shall inherit the earth." Christianity's emphasis on forgiveness, especially for one's enemies, also requires humility—in many ways, the opposite of narcissism. "Turning the other cheek" is not a narcissistic act. A number of studies have found that narcissists are less likely to forgive others. They see others' transgressions against them as a debt and want them repaid. Narcissists are also less willing to forgive God for problems or troubles in their own lives. Christianity and Confucianism both teach that you should treat others as you would like to be treated, another dictum counter to a narcissistic ethos.

Eastern religions also focus directly on egotism as a source of suffering. In the Hindu *Katha Upanishad*, Nachiketas meets Death, who offers him material wealth and social status if he will leave without asking questions about the mystery of life. Nachiketas, however, does not agree, noting that in the face of Death, material goods and social status are meaningless. Seeing Nachiketas's wisdom, Death relents and tells him the secret of the immortal soul. Buddhism takes these ideas a step further, arguing that there is not even an immortal soul (*anatman*). Zen also has several stories describing the negative consequences of egotism. For example, the prime minister of the Tang Dynasty once asked a Zen master, "What is egotism according to Buddhism?" The master shot back in a harsh tone, "What kind of stupid question is that!?" Insulted, the prime minister became angry. The Zen master then smiled and said, "*This*, Your Excellency, is egotism."

Originally, religions could enforce narcissism-reducing practices because they didn't have to compete for adherents: if you were born into a religion, you usually stayed. Now, however, people can select the religion that works for them—often the one that offers the most benefits with the least pain. To compete, religions have to give people what they want. Because reducing narcissism is not always pleasant, most people are not going to attend churches that demand humility.

Religious people are not necessarily less narcissistic than others. Religion is a big tent whose members display both self-sacrifice and rabid egotism. There have always been and always will be people who use religious belief to increase their own narcissism, the most egregious of whom start their own cults. The Branch Davidians of Waco, whose complex burned down in 1993, were named after their charismatic leader David Koresh (a name he gave himself; his real name was Vinnie).

When a group of University of California at Berkeley sociologists wrote *Habits of the Heart* in the 1980s, they were surprised to find a woman named Sheila who practiced her own religion. Not only did she construct her own system of beliefs and rituals, but she named the religion Sheilaism. Sheila explained her Sheilaism as "It's just—try to love yourself and be gentle with yourself." Human development professor Jeffrey Arnett found that "make-your-own-religion" was very common among the twenty-somethings he studied. One of them noted, "I believe that whatever you feel, it's personal. . . . Everybody has their own idea of God and what God is. . . . You have your own personal beliefs of how you feel about it and what's acceptable for you and what's right for you personally." What was once solely a collective exercise has become far more individual.

RELIGION AND SELF-ADMIRATION

Keith was raised in the Episcopal church. He went to traditional services (yes, a little boring), showed up because he felt compelled, and had absolutely no narcissistic needs met by the church. Like many in the Pew survey, and much to his mother's disappointment, Keith drifted away from the traditional church, instead spending his time studying religion, philosophy, and science and trying to figure out the universe for himself (he never really succeeded, and thus there is no Keithism). Recently, however, Keith had a very different religious experience—one that would have kept him attending church had he discovered it when he was younger. He went to a Southern California megachurch with his sister's family. Filled with options, the church was a giant, customizable religious emporium. Coffee stands (with high-end coffee, not the cheap stuff) were open throughout the expansive church grounds. You could watch the service from inside the stadium, from just outside, or in a coffee shop/bookstore on a flat-screen TV (an option Keith's sister called "church-lite"). The service itself started with a set by a talented and inspiring musician who sounded like Dave Matthews. The words to the music were projected on a screen, so you could sing along if you wanted (this was a choice, too). A motivational speaker followed, telling a fantastic story with a personal life message (with a reference to Paul from the Bible). After the service ended everyone had doughnuts—and more really good coffee—while the kids played on the lawn. Keith was happy, the kids were happy (there'd been video games and live music in the Sunday school building), and it was a beautiful Southern California day.

In one sense, the service demanded nothing. It was really entertaining. There was a huge degree of individual choice, and no kneeling—unless you wanted to. By adapting to today's self-oriented culture, this megachurch was able to bring people back to religion. Many of those who joined would start thinking about God more, some would study the Bible in detail, some would become better and more caring citizens, some would volunteer to help the world, and some would ultimately become less narcissistic. This odd bit of alchemy—taking narcissism and trying to turn it into altruism—is at the heart of much modern religion.

Joel Osteen is the pastor of Lakewood Church in Houston, Texas, the largest church in the United States, so big it now holds its services in a renovated sports arena. Lakewood is clearly giving the people what they want. "God didn't create you to be average," Osteen writes (leaving unanswered the pertinent question: If God doesn't want anyone to be average, doesn't that change the average?). "You were made to excel. You were made to leave your mark on this generation . . . Start [believing] 'I've been chosen, set apart, destined to live in victory,' " writes Osteen in his book *Become a Better You*, part of the new trend of religious books crossing over into self-help. One of his favorite movie lines, Osteen says, is "To win is to honor God." Winning, according to Osteen, can certainly include more money and a better job. "God may intervene in your situation, replacing your supervisor so you can be promoted," Osteen writes in *Your Best Life Now*. "Once you begin expecting more, a second key element to enlarging your vision is *believing God has more in store for you!*" Osteen clearly practices the self-admiration he preaches; the walls of Lakewood Church are covered with perfectly airbrushed pictures of Osteen and plaques quoting his words.

But there is a flip side to Osteen's message. The second half of *Become a Better You* is almost a course in antinarcissism: praise people as much as you can, swallow your pride and apologize, let strife out of your life, build better relationships. This sounds good, but to draw in Americans steeped in our self-focused culture, he begins with the contradictory premise that self-admiration must come first. "If you don't love yourself, you're not going to be able to love others," he writes, echoing the cliché proven wrong by all of the self-loving narcissists who make terrible relationship partners. Some of Osteen's advice skates dangerously close to narcissistic acquisitiveness. He gives the example of a couple who rented a small apartment but filled it with furniture made for the larger house they hoped to have in the future. "They were saying, 'We're not going to sit back and accept this. God has put bigger things in our hearts and we're making preparations to rise higher.' " He suggests that we should all be bold in expressing our wants, as his son was when he received the new guitar he wanted and then immediately asked, "When do you think we can get my new keyboard?"

Osteen also writes that "other people's opinions do not determine your potential," a version of the narcissist's belief that he's better than other people, no matter what others say. "God would not have put the dream in your heart if He had not already given you everything you need to fulfill it," Osteen writes in a passage that every terrible singer on *American Idol* seems to believe, even after Simon tells them they stink.

Many churches around the country now promote "prosperity Christianity," or the idea, as one book puts it, that *God Wants You to Be Rich*. George Adams, a former tile worker from Ohio, moved his family to the Houston area so he could attend Osteen's church. "God has showed me that he doesn't want me to be a run-of-the-mill person," Adams says in a *Time* magazine article. After taking a job selling cars, he says, "It's a new day God has given me! I'm on my way to a six-figure income!" Eventually, he believes, God will help him sell enough cars so he can buy his dream home with 25 acres, horses, a pond, and some cattle. Of the four largest megachurches in the United States, three teach some version of "prosperity"—the idea that God doesn't want you to be poor. "The tragedy is that Christianity has become a yes-man for the culture," says Stephen Prothero, chairman of the religion department at Boston University.

This is a very different view of God and religion than was common just a few decades ago. Back then, religion had expectations of you; it was not a vehicle for fulfilling your dreams. There were rules for behavior (no adultery, no idols before God, go to church, don't lie or steal, don't work on the Sabbath, don't covet your neighbor's stuff), and you'd better follow them or you would be doomed to hell (or, at the very least, you'd have to face up to your sins, confess them, and do penance). Many of today's preachers say that God still doesn't want you to sin, but he also wants you to have a big house.

Traditionally, religion also encouraged connections with other people and the community. Church members knew and helped one another. Many religious services include a part where congregants say "Peace be with you" to others. Even self-empowerment pastors like Osteen emphasize this. "Don't make the mistake of living your life self-centered, rushing through your day concerned only about yourself," he writes. "Take time for people . . . learn to appreciate them. When you go to the grocery store, encourage the cashier. Be friendly." The problem is that it's hard to be patient and friendly to everyone when you're overly focused on your own success and think you are special.

VOLUNTEERING AND SERVICE

In 1990, 64% of high school seniors volunteered their time at least once in the past year, but in more recent years more than 76% have. If narcissists are less willing to help people, less likely to feel their pain, and more focused on themselves, and narcissism is rising among young people, this finding seems paradoxical. "My generation is doing just as many positive things as the Boomers did when they were young, if not more," wrote JG on a *New York Times* comment board. "We may be less visible in our efforts but we're no less effective. Our entire generation is compassionate, volunteers, recycles, and is concerned for the welfare of others. Narcissistic my foot!" John was even more complimentary: "No generation in history has given more to help those in need, often to people in far away lands, people they may never meet, than we have. No generation." Eric, 25, agrees: "My generation has done more to help people in need than any that came before it."

Although we doubt that today's young generation has helped more people than, say, the World War II generation who liberated much of the world, volunteer service does seem to be on the rise among young people. This increase is caused by many factors, several of which demonstrate a growing compatibility between volunteering and the rise in narcissism.

First, many high schools have made community service a mandatory graduation requirement. In actuality, it's "involuntary volunteering." More high schools began requiring service in the 1990s, exactly when high school students started to report doing more volunteer service. "I had to volunteer 100 hours to graduate high school. If it wasn't required I would not have done any of it. It's sad, I know," wrote Scott, 25, in our online survey. Thus much of the rise in volunteering did not spring from altruistic feeling but from rules set by others.

With the college admissions picture more competitive, many high school students also volunteer because it looks good on their applications. When Jean spoke to students at a small college in Georgia, one of the freshmen said, "Our high school counselor explicitly told us to volunteer if we wanted to get into a good college." She admitted she probably wouldn't have done so otherwise. "I have done a lot of volunteer work in my short life," wrote Brittany, 19, from Canada. "I do it because I truly believe in the cause. Also it honestly looks good on a resume or college application."

The job search website monster.com advises, "Volunteer for Your Career. If ever there were a winning career-development strategy for college students, volunteering is it. Even if you have only a few hours a month to spare, you can make a significant difference. And *best of all*, you can boost your career at the same time" (italics ours). A flyer at Colorado College advertising a "Saturday of Service" asked the question "Why should I care about service leadership?" and answered it with five points about developing skills and experience useful for careers. There was no mention of the people who need help or the value inherent in helping them. And that makes sense given the narcissistic culture—if you want to recruit volunteers, focus on what's in it for them.

Although volunteering is often required for graduation and looks good on a college application, giving money to charity doesn't help with either—and, not surprisingly, charitable giving has decreased in recent years. In the '70s, 46% of high school seniors had contributed to one or more charities, but by 2006 only 33% had. So not all kinds of helping are increasing: only the most visible, and those that look good on an application.

But if you can donate to charity and get attention for taking off your clothes at the same time, that works. In July 2008, Virgin Mobile launched a charity campaign called "Strip2Clothe," which encouraged young people to make online videos of themselves stripping to music. Virgin Mobile would then donate clothes to homeless youth—one for each article of clothing removed, and one for every five times the video was viewed. It was the perfect confluence of narcissism and charity, especially since the only effort required was taking off your clothes and getting attention for it. Not everyone thought stripping for charity was appropriate, however, so a few weeks later the company gave the program the lame new label "Blank2Clothe," announcing that altruists could now film themselves doing whatever they wanted, not just stripping.

Natalie, 26, teaches high school in Pennsylvania and responded to our online survey. When a fellow teacher required her students to do two hours of community service and then write about it, "The kids were up in arms. A requirement that would take time away from their other activities, especially their jobs where they work to get money to buy the things they want? Never! Parents called the principal to complain that this project was ridiculous and unfair." When the teens did the service, though, they ended up enjoying it. "I'm almost certain that most students would not volunteer if they didn't have to do it for college, though," wrote Natalie. "I don't want to say that there are no kids that care. I just feel that there are very few who are willing to give back to the community if there isn't something in it for them."

One of the original motivations behind requiring community service for high school graduation was the idea that students would enjoy it and want to do it more. This may have worked in some cases. Between 2001 and 2005, the percentage of college students who did some type of volunteer work increased from 27.1 to 30.2%. Though a positive development, it does not yet "suggest the possible emergence of a new civic generation," as the group who did the survey declared.

After graduation, many young people work for organizations like Teach for America or AmeriCorps, and others have joined the military to serve their country. Most of the Americans killed in Iraq and Afghanistan were of the same generation that scores an all-time high on the narcissism inventory. Just as Baby Boomers joined the Peace Corps, the Greatest Generation fought bravely in World War II, and Gen Xers fought in the Gulf War, a segment of every generation dedicates itself to service. Even with the narcissism epidemic run rampant, our society benefits greatly from the exceptional young people who serve their country and serve others.

At the same time, the rest of us have been asked to do very little. During World War II, citizens planted Victory Gardens and gathered scrap metal to make military equipment. But unless you were close to someone serving in Iraq, the Iraq War had little impact on the daily lives of

Americans. After September 11, 2001, the country had a communal spirit for the first time in decades, and record numbers of people donated blood. But the president did not call for any collective action on the part of the American people—outside of telling them to go shopping to preserve the economy.

Service and awareness are clearly increasing in one area: more and more people know they need to do their part to help the environment. Awareness of climate change and carbon emissions is higher than ever, with "green" companies, cars, actions, and devices finally becoming cool. When Jean surveyed her undergraduate students about the good characteristics of their generation, awareness of environmental issues was the third most mentioned (the top two were better-educated and technology-savvy). Many also mentioned their generation's greater interest in global issues. Slowly, Americans are learning to look outside themselves.

MAKING A DIFFERENCE

So why do people volunteer and do community service? In the past, people who volunteered gave reasons like "It was the right thing to do" or "The people really needed help." Not so much recently. The 2006 Pew survey of 18- to 25-year-olds found that only 31% said "helping people who need help" was an important goal of their generation, coming in a distant third behind "getting rich" (81%) or "becoming famous" (51%). Instead, many young people explain their motivation for service by saying, "I want to make a difference." CNN's charity initiative is called "Impact Your World." *USA Weekend* magazine's national day of helping others was called "Make a Difference Day." Of course, any motivation for helping others is a good one, but this is an interesting change in attitude, shifting the focus from the society and the needy to the benefits to the self, especially if the benefit involves having a big impact, a personal role, or garnering praise.

Aynsley, 25, did extensive volunteer work in Africa. Although Aynsley did talk about helping when interviewed in a Lifetime TV special, her language is oddly individualistic for such a collectivistic cause. "I as an individual feel like I have to go out there in the world and make a difference myself," she said. We hope she does, but we also worry that less visible causes, and those without an immediate, tangible effect, might attract less interest.

A similar pattern is afoot in philanthropy and charitable giving. Giving has become cool, and although that has the upside of increasing donations, it has the downside of diluting the true purpose. As Robert Frank notes in *Richistan*, the business press now covers philanthropy "like a competitive industry." The new rich, Frank found, want to "give their money away now, while they can enjoy the praise and control the process. . . . Today's rich don't just want to do well by doing good: They want to be the *best* at doing good." Although these multimillionaires are truly helping others, their motives have the ring of narcissism: winning, competition, praise, attention, and personal impact are central. If this increases donations, all the better. Once again, organizations are evolving to do what they need to survive and thrive in a narcissistic culture.

More and more companies are incorporating social responsibility into their business plans, whether it's renewable energy or matching a product purchase with a gift. For example, the company Happy Baby Food donates money to feed undernourished children in Malawi. Now both the company that sells the product and the person buying it can feel they are making a difference. Some of this is about helping, but some of it is about having a bigger effect on the world than just buying or selling some baby food. Is that narcissistic? No, because it helps others. But it's not pure compassion, either.

The debate about whether true altruism exists is as old as philosophy itself. Immanuel Kant argued that people help others for their own selfish reasons, such as feeling good or getting praise. Our own view is that an increase in helping others is a good thing no matter what the cause. Organizations that have learned to gain support and volunteers from tapping into narcissism have ended up helping the most people, because they have stayed, or become, popular. The Lance Armstrong Foundation is a good example. By appealing to the desire to look like a good person by wearing a yellow wristband, they raised $180 million to fight cancer.

Helping and charity are usually not narcissists' first choices for getting attention (those are reality TV, the Internet, bars, and some workplaces). But with more Americans trying to support an inflated sense of themselves, not everyone can get the attention they'd like by going to work or posting a video on YouTube. With so many problems in the world, more and more people are recognizing that the best way to get attention is through helping others. The guy who posted his phone number on a Web page so he could provide a listening ear for others got on the *Today* show. *BusinessWeek* publishes a list of the 50 top givers. People who go to charity balls get their pictures in the paper. *People* magazine, which mostly focuses on the lives of celebrities, regularly runs feature articles on people who help others. This is good, because we need more attention paid to the good works that rein in the narcissism epidemic. If the easiest way to get attention is to help someone else, maybe narcissistic people will go that route—and perhaps become less narcissistic in the process.

Although it's not the normal course for a narcissist, the path of praise and attention for helping is one of the few possible upsides of the narcissism epidemic. It's also one of the solutions: if more people get involved in helping others, it's a useful reality check on the shallowness of narcissism. Karin, interviewed in Polly Young-Eisendrath's book *The Self-Esteem Trap*, was raised by missionary parents. Her encounters with AIDS and death in Africa were, she says, "a perfect antidote to all of the bullshit of high school pettiness, clothes, college applications, parties, drinking, sex, and gossip. Having something that was profound and spiritual—without preaching or dogma—was a perfect outlet. Those other things were silly. This was REAL."

SECTION 4

PROGNOSIS AND TREATMENT

CHAPTER 16

The Prognosis

How Far, and For How Long, Will Narcissism Spread?

When the first Baby Boomers were born in 1946, McDonald's was a barbecue stand with carhops who set a food tray on your car window. By 1953 it had become a franchise and was soon joined by other "fast-food" restaurants. Just two generations later, almost every town in the United States has at least one fast-food restaurant, and chains such as KFC, McDonald's, and Wendy's have expanded overseas into countries such as Saudi Arabia and China. In India, where Hinduism holds cows sacred, McDonald's burgers are made of lamb instead of beef.

It is much easier to spread narcissism than fast-food restaurants. There are no structures to build, no food to cook, and no workers to hire. As the most superficial part of American culture, narcissistic values are conveniently carried around the world in pop music, movies, television, and, increasingly, on the Internet. These media sources smoothly glamorize the narcissistic ethos, showing its shiny surface of prosperity and self-glorification without the downsides of alienation and social breakdown. When young people in Asia and elsewhere see cool American heroes beholden to no one, they may find it more difficult to accept the rigid, collectivistic rules of their more traditional societies.

Narcissism is the fast food of the soul. It tastes great in the short term, has negative, even dire, consequences in the long run, and yet continues to have widespread appeal. So, will American-style narcissism spread around the world, like the McDonald's that now sits in Tiananmen

Square in China? In other words, will the narcissism epidemic become a global pandemic? And will the narcissism epidemic continue to increase in the United States, perhaps even growing exponentially?

A disease model of narcissism gives a picture of how narcissism might grow and spread. Diseases need specific conditions to become epidemic: a host (a person or group who has the disease), a means of transmission (a way for the disease to move from one person to another), and a new host (a person or group who catches the disease). We already know that both individual Americans and our shared culture are becoming more narcissistic over time. Thus a host is in place. And narcissism has a means of transmission through the media and the Internet. The narcissistic behavior that brings attention to one person can, through the magic of the Internet, be spread instantly around the globe. Other cultures are increasingly becoming infected with narcissism, becoming hosts for the fast-moving virus of egotism, materialism, celebrity worship, entitlement, and self-centeredness. As epidemiologists can tell you, a virus that spreads from many people and many points can quickly overtake an entire population.

THE GLOBAL SPREAD OF THE NARCISSISM EPIDEMIC

The spread of Western ideas into formerly closed societies is relatively new. Keith remembers his first trip to China in 1980, when he was a teenager. Most of the people he met dressed in identical drab outfits, and few had seen a Westerner before. Riding on a bus one day, Keith (tremendously hip even in his younger years) played a cassette tape of the B-52's song "Rock Lobster" through some small speakers. A large crowd soon surrounded the bus to listen, enthralled with both the technology and the sound of rock music, which they had never heard before. Eventually, a Communist Party official broke up the crowd and told Keith to turn off the music. No more "Rock Lobster" for the Chinese—at least for another decade or so.

American ideas also sneaked in and infected the Soviet Union when it was a closed system. Some writers have claimed that the American TV show *Dallas* helped bring down communism in Eastern Europe. "Women lusted after the Ewing ladies' clothes and enormous kitchens, and men thrilled to the idea of having the freedom to make or break their own fortunes," wrote Matt Welch in *Reason*. In Romania, "a country where the waiting list for crappy Dacia cars stretched as long as 10 years if you didn't know the right person to bribe," Welsh writes, *Dallas* showed what life should be like.

Although countries such as China still restrict the flow of information to some extent, most corners of the world have been exposed to American ideas including celebrity, individual freedom, and materialism. Whether these societies will become infected with narcissism depends on the natural antibodies provided by their cultures. India and China, for example, may have a somewhat natural resistance to narcissism given their collectivistic cultural values, which emphasize group cohesion, rule following, and tight family structures. Nevertheless, even they have shown some symptoms of a disturbing change.

China has a strong sense of Confucian collectivism going back over two thousand years. This Confucian system is amazingly effective and resilient, and in China has been blended with communist values such as group cohesiveness and unity. The system specifies relationships and behaviors between individuals that encourage responsibility, hard work, and harmony, an antidote to a narcissistic culture. Yet narcissism has still gained a foothold in the land of Confucius.

Young Chinese born after the Cultural Revolution have earned the label "The Me Generation." A recent *Time* article profiled this group, who shock their elders by being much more interested in spa treatments than politics. They value material things, want to live away from home, and like to party with their friends at clubs into the wee hours. Over dinner at nice seafood restaurants, they discuss which islands have the best scuba diving, their skill at snowboarding, and which iPod is the best. One young man describes receiving six credit card offers in the mail. "Each one has a credit limit of 10,000, so suddenly I'm 60,000 yuan richer!" he says with a laugh. The pictures accompanying the article show Liu Yun, an actress, wearing tight shorts and a skin-baring belly shirt, and Barney, a fashion magazine writer, who poses in the whirlpool at his favorite spa. Vicky Yang recently spent $700 on snowboarding equipment. "I care about my rights when it comes to the quality of a waitress in a restaurant or a product I buy," she says. "When it comes to democracy and all that, well . . . That doesn't play a role in my life." Vicky's boyfriend, Wang Ning, espouses a similar attitude. "We are more self-centered. We live for ourselves, and that's good," he says. "We need to have the strength to contribute to the economy. . . . That's how our generation is going to help the country." Hong Huang, a magazine publisher, puts it this way: "On their wish list, a Nintendo Wii comes way ahead of democracy." Although the Chinese as a whole have probably not yet reached American levels of narcissism, they appear to be well on their way.

The rapid cultural change in China has led to some interesting conflations of Chinese tradition with American-style individualism and fame seeking. As *China Daily* reports, "Guoxue Spice Girl" is a Web celebrity in China who says she is descended from ancient scholars, but sings American-sounding hip-hop music and poses provocatively in front of Confucian statues. "I'm the best at attracting men. I could even attract Confucius," she says. Although this narcissistic behavior is popular, it has drawn direct cultural criticism. Liu Junyan, editor in chief of *China Youth Study*, admonishes, "Loving yourself is good as long as it's within reason. Unhealthy displays of private opinion or one's body is not civilized social behavior." Still, narcissism continues its spread to China through the Internet. After "Guoxue Spice Girl" became popular, wannabe Net celebrities like "February Girl," "Nasty Swallow," "Tianxian Sister," and "Megranate Brother" soon followed. As *China Daily* writer Li Qian put it, "Despite their differences in many aspects, [the wannabes] have a common characteristic—narcissism."

Regardless of these outbreaks of attention seeking, Asians as a group still score relatively low on measures of narcissism. Within the United States, Asian-Americans score lower on narcissism than any other ethnic group. But there are signs that the "narcissism gap" between the West and East might narrow. A 2005 *BusinessWeek* roundtable of experts from China and India noted that young people in these countries are increasingly more materialistic, independent, confident, and self-centered. One commented that China's one-child policy might have had the unintended consequence of raising a society of spoiled, arrogant youth. In other words, a top-down social policy designed to minimize the problems of overpopulation may have unintentionally increased narcissism. The Chinese say that each child is now the beneficiary of six people—four grandparents and two parents. All six are focused on making the child as successful as possible. In many cases, this has spawned "Little

Emperor Syndrome," in which children who receive too much attention and material things are becoming entitled, spoiled, and self-centered—even fat.

The Scandinavian countries of Northern Europe have a different type of immunity to narcissism. Traditionally very independent, Scandinavians are also very collectivistic, valuing their connection to their communities but fiercely opposing any one citizen rising to a place of power over them. The Scandinavian attitude is similar to the Australians' negative label "tall poppy"—someone who stands too high above others and needs to be cut down. This is a very foreign idea to Americans, who are taught from birth that standing out and being better than others is a good thing. With their egalitarian philosophy, countries such as Sweden and Denmark promote high levels of individual initiative and success, but also a very large social safety net. The system prevents a few individuals from amassing too much power, money, or influence and provides basic services such as health care to everyone.

This type of social structure is a buffer against narcissism, because it does not allow people to get too carried away with their own importance. Nevertheless, the narcissism epidemic has managed to sneak into Scandinavia through the power of the Internet. A Finnish young man who took the Web name "Naturalselector89" posted several YouTube videos of himself ranting about how stupid people are and expressing his admiration for the Columbine and Virginia Tech shooters and the fame they had attained. This young man from a nice, communal culture in Finland was infected with the idea of killing as a way to gain fame. In November 2007, Naturalselector89 killed eight people and himself in a mass shooting at his school in Tuusula, Finland.

Like many people who seek infamy, Naturalselector89 left behind a manifesto, never a good sign. Manifesto writing rarely ends well—just ask the Unabomber. Naturalselector89 clearly thought he was special. "Today the process of natural selection is totally misguided. It has reversed. Retarded and stupid, weak-minded people are reproducing more and faster than the intelligent, strong-minded people," he wrote. "Homo Sapiens, HAH! It is more like a Homo Idioticus to me! When I look at people I see every day in society, school and everywhere . . . I can't say I belong to same race as the lousy, miserable, arrogant, selfish human race! No! I have evolved one step above!" Naturalselector89 also spawned a copycat, a 22-year-old Finnish man who posted YouTube videos of himself shooting a gun and then killed nine people at a vocational school in September 2008. These episodes show the direct spread of destructive, narcissistic behavior in the United States—in this case, mass shootings—via the Internet.

The shifting priorities of Scandinavian culture go far beyond a few school shootings. One recent study looked at the language appearing in Norway's major national newspaper. Between 1984 and 2005, communal words such as "common/communal/shared," "duty/obligation," and "equality" were used much less often, while individualistic words such as "I/me," "freedom to choose," and "right/entitlement" were used more often. Thus the language of narcissism is spreading even to societies that once emphasized the importance of the group. As the authors of the study explain, this language use is a clear sign of the culture's shift toward more extreme individualism.

Some cultures also have strong shared religious identities that can serve as a buffer against the narcissism epidemic emanating from the United States. One of these religious buffers is Buddhism, which pro-

Communal and Individualistic Values in Norwegian Newspapers, 1984–2005

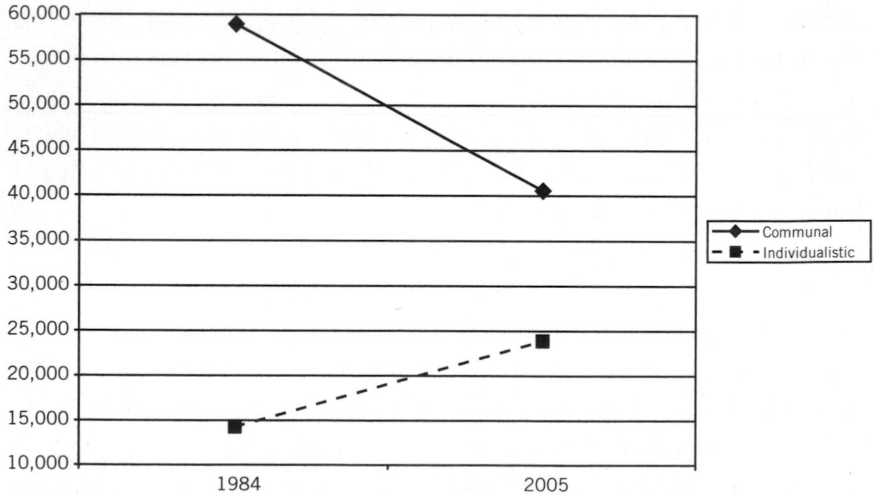

Source: Nafstad, H. E., Blakar, R. M., Carlquist, E., Phelps, J. M., and Rand-Hendriksen, K. (2007). Ideology and power: The influence of current neo-liberalism in society. *Journal of Community and Applied Social Psychology, 17*, 313–327.

vides strong values in countries and cultural areas in Southeast Asia and the Himalayas. It appears to work. Whereas narcissists in the United States favor "trophy partners" who help them look good over caring partners, narcissists in Thailand, for example, liked the idea of trophy partners but still preferred caring partners overall. Thus the collectivistic, largely Buddhist culture of Thailand has some capacity to buffer narcissism's effects. Of course, time will tell if this buffer will stay in place.

As another example, Bhutan has made a concerted effort to minimize some of the more materialistic aspects of American culture. The Bhutanese government has strictly limited the number of tourists allowed in the country, and has set economic policies that protect the culture of their Buddhist Kingdom. The result has been slow economic development in Bhutan, but also much less cultural upheaval and environmental degradation than seen in neighboring countries like Nepal. Even Bhutan, however, is changing, with its recent transition from monarchy to democracy. Its future will be fascinating to watch.

Finally, some of the most intense, religiously grounded opposition to the narcissism epidemic can be found in the Middle East. Many nations in the Middle East have Islam as a state religion and have adopted restrictive practices such as sharia law and the concept of surrender to God (in many translations, *Islam* means "surrender"). The ongoing conflict in the Muslim world between conservative religious beliefs and the forces of modernization is influenced by the narcissism epidemic, because the media prism makes Western culture look worse than it actually is.

The narcissism epidemic thus gives ample ammunition to conservative Islam to oppose modernization. America is seen as an exporter of self-absorption, materialism, sexuality, and vanity, and its values and practices are already spreading to the Middle East (though, given oil money, materialism was quite prevalent in some circles already). For example, rhinoplasty (nose jobs) are on the rise in Iran. According to ABC News, Iran is known as the "nose job capital of the world." And because the Iranian mullahs allow women to expose no skin except for their face, the face has become the focus of vanity efforts. Some women are even wearing bandages on their noses just so others will think they had a nose job. MTV Arabia is currently being launched from a base in Dubai. Apparently, efforts are being made to tone down the typical American fare with rules such as "close-ups of a bikini are O.K. for 1 sec.

but not 2; 3 sec. in a moving shot works but not 4." It seems safe to assume that for many in the Arab world, MTV Arabia will be a source of concern.

Like many cultures, the Arab world has its share of narcissistic leaders and celebrities. Saddam Hussein plastered his face on every billboard he could find, had more than 100 homes, and killed those who defied him. One could argue that Islamic terrorists are incredibly narcissistic, willing to kill innocent people to advance their worldview. Between the forces of shallow Western materialism and extreme religious righteousness, much of the Muslim world has already been infected by narcissism.

HOW THE NARCISSISM EPIDEMIC SHAPES THE VIEW OF THE UNITED STATES AROUND THE WORLD

Due to global media coverage and the Internet, when the world's citizens see America, they see narcissism. This clearly isn't all that there is to America, but how would the rest of the world know?

Consider this example. When Keith teaches undergraduates about "cognitive schemas" (a fancy term for knowledge structures), he asks them to list whatever comes to mind when they think of Scotland. The list typically goes something like this: kilts, bagpipes, whiskey, *Braveheart*, the Loch Ness monster, and leprechauns. Although these students are largely of Scotch Irish decent, this is a list twisted by popular perception. The Loch Ness Monster probably doesn't exist, leprechauns don't exist and are Irish and not Scottish, and *Braveheart* is a U.S. movie directed by an Australian. The students never name the great Scottish thinkers, such as Adam Smith and David Hume, the role of Scotland in European politics, Scottish art (even though the word *picture* derives from the Picts, an early Scottish people), or the recent economic revival of Scotland. The students know a caricature of Scotland shaped by media portrayals.

Even within the United States, what we know of a region is often warped by TV. Jean's family, originally Minnesotans, moved to Dallas in the early 1980s. Their midwestern friends were surprised that everyone in Dallas didn't wear cowboy hats, spend lavishly, and live on a ranch—after all, that's what everyone did on *Dallas*!

Now imagine what the rest of the world sees of America. They don't see our historic great leaders, or political philosophy, or achievements in the arts and sciences. Instead they see blockbuster movies (especially action movies), our TV shows (Jean's brother once watched *Full House* dubbed in Swedish and subtitled in Danish), our pop music, and Paris Hilton. The face we present to the world is largely made up of gossip and trash. Keith was recently on a radio show in Australia talking about the spread of narcissism in Australia. When talking about the role of narcissism in leadership, Keith mentioned former New York governor Elliot Spitzer's fall from grace (via the discovery he frequented high-priced call girls). Keith began to explain the details, assuming that news of a U.S. state governor would not have made it to Australia. But of course it had, and the host assured him they were familiar with Spitzer's expensive proclivities. Fantastic—more great press for the United States. When citizens in other nations see how their children are drawn to these American cultural ideas, and how they turn their backs on their own culture and history, they are understandably not very happy. Think about it this way: If you only saw American movies, TV shows, and websites, would you like us?

A SPIRALING EPIDEMIC IN THE UNITED STATES

People often ask us if narcissism will continue to increase in the United States. In the first half of 2008, we said yes without much hesitation. All the arrows pointed upward, and some even seemed to be accelerating. After many financial institutions failed and the country became mired in an economic crisis later in the year, however, we stepped back from that prediction somewhat: Perhaps the system was correcting itself? The flights of narcissistic fantasy were crashing to earth as risky mortgages failed and the money stopped flowing. In an economic downturn, the first person to get fired would be the praise consultant. Next to go would be the whiny, entitled people and the narcissistic underperformers. With home equity lines of credit drying up, it became harder to finance a nice car or plastic surgery. Fewer people can afford expensive consumer goods. The bursting of the credit bubble might suck the oxygen out of the system that narcissism needs to survive. While we don't think this will stop the narcissism epidemic, it could slow its growth for several years.

Yet even with economic bad times, many of the root causes of narcissism are relatively unaffected. Earlier, we identified five key causes of the rising narcissism in American culture: A focus on self-admiration, child-centered parenting, celebrity glorification and media encouragement, the attention seeking promoted on the Internet, and easy credit. The first four of these are continuing to grow and might do so even in a struggling economy; only the last, easy credit, is contracting.

Self-Admiration

As we explored in chapter 4, the focus on self-admiration has been growing for a long time. With the possible exception of the 1950s, each passing decade of Western history placed more emphasis on the needs of the individual and less on the needs of the society. In place for centuries, this trend goes all the way back to the Renaissance, and we don't think it's peaked. Because narcissism has benefits in the short term, it takes a while for the disadvantages to appear, and in our fast-moving society most people aren't around anymore when the suave but dishonest charmer finally gets his comeuppance. The one cause that might mitigate the focus on self-admiration is the green movement, though it remains to be seen whether people will significantly disrupt their lives to go green. At the moment the focus seems to be on things people can do without much cost to themselves—or even with savings to themselves, as in buying a Prius and saving lots of money on gas. Many people have argued that environmental change will happen only when it's in people's self-interest, a conclusion very consistent with the narcissism epidemic. Economic hard times will do little to change Americans' core belief in self-admiration; in fact, many people will be told they just have to believe in themselves *more* to succeed during tough times. With the common belief that narcissism helps one succeed in a competitive world, narcissism might be seen as even more necessary.

Parenting

Parents have begun to realize that they can praise their children too much, thanks in part to an excellent *New York* magazine article in 2007 on studies finding that praising a child's work ethic is better than telling her she's smart or the best. Yet when Jean does radio call-in shows, parents and teachers are shocked when she says we shouldn't tell kids they are special. Parents still commonly tell their children that they are unique and should stand out. *Discipline* is increasingly a dirty word, and indulgent parents seem to populate every grocery store, zoo, and park. As we enter the next decade, more and more people born in the '80s will become parents, a generation that has only known a narcissistic world and takes it for granted that it's important to admire yourself.

Although one might expect self-centered parents to neglect or marginalize their children, many seem to instead transfer their narcissism onto their kids. They feel it's OK to spend lots of money on designer clothes when the clothes are for your child. It's OK to obsess about the perfect bedding if it's for a crib. And it's not just OK but expected that parents buy "educational" toys and videos to prepare children early for the cutthroat competition they will inevitably face. Overall, there is little discernible backlash or turning in parenting styles in response to the narcissism epidemic, at least not yet. If anything, things are getting worse as a new generation of parents thinks that a "Pawparazzi celebrity pet" is "cute." The transformation is complete, and it will take a considerable opposing force for the stricter parents of the past to make a comeback. That opposing force is not likely to be the economy. Money troubles might mean that parents buy children fewer things, but it is unlikely to change deeply rooted parenting philosophies.

Celebrities and Media

America's celebrity obsession is growing by leaps and bounds. The new twist is the idea that ordinary people should act like the famous, which was unheard of just three years ago (the fake paparazzi companies, for example, were founded in 2007). The explosive growth in plastic surgery also seems to be rooted in the growing acceptance of celebrity images. Interest in celebrity lifestyles has not yet reached a saturation point or anywhere close to it. Challenging economic times are unlikely to dampen the interest in celebrity; economic down times often coincide with an interest in escapism. During five of the last seven recessions, movie admissions increased. During the Great Depression, many people spent what little discretionary income they had going to the movies. The year 2008 followed the pattern, with movie revenues setting new records. Fewer people will be able to afford fake paparazzi, but the desire to be famous will not go away.

Media influences such as reality TV shows are another area of growth. TV is well-known for fads coming and going. For all its popularity, *American Idol* won't be on the air forever. "Slice of life" reality shows, on the other hand, are popular among the young people who watch MTV and continue to be slavishly followed. These shows tend to showcase the most blatant narcissism, as the people who star in them are, as Pinsky and Young's study showed, highly narcissistic. The "slice of life" shows such as *My Super Sweet 16* also allow their stars free rein to behave however they want and say whatever they want (much more than a show like *American Idol*, which is mostly about singing on stage). It remains to be seen what the next great pop culture influence will be, but it's highly unlikely to be about poor, unattractive people who have no interest in promoting themselves.

Internet

The Internet has the potential to serve as a giant narcissism multiplier. Of course, people can use Internet tools for good or for ill. The Internet doesn't care if you focus on promoting yourself, making art, or helping the world; it facilitates all of these things. We suspect, however, that many of the ways people use the Internet will continue to increase narcissism.

There are at least five reasons for this. First, the Internet allows individual narcissism to be reinforced. For example, you can have your own Web page, blog, YouTube channel, and movie company. As we discussed in Chapter 7, narcissistic individuals are more likely to use these to enhance and reinforce their own inflated self-images. Second, the Internet promotes narcissistic behaviors. There is an intense emphasis on the self and self-promotion. With MySpace, for example, a user can spend a good chunk of his day refining his public image. There is also competition on the Web to get noticed, and one way to "win" this competition is through narcissistic self-promotion, including showing yourself scantily clad, having "hot" friends, claiming significant knowledge of a topic (even if you don't have it), or releasing images of yourself engaging in acts that are rude, disgusting, or bizarre (or all three). Third, some people become addicted to Internet use. Many people talk about "MySpace addiction" or use the term "Crackberry" to describe their experience with checking e-mail on their BlackBerries. This addiction can also be linked to fame or notoriety. People can get hooked on the attention-seeking aspects of the Web. Fourth, standards of "normal" behavior are changing. Thanks in part to the Internet, "normal" behavior now includes the public expression of private thoughts and moments; provocative and self-promoting public dress; and somewhat crude discourse (go read the comments sections to a YouTube video—they would make sailors blush). Thus the norms for social behavior have become more narcissistic. Fifth, and perhaps most importantly, the Internet has enormous reach. At any moment millions of people can potentially look at you and see your message. This spreads narcissism as effectively as fleas spread the Black Death.

Studies suggest that the rise in individual-level narcissism has been accelerating since 2000, possibly because more and more young people have structured their identities using MySpace and Facebook. The generation of young people who used MySpace and YouTube all through high school is just now beginning to enter college, and their narcissistic traits may set a new record. In short, Internet-fueled narcissism is not going away. Even in bad economic times, an Internet connection is considered a necessity. Most young people, and many older people, would eat Ramen noodles every night or move back in with their parents before they would go without the Internet.

Easy Credit

Credit is the one area that has been contracting—but only in some areas. In 2008, banks began to tighten their lending standards for home mortgages as foreclosures mounted. If your credit isn't the best, it's now harder to get a mortgage than it used to be. But banks are still offering many mortgage products not available 20 years ago, such as interest-only loans and 40-year loans. People who want to stretch their credit as far as possible to buy a big house can still do so. This was even temporarily made easier in 2008 when the cap for a "conforming" loan was raised in many markets to $729,750, making it easier to get a big loan for a lower interest rate.

With housing values decreasing, the spigot of credit previously provided by home equity lines of credit (HELOCs) has gone dry, at least for people who bought their houses in the last few years. This should put a damper in some narcissistic spending, as many people used these loans for status purchases like new cars. Apparently some people used HELOCs to gain another type of status—getting their breasts enhanced. As the website breastenhancementfacts.com advises, "The most sensible financing option, if it's available to you, is to try to get a HELOC, [as they have] the lowest interest rates and may be income tax deductible. Lenders [are] more flexible with the purposes of HELOCs, meaning they can be used for purposes other than home improvement." A society that encourages tax-deductible loans for breast enhancement clearly has problems. But with HELOCs less available, plastic surgery rates might start decreasing.

But maybe not, if people put their plastic surgery on a credit card as the postal worker from Chapter 9 did. It is still enormously easy to run up debt on a credit card. As James Scurlock documented in *Maxed Out*, Congress shows no signs of reforming anything about the credit business. Banks will continue to hand out credit cards, knowing that high interest charges will make them rich even if some people default. The U.S. government continues to set the example for its citizens, with the national debt rising higher each day. The credit problem is not going away, and a new generation of Americans is more comfortable with credit than ever. Many had a credit card when they were still in high school, courtesy of their parents, who are also comfortable with credit. Not that long ago, the parents of twenty-somethings had much more ambivalent attitudes toward credit. Jean's parents, for example, did not get a credit card until 1990. But the rising generation, born in the '80s, were raised by parents who charged their diapers on MasterCard. Just as their parents did, they will continue to use credit to make themselves appear better off than they actually are. This is true in challenging economic times as well; as we noted in Chapter 10, people in poor neighborhoods are actually more likely to spend money on conspicuous consumption than people in affluent neighborhoods. If the nation becomes less economically prosperous as a whole, Americans may become even more interested in proving their status through consumption. If people were entirely logical, they would stop spending their money on bling and would instead save their money for the future. But unless credit cards disappear entirely, it is still going to be possible to look high-status now and pay later.

THE OBSESSION WITH SELF-PROMOTION

Other influences are also pushing narcissism continuously upward. Self-promotion and individuality are seen as essential to getting into the right school or hired by the right employer. This type of flagrant self-promotion is actually difficult for many people, and it is common practice to have a colleague read your résumé and "punch it up" a little bit by making it more self-promoting. There are books (for example, *Brag!*) that tell you how to promote yourself just the right amount. This type of self-promotion may grow even more accepted if unemployment rises and more people are fighting to get jobs.

The irony is that all of this self-promotion doesn't work very well at a societal level. The exact same number of students get into elite universities, the same number of people get plum jobs, and the same number of faculty get tenure. All the self-promotion results in absolutely *zero* increase in overall success. The only difference is that everyone self-promotes—the standard rises for everyone. Nevertheless, as long as self-promotion is seen as an advantage, people will continue to self-promote, and continue to encourage their kids to self-promote. Who can blame them?

The narcissistic young person in particular has little reason to change, as many negative consequences of narcissism do not appear until later. Diseases that kill their hosts too quickly usually do not spread very far. For example, Ebola and other hemorrhagic fevers rarely spread to many people: your eyes start bleeding, and people run away from you. But, like narcissism, many diseases damage the host only after the virus has spread. AIDS, for example, has spread so far because it kills so slowly and has little outside sign, giving its carriers plenty of time to infect others.

The course of the epidemic of narcissism looks more like AIDS than Ebola. The damage that narcissism causes to the individual "host" often does not show up for a long time. Narcissists typically look healthy and appealing from the outside, at least in young people and strangers. Narcissism, however, is a destructive trait in old age. You lose your looks and your behavior drives away your family and friends. The 65-year-old man who still primps in the mirror and drives a flashy car is semipathetic. Senior citizen narcissism is not a good way to end your time on earth. But if you are young, attractive and ambitious, narcissism works better for you (although not necessarily for your friends and family).

Consider, for example, a story about a football coach (some say it was Tom Landry). When a young player scored a touchdown and started dancing around in the end zone, the coach looked at him and said, "Act like you've been there before." This is great advice for appearing mature—or at least it used to be. In today's culture, though, the silly end zone dance gets you the endorsement deal. When Jamaican sprinter Usain Bolt beat his chest in celebration 20 meters from the finish line during his 2008 Olympic victory, International Olympic Committee president Jacques Rogge complained about his lack of sportsmanship. The press in the United States and United Kingdom promptly ridiculed Rogge, with the *Times* of London calling him "out of touch" and holding to a "draconian code of ethics." A U.S. newspaper reader commented, "Jacques Rogge should stop criticizing Usain Bolt. Bolt is just celebrating, showing a lot of confidence that he believes in himself. Usain was just proud of his accomplishment," apparently forgetting that the pride is supposed to come *after* the accomplishment, not during. A columnist in the *Los Angeles Times* referred to Bolt's premature showboating as "crowd-pleasing theatrics" and called Rogge an "effete old man" and a "fuddy-duddy." The same article theorized that this is why the Olympics are losing young viewers. The virus has accomplished its goal: narcissism is now seen as normal, even good. If you're not narcissistic, you're not with it. In the old days it was enough just to win an Olympic gold medal in front of a crowd of millions—today, you need to stick an exclamation point on it.

As long as narcissism doesn't grow so rapidly that hosts are harmed before they have a chance to spread the disease, narcissism should continue to thrive. If the acceleration in the rise of narcissism continues, the results could be much worse.

WHAT THE FUTURE HOLDS

When we authors began to assemble our predictions for the future, we guessed that in the future the United States might have a "national self-esteem day." Just to make sure we weren't predicting an event that had already happened, we Googled it. Sure enough, somebody had beat us to it—not only in the United States, but also in New Zealand, a country of self-reliant individuals that we'd hoped hadn't bought into this whole mess. New Zealand Self-Esteem Day was the proud (of course) creation of a woman named Janice Davies. Recently, Janice decided to rename it International Self-Esteem Day. (And why not? As Stuart Smalley would say, the day is good enough, smart enough, and doggone it, people like it.) Her Web page declares that International Self-Esteem Day is now "one step close [*sic*] to the Oprah Show . . . and one step closer to becoming a world wide phenomenon." As usual, the United States is number one in thinking we're number one: New Zealand has a self-esteem day, but the United States has a whole Boost Your Self-Esteem Month (February . . . too bad it's not Boost the Temperature Month).

We also suspected that the narcissism epidemic would spawn a National "Me" Day, which would only be fair given that we have Father's Day, Mother's Day, and even Secretaries' Day. Apparently this has not happened yet, although we found a few people on the web suggesting it.

This silliness aside, the big question is, What will America look like if the narcissism epidemic proceeds unabated or continues to accelerate? Given the dramatic cultural changes of the last 30 to 40 years, we can assume that the changes of the next 30 to 40 years will be just as large and, to our eyes, look absolutely extreme. Think about how much can happen in only a little time. E-mail has only been widely used for about 15 years and now takes up a significant percentage of our lives (and many young people consider e-mail outdated, preferring texting, chat, and social networking site postings). Twenty-somethings and teens spend a significant part of their lives on social networking websites like Facebook and MySpace, neither of which existed before 2004. Not that long ago, kids freely rolled around in the back of cars (even lying on the shelf under the back window), and now parents practically get waterboarded for letting an eight-year-old ride in a car without a booster seat. Suffice to say that culture can change rapidly. But, like our own aging, we don't really notice the changes until we look back at our wedding pictures or our hair in our high school yearbook. (Jean's from 1989 was particularly stellar, with her hot-rollered hair whipped up into a hair-sprayed crown and backlit. Yes, that was actually "in" at one time.)

If the narcissism epidemic continues, there will be even more entitlement, materialism, vanity, antisocial behaviors, and relationship troubles. As long as the trend is not too rapid, Americans might not even notice it. Perhaps parents will routinely suggest plastic surgery to their kids to "boost self-confidence" in the same way we now encourage braces and the right clothes. Young people will each have thousands of friends but will spend so much time tending those shallow relationships that they will spend much less time on deeper connections with others. Home mortgages will get longer and longer so homeowners will never get out of debt but can have the fine lifestyle that they feel they deserve. We might eventually become a giant "leased society," where we get our grand lifestyle up front rather than having to save for it, and then get saddled with a lifetime of debt to pay for it. This would in some ways be a return to the past, as we would be creating a society of indentured servants. Future Americans will be extraverted and socially confident—even the shyest people will have appeared on the Internet many, many times—and many will be looking for the next hit of fame or excitement. There will be widespread use of technologies like "Twitter," which broadcasts people's every action from their cell phones to their personal websites and blogs. Virtual identities may become as important as real identities.

The narcissism epidemic has already had serious consequences. First, there has been a giant transfer of time, attention, and resources from reality to fantasy. Rather than pursuing the American dream, people are simply dreaming. Our wealth is phony, driven by credit and loose lending; this part of the narcissistic dream has already been dashed. Second, narcissism has corroded interpersonal relationships. There has been a switch from deep to shallow relationships, a destruction of social trust, and an increase in entitlement and selfishness.

More people are pursuing fleeting, insubstantial fame rather than making a solid contribution. Even people with real skills are now going for the sizzle instead of the substance. The number of plastic surgeons, for example, has tripled since the mid-1970s while the number of physicians has merely doubled. Ten times as many medical students in 2002 chose dermatology as did in 1996—there's money to be made in Botox, and no middle-of-the-night calls. At the same time, the popularity of less sexy specialties has declined. In 2008, only 2% of medical students planned to go into general practice. This will most likely lead to a serious shortage of doctors in primary care.

These two processes—a corrosion of close relationships and a substitution of fantasy for reality—paint a bleak image of the world. It looks like an upside-down birds' nest: a hollow vessel with an empty interior and a rotting structure.

The lifecourse of the generation of Americans just now entering the workforce will be especially interesting to watch. Their parents and teachers gave them inflated feedback and much of what they saw on TV featured the pleasures of the rich. They got trophies just for showing up as kids, but as adults many of them might be struggling just to find a job. The culture of the last few decades has not prepared this generation for the challenges they will face. Many will rise to the occasion, buckling down to work harder. The rest will be angry and depressed at their lot in life, so different from the comfort and ease they were led to expect would be theirs. Despite all of the attention paid to thrift shopping and pinching pennies during the economic downturn, the desire for material things and riches has not gone away. This has happened before: the song "We're in the Money" was written at the height of the Great Depression.

At base, the culture and the economy have to be about something real. Much of what is "real" is moving overseas. The sovereign wealth funds of Russia and Dubai are buying our assets with money we sent them when our SUVs guzzled foreign oil. A large study by the National Science Foundation found that science and engineering research output in U.S. universities has slowed down just as it is growing in Asia and Europe. Even the fantasy—the stuff the United States is really good at, like making movies and music—is moving overseas, with the ascendance of "Bollywood" and other homegrown movie machines. More automobiles are being made overseas now that U.S. companies are hung over from their binge of making SUVs. Not that long ago, the U.S. economy was the envy of the world. Then came the age of easy credit for individuals and massive government deficits. As Justin Cox noted in *Time*, we have borrowed so much from overseas that the number-one export of the United States is now debt.

As long as people continue to be pumped up with false feedback, connected in illusory close relationships, and driven by flash rather than substance—that is, as long as fantasy can trump reality in the game of life—narcissism will thrive. And as long as narcissism thrives, we can expect a culture that is more and more built on the faulty ground of inflated self-perceptions, shallow relationships, shameless self-promotion, and excessive attention seeking.

But what about a backlash? The liberal 1970s created the conservative '80s, as exhibited perfectly in Michael J. Fox's character on *Family Ties*—the son was conservative, the parents liberal. But cultural change usually moves in a linear direction, not in backlashes. Despite the reversal in politics in the '80s, the decade actually continued more '70s trends than it reversed (for example, women working, civil rights, the shift of the American population toward the Sunbelt). Similarly, we have not yet seen any real backlash against the narcissism epidemic. Most people don't even realize it exists. They see bits and pieces—a celebrity here, a mass murderer there—but not the entire structure. However, it is possible that the epidemic will go so far that it will be solidly rejected by the masses. A few small countertrends hint at such a backlash, such as the "simplicity movement," the "not so big house," and YAWNs (young and wealthy but normal). Bad economic times may beat back some symptoms of the epidemic, such as plastic surgery and outsize materialism. But if we had to wager, we would bet against the countertrends and on the spread of the narcissism epidemic. Most of the root causes of the epidemic are well-entrenched.

There is another possibility, however—one that is even more frightening: The narcissism epidemic could be reversed during a major economic and social upheaval. The narcissism epidemic itself might cause this social collapse. The financial crisis of 2008 might be only the first step of narcissistic overconfidence bringing down long-established institutions. So far, it has only spawned a new era of entitlement with government bailouts, but if these don't work and the whole economy is infected, things could get very ugly.

But maybe such a collapse will actually turn things around. The

Great Depression forged a generation of hardworking, collectively focused citizens, who were further shaped by the fight against tyranny during World War II. Some of America's greatest moments were also its most challenging. These bad times brought America a long way from the culture of the roaring 1920s—also a narcissistic era, but nothing that approached today's culture. Another economic collapse could have a similar effect. Or there could be a disease epidemic (like the flu in 1918) or an environmental catastrophe. There have been hints of all three possibilities lately. We have no idea if such a collapse will happen, and we are certainly not pulling for it, but these types of upheavals might temper the narcissism epidemic.

So if the narcissism epidemic is accelerating in the United States and spreading around the world, are things completely hopeless? Do we have to go through societal collapse for things to change? We are happy to say that the answer is no. There are many things that Americans can do—as individuals and as a society—to temper the narcissism epidemic, and most of them don't even cost any money.

CHAPTER 17

Treating the Epidemic of Narcissism

In the movies, narcissistic characters are miraculously cured. Self-centered people get hypnotized (*Shallow Hal*), shocked with electricity (*What Women Want*), shown their future (*A Christmas Carol*), caught in a cycle of time (*Groundhog Day*), threatened by a sniper (*Phone Booth*), or captivated by cute young children (*Jerry Maguire*; *The Grinch Who Stole Christmas*). *Regarding Henry* is the most direct: the narcissistic character is shot in the head and suddenly becomes a nice person. These are effective plot devices, but do not work in the real world—we do not recommend shooting your favorite narcissist in the head to try to cure him.

There are good and bad ways to respond to epidemics. When SARS (severe acute respiratory syndrome) first appeared in China, the slow response to the epidemic allowed it to spread fairly rapidly to several provinces. But when SARS began to spread around the world in 2003, other countries acted quickly, identifying the virus, quarantining victims, and encouraging people to wear masks to prevent further infection. As a result, the disease has virtually disappeared. Compare that to the course of AIDS, where the disease spread for years before anything was done. The gay community fought to keep the bathhouses open in San Francisco. The straight community ignored the problem because it was "a gay disease," paying very little attention to the epidemic until actor Rock Hudson died of it in 1985. Other countries also denied the existence of AIDS or disputed its cause. By the end of 2007, more than 25 million people worldwide had died of AIDS.

The disease model provides some useful guidelines for combating the epidemic of narcissism. First, people need to know how to identify narcissism and its symptoms. Americans also need to understand that narcissism is ultimately not a good trait for society or the individual. It might feel good, and it might result in the perception of success (and perhaps even some short-term successes), but it is not worth the longer-term costs. Confidence is fine, but too many have crossed the line into overconfidence.

Awareness of the narcissism epidemic may be growing (though slowly), and we hope that this book helps in the process, but the biggest obstacle to understanding narcissism is its wide array of symptoms. Vanity, self-promotion, materialism, and poor social behaviors are all linked. The increases in plastic surgery, credit card debt, videotaped violence, crass materialism, and the desire for fame are interconnected trends. The key to seeing the narcissism epidemic is knowing that narcissism underlies each of these trends.

Once you've recognized the symptoms of the epidemic, take action to avoid or stop the spread. For many diseases, quarantine is the first line of defense. We are not nutty enough to suggest narcissist internment camps (would they have mirrors on every wall?), but quarantine seems to occur naturally. Narcissistic people eventually become isolated from their families, friends, and professional colleagues as their self-centeredness becomes apparent. Narcissism still thrives, however, because these isolated narcissists go on to find new lives to mess up. A natural quarantine might occur if it became more difficult for narcissists to start relationships or get hired. We can each do our part in this department. Don't date the charming guy who yammers on about his expensive watch (even if he is cute), and don't hire the confident, accomplished job applicant who wants to know all about what the company can do for *her* but doesn't show much interest in what she can do for the company.

The other version of quarantine is to avoid sources of narcissism. This might mean protecting yourself from celebrity gossip and from high-status, narcissistic people. On the Internet, it might mean using Web 2.0 to strengthen and maintain important relationships in your life, but not creating many shallow "friendships." This also means involving yourself in activities that support the values of community and charity, or those that give you an accurate assessment of your abilities without garnering adulation.

Quarantine, however, is not a fully effective solution to the narcissism epidemic. Like AIDS, the clearest symptoms of narcissism are often not seen until later in life, so quarantine isn't really an option. Second, the social forces that promote narcissistic values, such as the media or the consumer economy, are nearly impossible to hide from, unless, of course, you move to an isolated community like those of the Amish. Even then you will not necessarily be safe. One group of Amish was part of a reality TV series called *Amish in the City*. We're not kidding.

CHANGE FOR YOURSELF AND YOUR CHILDREN

With cultural-level narcissism accelerating, many people with merely average levels of narcissism are getting sucked into the maelstrom of vanity, materialism, and entitlement. Even when you're not all that vain, Botox is tempting when everyone is doing it. Having a simple wedding makes you feel cheap and unimportant when lavish weddings are in. Your plain pictures look sad on Facebook when everyone else's page is so flashy. Take a step back and realize what you're getting drawn into. If you have a relative from a humble background, consider what she would think about the indulgence you're considering. Also, think about what personal finance experts call a "latte factor"—how you could use that money to save for your future. In an episode of *Sex and the City*, Carrie complains that she can't afford to buy her apartment now that it's turning condo. Miranda asks how much she has spent on shoes over the years she's lived there. Carrie does the math and it hits her—that's where her down payment went.

Quieting the Ego

In late 2006, a group of psychology researchers met in Flagstaff, Arizona, for a conference on "Quieting the Noisy Ego"—in other words, strategies for quelling narcissism among individuals. Keith, who spoke at the conference, remembers discussing ideas with colleagues in front of the fireplace as a light snow fell outside—a definite upgrade from his usual life of sitting at a computer in a lab with asbestos floor tiles. The researchers used words now considered quaint, including *humility*, *self-compassion*, and *mindfulness*.

In many ways, humility is the opposite of narcissism. Some people misconstrue humility as bad, equating it with shame or self-hatred.

Humility is not the same as humiliation. True humility is a strength: the ability to see or evaluate yourself accurately and without defensiveness (notice we said "accurately," not "negatively"). Our friend and colleague Julie Exline, who researches humility, found that humble people are often surrounded by friends and family who support them and allow them to see themselves accurately. Sometimes this support comes through religion, as many religions emphasize humility. Overall, humble people are more connected to others. When you don't concentrate on pumping up the self, it is easier to relate to other people and the wider world. Many people think that humility is a virtue that only great leaders possess, like Gandhi or Mother Teresa, but everyone can practice humility by honestly appraising themselves, remembering the people who have helped and supported them, and truly valuing the lives of others.

Another treatment for narcissism comes from a surprising source: compassion for yourself. Kristin Neff, who did some of the first research on the concept, writes that compassion for yourself works because "people cannot always be, or get exactly, what they want. When this reality is denied or fought against, then suffering increases in the form of stress, frustration and self-criticism. When this reality is accepted with sympathy and kindness, then greater emotional equanimity is experienced." Compassion for yourself isn't about admiring or esteeming the self or making excuses for shoddy behavior—it means being kind to yourself while also accurately facing reality. "With self-compassion, you don't have to feel better than others to feel good about yourself," writes Neff on her website, www.self-compassion.org. People who practice compassion for themselves experience less anger, fewer uncontrollable thoughts about themselves, less self-consciousness, more positive emotions, more happiness, and more constructive responses to criticism. It also predicts curiosity, wisdom, the motivation to master academic tasks, and a growth in compassion for others.

Neff believes that compassion for yourself can be learned, primarily through meditation. She lists a range of more straightforward practices on her website that directly target being kind to yourself. For example, she suggests drawing on our sense of common humanity, realizing that "all humans are vulnerable, flawed, make mistakes, have things happen that are difficult and painful." She also suggests stepping back from the drama of your situation and realizing that the difficult emotions you are feeling will only last a short time.

Mindfulness, an outgrowth of traditional Buddhist practice, may also reduce narcissism and quiet the ego. Mindfulness is the awareness of the present moment—the thought, the feeling, and the physical experience—without negative judgment. This sounds simple but isn't. When you eat, you might be thinking about what you have to do for work the next day; when someone walks by without saying hello, you might become lost in concern about your appearance or fantasize about retaliation. Not only do your thoughts jump around, but they are accompanied by a heaping dose of self-concerned judgment. Why didn't that good fortune befall me? I am smarter than so-and-so. How dare he say that—I want to kick his ass.

Practicing mindfulness keeps the self from entering every experience in your life. Not only do you see the world more as it is, but the practice has clear benefits for your relationships, reducing conflict and keeping it from getting out of hand. When someone says something that you could interpret as critical or confrontational, you can learn to react more calmly. Fewer fights with your spouse, coworkers, or children are reason enough to practice mindfulness.

If you are religious, drawing on the compassionate, mindful aspects of your faith is a great way to quiet the ego. Almost all world religions teach love, compassion, and forgiveness. "Do unto others as you wish them to do unto you" is a classic Judeo-Christian principle that appears in many other religions as well. Islam's prophet Muhammad said, "Not one of you truly believes until you wish for others what you wish for yourself." The Buddhist *Udanavarga* says, "Treat not others in ways that you yourself would find hurtful." The Talmud of Judaism says, "What is hateful to you, do not do to your neighbor. This is the whole Torah; all the rest is commentary." Atheism and secular humanism also encourage harmonious, ethical relations with other people.

Many of these strategies require practice and patience. Personal change takes work. In our culture, we are comfortable with the idea of practice for sports like golf—we know we will never be Tiger Woods, but we strive to improve. We're also fairly accepting of the idea that it takes practice to improve at school and at work. However, the idea that changing ourselves also takes practice is not as accepted. The culture of self-admiration tells us to love ourselves unconditionally just as we are. This is unfortunate, because most personal change takes practice and time—and we won't always reach our goals. As the Serenity Prayer says, "God grant me the serenity to accept the things I cannot change; the courage to change the things I can; and the wisdom to know the difference." We can change some things about ourselves, and knowing that is wise.

The key to practicing personal change is to set a goal ("I want to put others first" or "I want to experience the world without always thinking about myself") and establish a set of action steps ("I will work in a charitable organization for two hours per week," "I will take up a sport that is so difficult that I cannot think about myself," "I will not interrupt others when they talk," or "No more shopping except for necessities"). If possible, enlist some social support toward this goal. It's more embarrassing to fail at self-improvement when your daughter or your husband knows about your goals—and, on the positive side, friends and family can encourage and support you. Stick with it, keeping a record of your efforts. This is not a quick fix, but it can be very effective.

The bestselling book *Me to We* provides many great suggestions for making the world a better place and changing your life philosophy in the process. Some of these involve changing your thinking. "The things you worry about can be a good indication of where your priorities lay," write authors Craig and Marc Kielburger (Craig founded an organization to fight child labor around the world when he was just 12 years old). "Are you focusing on your family? Fashion? Community? The global community?" Focus on being grateful for what you already have instead of thinking about what you don't have (as a bonus, feeling gratitude increases happiness). Other strategies are simply ways of providing help and creating community. Babysit for new parents, they suggest, or organize a reunion for family and friends. As the authors point out, helping others has benefits for the self as well—not only in becoming less narcissistic, but also in becoming happier. Research consistently finds that people who focus on status and materialism are more likely to be depressed, and those who focus on close relationships are happier.

Another practice for minimizing narcissism is paying attention to the wider social connections in the world. No one can exist without massive amounts of support from others. Writer Rebecca Walker was mesmerized when she saw the Dalai Lama speak on this topic. As Walker relates, His

Holiness "was talking about the myth of independence. If you are so independent, he asked, who grows your food? Who sews your clothes, builds your house, makes sure that water comes out of your showerhead? How were you even born? The fact is, he said, we have not done one single thing alone, without the help of a small army of others, and yet we walk around talking about the necessity and supremacy of independence. It's completely irrational."

Finally, if you can't stop feeding the ego, you can align your narcissism with behaviors that help the community. It would be great if beneficial forms of self-promotion (for example, donating enough money to have a hospital wing named after you) became more admired than other forms (looking rich by having expensive clothes, jewelry, and cars). Become a highly visible crusader for some positive change in your community; start a foundation named after yourself (or just donate several park benches to the community with small brass plaques featuring your name); become a leader in your religious organization's volunteer programs. All these things can get you attention and admiration—and help the community.

How to Create Connection—and How Not To

One way to reduce the negative behaviors that so often stem from narcissism is to acknowledge connections and commonalities with others. In two experiments conducted by Sara Konrath, Brad Bushman, and Keith, participants were insulted by someone and then given the opportunity to retaliate by blasting that person with painful noise. As several other studies have also shown, narcissists were significantly more aggressive in this situation. These new experiments added a twist, however: half of the participants were told that the other person was similar to them in some way—either they shared the same birthday or they had the same rare type of fingerprint. When narcissistic people had something in common with their opponent, they were no more aggressive than non-narcissists. When we see ourselves as connected to others, egotism dissipates.

This is great news: there is a potential cure for narcissistic aggression if we can teach children how similar they are to one another. However, many schools, parents, and TV shows instead emphasize to children that everyone is unique and different. Incredibly, one school program teaches the exact opposite of the narcissism cure. Called "I'm Thumbody," the program is standard in grade three in public schools in Ontario, Canada (yet another sign of the narcissism epidemic's spread beyond the United States). Sponsored by the Canadian Mental Health Association, it announces, "I am me! There's not another person in the whole world like me. I have my very own thumbprint. *I am special.*" Telling people how similar they are reduces aggression, yet this program emphasizes to kids how *different* they are from one another. This program even tells kids they have unique fingerprints—the exact opposite of the message that reduced narcissism (that your fingerprint type was similar to someone else's). The program claims it aims to "increase skills that promote personal development and successful relationships," but it potentially encourages attitudes that could undermine relationships through narcissism and aggression.

This is far from the only school program (or media message) that emphasizes how different we are from one another. A guide for child-care providers on self-esteem emphasizes telling children, "You are a very special person. There is only one you in the world." A website called "manifest your potential" asks, "Do you wonder what makes you different from everyone else? Are you looking for an answer to 'What makes me special and unique?' Understanding how each of us is unique is an essential part of questioning who we are and why humanity exists." Some preschools have kids look in the mirror to see how they are different from their classmates.

Not only does this go against the research on reducing aggression, but it defies centuries of history. Almost every war and every atrocity in the history of the world has been based on differences among people. Tribal factions always say the other people are different, wrong, less than human. Hitler singled out the Jews as different, and turned them into a common enemy to be killed. The Tutsi killed the Hutu, Shiites kill Sunnis, and Serbs killed Croatians. White people enslaved black people. Men prevented women from working and voting. The powerful side always claimed the others were too different, not like us.

Not only does teaching uniqueness have the potential to increase aggression, but it emphasizes relatively trivial differences. The Dalai Lama has some very wise words on this topic as well. "Human beings have different hair and different eye colors, we wear different clothes and come from different places," he said. "But really, at the fundamental level, we are all the same." In other words: Yes, each human being is unique, but we are much more alike than different in our feelings and challenges. Recognizing the common humanity in your enemy is often the first step to stopping a war or other conflict.

Instead of allowing schools, parents, and TV shows to teach children that they are all different and unique, support programs fostering conflict resolution and friendship skills. Teach children how to get along with others with polite, civil conduct, and how to resolve conflicts with their friends. After Washington Elementary in Lancaster, Pennsylvania, an inner-city school where frequent conflicts occurred among students, taught children how to resolve conflicts through mediation, fighting diminished considerably. Instead of singing songs about how special they are, children at the school beat drums and chant, "As a drummer for peace / I will live at peace with others."

Other programs focus on friendship skills, such as Jared Curhan's book, *Young Negotiators*, which teaches preteens how to keep drama at bay and resolve conflicts peacefully. Corinne Gregory, who entered the education field with manners courses for children called PoliteChild, now has a program called SocialSmarts. Adopted in some public schools, the program teaches social skills that benefit everyone. The program, Gregory says, "makes kids aware that it's not 'all about you' and that they have to consider the needs, wants, and feelings of others if they intend to have friends, be successful, and be happy in life. Ironically, by thinking of others and leading with courtesy and respect, they get a lot more of what *they* want, more easily, and a lot less of what they DON'T want, so it helps all stakeholders in the interpersonal equation." Gregory reports that schools using the program have seen decreases in disciplinary problems and bullying and increases in teacher and student morale. Academic test scores even rose, with reading skills up by 20%.

When we all get along, it benefits individuals as well as the group. At base, these programs teach empathy: being able to take someone else's perspective and, when things are bad, feel compassion for his or her pain and suffering. That is the most important lesson to teach our children—not how special they are.

One school program, called Roots of Empathy, focuses specifically on these skills. Designed for elementary school children, the program brings an instructor, a parent, and a baby into the classroom. By interacting with the baby, the children come to understand the baby's feelings and needs, and realize these are similar to their own. Schools using the program report fewer fights and discipline problems, more helping, and better social skills.

Some schools that teach social skills and conflict resolution also teach "I am special." This is a bad idea—the two can potentially cancel each other out. It's important to remember that it's usually not low self-esteem that causes a kid to become a bully. Much more often, it's narcissism: narcissistic kids fight when insulted, not the low-self-esteem kids (who are likely to do nothing). Teaching kids how special they are makes things worse, not better.

CHANGING AMERICA'S CORE VALUES

Two core cultural ideas are at the root of the narcissism epidemic: that self-admiration is very important, and that self-expression is necessary to establish one's own existence. To slow the narcissism epidemic, these values need to be modified.

One option is to counteract cultural solipsism—you don't need to admire yourself, and you don't need to express yourself to exist. A direct attack on these now well-established values, however, is likely to be met with intense resistance. Many people are incredulous when we suggest that all people are not special. The emotions involved in this are so strong that arguing against the importance of self-admiration is often a nonstarter. Sometimes people come around when we point out it's better to simply tell your child you love her, but even then people argue that children have to like themselves or they will suffer dire consequences. These views are so ingrained in American culture they are hard to fight. It's kind of like telling people they don't really need to wear pants.

Likewise, the importance of self-expression is enmeshed in our culture. When people discuss taking an art class, or creativity, or voting, these activities are often framed in terms of "self-expression." This is a new phenomenon. Art was not historically about self-expression, nor was creativity, nor was voting—but removing self-expression from the discussion will be met with resistance. Thomas Edison said that creativity was 10% inspiration and 90% perspiration, but today's culture suggests that it is 50% inspiration, 10% perspiration, and 40% self-expression. Americans love the idea that they can express themselves, and it is difficult to convince people that this isn't really necessary.

A more reasonable approach might involve redirection and substitution. We can try to lower the amount of attention paid to self-admiration and self-expression, and instead increase the attention paid to our common American cultural ideals, such as freedom, self-reliance, and equality. When we were growing up in the 1970s, kids' television shows were mixed with public service messages about American history, politics, math, and grammar. *Schoolhouse Rock* included America Rock, Grammar Rock, Science Rock, Multiplication Rock, and Money Rock. Each topic was covered with catchy songs about, for example, "the shot heard 'round the world," "I'm just a Bill," "Great American Melting Pot," and "Conjunction Junction." If you're in your 30s or 40s, you might still know these tunes. Notably, there was no *Schoolhouse Rock* for self-esteem, loving yourself, or expressing yourself.

Today's public service announcements (PSAs) are different. American history, grammar and science have been dropped for PSAs on scary stuff like child abuse, depression, prejudice, and teen drug use, plus more positive stuff like expressing creativity and having high self-esteem (NBC's collection of PSAs are a good example). When government and voting are mentioned, their importance is often tied directly to the self. A PSA from the League of Women Voters that urges people to vote uses the phrase "Express yourself and be heard"—very different from a previous era's notion that voting was a civic duty. The spot even ends with the same slogan used to sell Botox: "It's all about freedom of expression." Jean thought this was a coincidence until she saw a Botox commercial featuring the same actress as the voting PSA (Virginia Madsen) and read the description on the League of Women Voters website, whose campaign "aims to encourage women to express themselves in life, politics and beauty—specifically by voting for what they believe in and taking care of their health and skin." So vote, but don't miss your Botox appointment!

These PSAs vividly illustrate what Americans are now concerned with (ourselves) and what no longer gets much attention (knowledge and the larger world). Today's PSAs contain little American history (but plenty on personal issues), little about grammar, math, or science (but several about creativity—not scientific creativity, but self-expression), and few on self-discipline and self-control (but several about self-esteem).

These PSAs paint a worldview for kids that goes something like this: the world is filled with really scary things; be tolerant, be creative, express yourself, and admire yourself. To cure the narcissism epidemic, it would be better to dial back on the fear and expressing yourself, and add back the grammar, math, science, history, and civics lessons. We might even toss in spots on the virtues of self-control and saving your money. How about a *Schoolhouse Rock* on compound interest? If PSAs are going to positively influence Americans, they need to start by focusing on things outside ourselves.

THE POLITICS OF NARCISSISM

Discussing cultural change inevitably leads to the world of politics. In general, we have tried to avoid politics in this book because we don't want the discussion of narcissism to get transformed into the typical political debate. On the surface, both liberals and conservatives are opposed to narcissism. Those on the left believe that the country would be better off with more communal values and programs (for example, universal health care) and oppose greedy corporations who squash the little guy to get ahead. Those on the right see narcissism as destroying the traditional values of hard work and self-reliance that made America great. Conservatives oppose the culture of self-admiration when it pushes self-esteem over performance or refuses to reward individual initiative.

Both parties cherish historic American cultural ideas, with the left emphasizing equality and the right emphasizing self-reliance. The left doesn't like the materialism and unequal social status favored by narcissism, and the right doesn't like the phoniness of narcissism. Both groups want stronger communities, although the left emphasizes the organization at the community level ("it takes a village"), and the right emphasizes organization at the family level ("family values"). Both parties would like to see greater civic engagement, although perhaps at somewhat different levels of government and for different levels of government and for different ends.

We authors have discussed these issues at length, partially because we belong to two different political camps. Jean's political beliefs fall more on the Democratic side, and she sees narcissism as part of a trend toward the breakdown of communal values in the country. Keith's political beliefs fall more on the Republican/Libertarian side, and he sees narcissism as part of a troubling trend away from personal responsibility. Despite these differences in perspective, we are both deeply troubled by the narcissism epidemic.

At base, the narcissism epidemic was not caused by either political party, and neither actively encourages it. But both could do more to fight it. They could start by pushing for increased civic engagement. More than two-thirds of citizens voted in 1960, but now just over half do. Knowledge of civics has dropped. A comprehensive review of the data notes that for most categories of political knowledge, "today's high school graduates are roughly equivalent to the high school dropouts of the late 1940s, and today's college graduates are roughly equivalent to the high school graduates of that earlier epoch." Although the 2008 election revived interest in politics across the country, there are still more people who vote for the next *American Idol* than who vote in presidential elections. Even worse, more people know the contestants on *American Idol* than the names of the justices of the Supreme Court. The average American is more interested in singers vying for celebrity than in politics and civics.

We also need both parties to push for shared American values: the fundamental equality of all citizens and the freedom of all citizens to pursue the things they want to pursue. How these beliefs are balanced out, as well as the struggle over issues like wars or tax rates or gun laws or freedom of speech, can be hashed out in a political debate among an informed citizenry. These are important issues that affect all of us. Sticking a clip of yourself on YouTube sitting underwater and playing "Stairway to Heaven" on a pennywhistle is not. Our culture has descended into minutiae—as long as it's minutiae that will get you famous.

We realize that this level of change is probably a pipe dream. We hope some people on both sides of the aisle care about the country and secretly want serious political discussion or involvement. Whatever decisions are made by more civic involvement, it is tough to imagine that they will be worse than they are now, and there will be the added benefit of a civic-minded, engaged populace.

CHANGING SOCIAL PRACTICES

Changing core ideas is important, but even if these changes are possible they will be for naught if we do not also change our social practices in parenting and education, celebrities and media, the Internet, and economics.

Parenting and Education

Parenting is a good place to begin to slow the narcissism epidemic. Parents need to abandon the notion that their child is the center of the universe. This is a tough pill for parents to swallow sometimes, because they have been told that being special is necessary for being loved. But that's not really true. You can love a child without thinking that he or she is by definition the greatest child in the world. In a way, that is the definition of mature love. When romantic relationships form, there is often a sense of idealization and passion. People think that their significant other walks on water. This is a wonderful state to be in, but it doesn't last because it is not real. In more mature relationships, there is love for the partner despite his or her flaws. This type of love is often more enduring and more satisfying. In fact, it feels more substantial to be loved despite your flaws than because your partner has no idea who you actually are, flaws and all.

In addition, love emphasizes connection, but specialness emphasizes difference. People who truly think they are special have trouble with connecting to "normal" people; likewise, "normal" people have problems connecting to "special" people. Imagine if you were a celebrity trying to form a relationship with a "normal" person. Even if you didn't see yourself as that special, it would still be hard to form the relationship if the other person saw you as special or remarkable. In contrast, love in conjunction with true knowledge of a person's strengths and weaknesses is the doorway to emotional intimacy. And these deep connections with others are inoculations against narcissism. True friends don't let their friends be arrogant jerks.

Focus on teaching your children empathy and compassion. Praise them when they help others ("That's so nice you helped your brother"). Punish mean behavior quickly, and not by spanking, which undermines the whole point, but by time-out or taking away privileges. Talk about how other people are feeling so kids can see that everyone experiences the same emotions. If your toddler says, "Baby crying," comment that the baby might be hungry or tired, just as your child is sometimes. Teach children to admire true heroes—those who help others—instead of the shallow role models on TV. And be a good role model yourself, showing empathy for your child's feelings and, just as importantly, those of other children and adults.

Parents should also set limits. There's a simple rule of parenting many seem to have forgotten recently: Kids should not always get what they want. Parents are still fairly good at drawing the line on things we know are bad, such as too much candy, hurting other children, or too much sexuality too young. But our narcissistic culture has made the lines around other things fuzzier. Preschool girls are watching shows like *Hannah Montana*—free of sex and violence, yes, but selling the seductive narcissistic dream of fame, riches, and vanity. Young boys are playing violent video games in which they show no regard for others' lives—and contrary to the idea that this helps them "blow off steam," those who play violent games are more aggressive in real life. Young teens, and even 11- and 12-year-olds, are clamoring to have a MySpace page. Parents insist it be friends-only to ward off predators, but may not realize that these sites can shape children's identities into narcissistic packages even when only "friends" have access.

College students with higher narcissism scores report that their parents were more indulgent. Despite the short-term pulls for giving in, cutting indulgence to reasonable levels is likely to minimize narcissism. Sometimes what your kids want and what they need are two different things, and giving them what they want will not always lead to the self-control they will need later in life.

The last thing we want to do is come off as "know-it-all" parents or, worse, get concerned parents even more obsessed with their own behavior. We both struggle with these issues and often come up short. Keith's older daughter had five pairs of princess pajamas, several replete with multiple princesses. (He liked to comfort himself with the thought that they at least don't announce that she *is* a princess.) Jean finds herself asking her toddler what she wants, and then realizing her toddler might not know—and definitely won't always know what is good for her. (Kate could say the word *pizza* very clearly by 17 months, and said "cookies" by 21 months. Fortunately, she also eats broccoli, a possible sign of the apocalypse.) We also both realize that, as parents, we can only do so much because there are many other powerful sources that shape our children, from peer groups to education to the media. We do the best we can, but have given up on perfection.

Giving up on parenting perfection may actually be a good way to fight narcissism, too. Bombarded with information, many parents today want to mold every aspect of their children's lives to keep them safe and help them succeed. This is a good impulse, but it is often taken too far. We've lost sight of the idea that it is OK for kids to fail once in a while. Ask a room of adults, and most will tell you they learned the most when they did poorly at something. Children who always win develop the idea that they are invincible and better than everyone else. The real world will come as a shock, and they will be too full of themselves to learn from the feedback.

Education reform is also necessary to combat the narcissism epidemic. In schools, the emphasis on self-esteem has to go. No more "I am special" songs; no more "everyone is a winner." Keith's daughter has been coming home with papers stamped "A+." He's guessing that there aren't stamps for the rest of the grades from F to A. We are not saying that children need to be told they are not special or are losers—just drop the whole issue. If you want a child to be physically fit, you don't make him sing songs about how muscular he is. You have him get lots of exercise. The same is true of success. Beyond learning itself, the focus should be on developing a love for learning, a sense of efficacy (if I work hard, I can master a topic), the ability to get along with others, and a high level of self-discipline and emotional resilience. It is relatively easy to succeed in life with low self-esteem, but very difficult to succeed without self-control, self-discipline, or emotional resilience in the face of setbacks.

It is OK for a child to feel somewhat bad if he or she underperforms in academics, sports, or personal conduct. The child can then learn from the poor performance and be given the opportunity and encouragement to strive to improve. (Note that this does not mean the child feels unworthy of living, just that she feels bad about how she did.) This ability to learn from failure is crucial in life, and is much, much easier in a culture that does not push "specialness." Children's sports programs should stop giving trophies to everyone who participates; it is perfectly fine for only the top one or three teams to get trophies. This issue sparked debate in Keith's daughter's soccer team recently. During one of the final games, the children were lying down on the field (or, in the case of Keith's daughter, dancing with her own shadow) instead of trying to play soccer. As the other team (not surprisingly) scored, one of the parents asked who was picking up the trophies this year. With the children out of earshot, Keith commented that the team kind of sucked and the kids didn't really deserve trophies. One parent high-fived Keith in agreement, while another thought the kids needed trophies for encouragement. The mini-outbreak of the narcissism epidemic was put down with a compromise: all of the kids got a framed team picture. This would help the children remember the team experience with their friends and celebrate the soccer season. If they'd all gotten trophies, it would have taught the lesson that you win even when you don't try.

Real life—such as getting into college, getting promoted, or playing sports after childhood—does not operate on the "trophies for all" policy. Instead of telling kids what winners they are, it's better that they learn how to fail with grace and resilience. In academia, we've found that this "learning to fail" lesson has been much more useful than the "you're special" message. We tell our students that academics is a war of attrition. Many journals reject 80% or more of submissions, and a job opening for a faculty position usually gets one hundred or more applications. But if you keep pushing forward and continue fighting after failures, you will eventually win a decent career for yourself. If you crave constant attention and positive feedback, however, you might have to find a different career. This message holds for many other careers as well.

Of course, parents should still encourage children. The key is to give praise that is specific and emphasizes working hard. Instead of saying "You're so smart," say, "You really did well on those math problems. I can tell you tried really hard." When a child feels discouraged and thinks she can't do something, focus on the specific skills involved and self-talk needed. Many athletic coaches use this technique. For example, a swimming coach might say, "Keep practicing your flip turns—think about starting a little closer to the wall this time. I know you can do it!" rather than "You are an awesome swimmer—you are the best!" Focusing on specific skills and trying hard fosters self-efficacy, which is different from self-esteem and specialness. Self-efficacy is linked to successful performance, but global praise is typically worthless or counterproductive. Thinking you're great and believing you can do something are two different things. Instead of everyone getting a trophy, it's better for kids to get specific encouragement so they can build their skills, and actually *earn* a trophy. And if they don't—maybe soccer just isn't their talent—that's an OK lesson, too. That doesn't mean they have to quit, just that it may take more work for them to play well. Or they can find another sport and discover where their talent lies.

Media

Combating the epidemic of narcissism will also require a change in the media. We know this is a tougher sell—after all, the media's job is to get attention and thus advertising dollars. However, there is room for some responsibility. Britney and Paris are not central to the functioning of our country. A few unabashed celebrity news outlets are OK. TMZ, for example, never pretends it is a serious news outlet. It's kind of like the cereal shaped like little cookies—no one is really getting fooled. But it is getting more and more difficult to find hard news on the so-called news channels. In place of hard news we have endless discussions of the latest celebrity trial, death, drunk driving charge, murder, or stupid behavioral episode. It's like opening a box of All-Bran to find it half filled with those little cereal cookies.

Even more troubling is the media coverage of mass shootings. Although the media must of course cover such events, the amazing amounts of coverage given to the Columbine killers and Seung-Hui Cho from Virginia Tech sends the message that committing a spectacular act of murder or killing is a great way to get attention. The troubled young man who shot shoppers at a Nebraska mall in late 2007 left a suicide note saying he'd now be famous. For a few weeks afterward, he was. For the cycle to be broken, the tone and content of media coverage of killings needs to change. Rather than paint these mass murderers as highly sophisticated agents of evil, news coverage should portray them as what they are: pathetic individuals who sought fame by brutally killing other people. We should view these killers with shame, not awe.

When the U.S. media was busy talking about Virginia Tech shooter Cho's grand evil plan and every detail of his short life, Korea, where Cho's parents emigrated from, reacted with a culture-wide feeling of shame. The South Korean ambassador apologized for Cho's actions. Imagine being a teen in South Korea and hearing this. You would think that this mass murder was a source of shame for the nation, not something that made you an outlaw or a cool killer. Teens thinking that they might like to go out in style by becoming infamous would realize they would only bring shame on themselves, their families, and their entire country. It is difficult to imagine an American teen thinking twice about his scheme to shoot up his school because it would bring shame on his family. He'd be more likely to think about his brilliant plan being discussed on NBC, especially after he sends them a media package with cool pictures of himself holding guns, as Cho did.

The other media trend of our times that could be quelled, or at least modified, is reality TV. Consider what today's tweens and teens watch: mostly reality TV, from *American Idol* to *My Super Sweet 16* to *Hell's Kitchen*. Many of these shows rely on drama provided by self-absorbed characters engaged in confrontational behaviors and/or self-aggrandizement. As Drew Pinsky's study found, reality TV stars were the most narcissistic of all celebrities. Much reality TV is a shallow and pathologized portrayal of human nature, presented as "reality" and made worse by the fame and fortune attained by many of the "stars" of these shows. Reality television is clearly here to stay, but moving shows away from narcissism toward something a little more mature would help. Instead of contests promising fame, how about contests rewarding the team that can design the most environmentally friendly car, or those who come up with the best volunteer plan to help flood victims? For the slice-of-life reality shows, there's plenty of drama in poor and middle-class families struggling to pay the bills every month—that would be reality TV much closer to reality and would still satisfy the genre's requirement for peering into people's lives. Watching regular families decide whether they can afford the nice day care or the better college for their kids is much more dramatic than watching rich kids whine that they got the $50,000 car instead of the $100,000 car—and it would allow viewers to realize how many families struggle with the same issues they do.

There are some antidotes to narcissism already on TV. *The Colbert Report* features a humorously narcissistic host who tries to steal the audience's applause from his guests and coins new words to alter reality to fit his own agenda. *South Park* aired a vicious parody of Paris Hilton that directly asked parents to teach their kids to admire better role models. (One of the girls in the episode buys a Hilton-endorsed toy called the "Stupid Spoiled Whore Video Playset," which contains "a night vision filter, fake money, a loseable cell phone, and 16 hits of ecstasy!") For the younger set, *High School Musical* 2 parodied Paris Hilton and her ilk through Sharpay, who carries a small dog and schemes to steal the sweet girl's boyfriend. Teens watching this probably get the point, but the 3- to 11-year-olds who are the movie's main audience don't. A direct statement about the negatives of narcissism is necessary if younger children are going to get the message.

Internet

For better or worse, sites like YouTube take out the media execs and let you "broadcast yourself." The upside is that we can watch old clips of Van Morrison or the Stanford Prison Experiment; the downside is you have thousands of people gunning for their 15 seconds of fame by crossing the street like a caterpillar, letting their dog drive an SUV, or, much worse, beating up the class loser so everyone can see how powerful they and their friends are. The enormously popular social networking sites like Facebook and MySpace have the same issues, where popularity is linked to self-promotion. These sites are not going away. Our best hope is that by making people aware of the narcissism epidemic, the most transparent grabs for attention on the Internet will be ignored, and their frequency will drop. But it does little good for YouTube to remove the videos of teen beatings when network TV airs them. A better approach is to ignore this type of attention seeking—right after you arrest the perpetrators because you can identify them from the video they so stupidly made.

It is also important to educate young people, and even older people who should know better, about the downsides of Internet interactions. Your friends might think your weekend party pictures are pretty cool, but your prospective employers might not. The CEO of Whole Foods thought he was helping his company by allegedly posting anonymously on message boards until he got caught and looked like a complete fool. Maybe when people realize the costs of Internet self-promotion, some of the narcissistic behaviors and posts will decrease and the more tasteful or interesting or friendly ones will increase.

As the generation who inaugurated MySpace and Facebook matures into their 20s, their pages might become less about skin and popularity and more about causes and ideas. If twentysomethings change the standard of cool on social networking sites, friending and commenting on sites that are thought provoking or society enhancing, perhaps teens will follow their lead.

Credit and Economic Policy

American society actively promotes living beyond your means. You want to appear to be richer, cooler, or more successful than you are? There are no payments for the first 12 months! The result is a country full of people in tremendous debt for goods that decrease in value the moment they are bought. This consumption binge has been accelerated by the cultural emphasis on self-promotion. Try to look beyond the superficial trappings of success and judge people more for who they are—their character, skills, and contribution to society. The 2007–2008 collapse of the real estate and mortgage markets may have some positive effect in the longer term, making savers and fixed-rate mortgages cool again, but it is unfortunate that this lesson required so much pain and suffering.

The biggest problem is that the policies of the U.S. government reward people who go into debt and spend, and punish people who save. If you borrow a million dollars to buy a McMansion using an interest-only mortgage, you get to deduct the entire amount from your taxable income. If you decide instead to save a thousand dollars a month so that you can pay cash for that McMansion, the government taxes the interest on that savings. It also taxed the money when you first earned it. In short, the government pays Americans to take significant financial risk and live beyond our means.

More generally, the government taxes savings but not spending. If you buy a new car, you pay zero federal tax (only local sales tax). The federal government puts no barriers between you and buying a car. If you put $30,000 in the bank instead, you get taxed on your interest, even though that interest is primarily making up for inflation. At the current low interest rates, if you put money into a standard savings account you are actually *losing* money in real terms every year as a result of inflation and taxes. No wonder people don't save.

One big solution is to stop taxing savings, stop paying people for going into debt, and start taxing consumption. Called the "fair tax" by supporters, this tax plan advocates replacing the income tax with a national sales tax. Most proposals allow some nontaxed consumption to make sure that lower-income people are not unfairly taxed. Dismantling the IRS is a tough sell, but the fair tax would reward success instead of punishing it with higher taxes. Taxes would incur only when you consumed goods. As a Democrat with a high mortgage tax deduction, Jean initially tried to talk Keith out of praising the fair tax, but she came to agree that it is one of the only ways that Americans could be instantly incentivized into saving instead of spending. At the very least, the income tax on savings accounts should be eliminated. Why punish saving? It's not even cool. But it is beneficial in the long run—otherwise known as the time when even the narcissists wish they hadn't blown their cash on a BMW.

Congress has done relatively little to regulate the credit card industry. One simple change would make a big difference: don't give credit cards to people who can't afford to pay them off. At the moment, low-income people and students with little to no income can easily obtain credit cards with fairly high limits. In addition, regulators should outlaw the riskiest mortgage loans, such as negative amortization (where you owe more on the house later) and no-doc "liar" loans (which allow people to get mortgages without any proof of income). There should also be some regulation of riskier loans like adjustable-rate interest-onlys. These types of loans result in the financially irresponsible party buying the nice house while the financially responsible family who wants a 30-year fixed cannot afford it. It's fine for people to have choices other than a 30-year fixed, but no one should be able to get a mortgage without some proof of income. More regulation of mortgages is clearly needed, because risky loans are so attractive in the short term: the buyer gets the house, and the lender makes money. In the long term, they cause harm to everyone. Banks themselves began to tighten standards in 2007, but more oversight is needed. There will always be some small outfit willing to take big risks to make a fast buck.

Even if Congress doesn't act, smaller institutions can still make a difference. Colleges should reduce credit card advertising on campus. College students are easy prey for the lure of a credit line, and many end up dropping out when they can't pay their bills. Churches and foundations could give short-term loans so people short a few hundred dollars don't have to pay the exorbitant interest rates of payday loan outfits. Financial literacy should be taught in schools; it might be the most useful class the students ever take in high school. Parents can also teach these principles at home beginning fairly early. One program, called Share Save Spend, teaches children to develop healthy money habits. Using the program's tools, parents and kids can start discussions on such topics as "When is buying things on sale a good idea? When is it a bad idea?" "What's an interest rate?" "When have you bought something because someone else thought you should?" and "How much does a vacation cost?" It also encourages sharing and charity through such questions as "How does sharing money with others make you feel?" and "Is it easier to name your favorite store than your favorite charity? Why—or why not?"

The most important goal should be to shift away from the narcissistic idea that we deserve everything we want and don't have to wait to get it. Americans have grown far too comfortable living in the fantasy of endless debt. Reality always intrudes eventually—and when it does its wrath is swift and final.

AND IF WE DON'T . . .

As a society, we have a chance to slow the epidemic of narcissism if we learn to identify it, minimize the forces that sustain and transmit it, and treat it. If we are unwilling to make these changes, reality *always* wins in the end. The only question is how long it will be before our nation buckles under the strains of narcissism.

The economic foundations of the United States are already cracking, with the failure of many large companies and financial institutions and the government bailout of others. But the fantasy persists in other areas, with many Americans still bent on self-admiration, getting attention, and looking hot. Many people still buy lots of stuff and put it on their credit cards. If this continues, there will be massive environmental damage as more people feel entitled to whatever they want and global warming skyrockets. Our social fabric will tear under the weight of egotism and incivility. The Chinese will eat our lunch economically as narcissistic American consumers spend themselves into permanent debt and entitled employees demand more money for less work.

We hope there will not be such a dramatic crisis caused by narcissism. For the sake of our children, we hope we are wrong. We hope people will change their narcissistic focus without a major collapse, and wish for a rapid recovery if there is a collapse. A few years from now, we would love to write a book titled *The Retreat of Narcissism and the Rebirth of America.*

BIBLIOGRAPHY

We have placed a thorough notes section documenting all of our sources as a downloadable PDF file on our website, www.narcissism epidemic.com. The website also includes a PDF file of appendices (for example, a model of how culture affects individuals, more examples of self-admiration in American culture, and more on the history of self-admiration). Below we list most of the academic journal articles and book chapters reporting the research studies mentioned in the text. These are available at university libraries and some public libraries.

Aalsma, M. C., Lapsley, D. K., and Flannery, D. J. (2006). Personal fables, narcissism, and adolescent adjustment. *Psychology in the Schools*, *43*, 481–495.

Alwin, D. F. (1988). From obedience to autonomy: Changes in traits desired in children, 1924–78. *Public Opinion Quarterly* 52, 33–52.

Alwin, D. F. (1996). Changes in qualities valued in children in the United States, 1964–1984. *Social Science Research*, *18*, 195–236.

Baer, R. A. (2003). Mindfulness training as a clinical intervention: A conceptual and empirical review. *Clinical Psychology: Science and Practice*, *10*, 125–143.

Baumeister, R. F., and Vohs, K. D. (2001). Narcissism as addiction to esteem. *Psychological Inquiry*, *12*, 206–210.

Baumeister, R. F., Campbell, J. D., Krueger, J. I., and Vohs, K. D. (2003). Does high self-esteem cause better performance, interpersonal success, happiness, or healthier lifestyles? *Psychological Science in the Public Interest*, *4*, 1–44.

Baumeister, R. F., Smart, L., and Boden, J. M. (1996). Relation of threatened egotism to violence and aggression: The dark side of high self-esteem. *Psychological Review, 103*, 5–33.

Blair, C. A., Hoffman, B. J., and Helland, K. A. (in press). Narcissism in organizations: An empirical look at managerial integrity and effectiveness. *Human Performance*.

Bleske-Rechek, A., Remiker, M. W., and Baker, J. P. (2008). Narcissistic men and women think they are so hot—But they are not. *Personality and Individual Differences*, *45*, 420–424.

Blickle, G., Schlegel, A., Fassbender, P., and Klein, U. (2006). Some personality correlates of business white-collar crime. *Applied Psychology: An International Review, 55*, 220–233.

Boden, J. M., Fergusson, D. M., and Horwood, L. J. (2007). Self-esteem and violence: Testing links between adolescent self-esteem and later hostility and violent behavior. *Social Psychiatry and Psychiatric Epidemiology*, *42*, 881–891.

Boden, J. M., Fergusson, D. M., and Horwood, L. J. (2008). Does adolescent self-esteem predict later life outcomes? A test of the causal role of self-esteem. *Development and Psychopathology*, *20*, 319–339.

Bosson, J. K., Lakey, C. E., Campbell, W. K., Zeigler-Hill, V., Jordan, C. H., and Kernis, M. H. (2008). Untangling the links between narcissism and self esteem: A theoretical and empirical review. *Social and Personality Psychology Compass*, *2*, 1415–1439.

Brunell, A. B., Gentry, W. A., Campbell, W. K., Hoffman, B. J., Kuhnert, K. W., and Demarree, K. G. (in press). Leader emergence: The case of the narcissistic leader. *Personality and Social Psychology Bulletin*.

Buffardi, L. E., and Campbell, W. K. (2008). Narcissism and social networking websites. *Personality and Social Psychology Bulletin, 34*, 1303–1314.

Bushman, B. J., and Baumeister, R. F. (1998). Threatened egotism, narcissism, self-esteem, and direct and displaced aggression: Does self-love or self-hate lead to violence? *Journal of Personality and Social Psychology*, *75*, 219–229.

Bushman, B. J., Baumeister, R. F., Thomaes, S., Ryu, E., Begeer, S., and West, S. G. (in press). Looking again, and harder, for a link between low self-esteem and aggression. *Journal of Personality*.

Bushman, B. J., Bonacci, A. M., Van Dijk, M., and Baumeister, R. F. (2003). Narcissism, sexual refusal, and aggression: Testing a narcissistic reactance model of sexual coercion. *Journal of Personality and Social Psychology*, *84*, 1027–1040.

Buss, D. M., and Chiodo, L. M. (1991). Narcissistic acts in everyday life. *Journal of Personality*, *59*, 179–215.

Butz, D. A., Plant, E. A., and Doerr. C. E. (2007). Liberty and justice for all? Implications of exposure to the U.S. flag for intergroup relations. *Personality and Social Psychological Bulletin*, *33*, 396–408.

Cain N. M., Pincus, A. L., and Ansell, E. B. (2008). Narcissism at the crossroads: Phenotypic description of pathological narcissism across clinical theory, social/personality psychology, and psychiatric diagnosis. *Clinical Psychology Review*, *28*, 638–656.

Campbell, W. K. (1999). Narcissism and romantic attraction. *Journal of Personality and Social Psychology*, *77*, 1254–1270.

Campbell, W. K., and Baumeister, R. F. (2001). Is loving the self necessary for loving another? An examination of identity and intimacy. In M. Clark and G. Fletcher (Eds.), *Blackwell handbook of social psychology (Vol. 2): Interpersonal Processes*. (pp. 437–456). London: Blackwell.

Campbell, W. K., Bonacci, A. M., Shelton, J., Exline, J. J., and Bushman, B. J. (2004). Psychological entitlement: Interpersonal consequences and validation of a new self-report measure. *Journal of Personality Assessment*, *83*, 29–45.

Campbell, W. K., Bosson, J. K., Goheen, T. W., Lakey, C. E., and Kernis, M. H. (2007). Do narcissists dislike themselves "deep down inside"? *Psychological Science*, *18*, 227–229.

Campbell, W. K., and Buffardi, L. E. (2008). The lure of the noisy ego: Narcissism as a social trap. In J. Bauer & H. Wayment (Eds.), *Transcending self-interest: Psychological explorations of the quiet ego*. Washington, D.C.: American Psychological Association.

Campbell, W. K., Bush, C. P., Brunell, A. B., and Shelton, J. (2005). Understanding the social costs of narcissism: The case of tragedy of the commons. *Personality and Social Psychology Bulletin*, *31*, 1358–1368.

Campbell, W. K., and Campbell, S. M. (in press). On the self-regulatory dynamics created by the peculiar benefits and costs of narcissism: A contextual reinforcement model and examination of leadership. *Self and Identity*.

Campbell, W. K., and Foster, C. A. (2002). Narcissism and commitment in romantic relationships: An Investment Model analysis. *Personality and Social Psychology Bulletin*, *28*, 484–495.

Campbell, W. K., Foster, C. A., and Finkel, E. J. (2002). Does self-love lead to love for others? A story of narcissistic game playing. *Journal of Personality and Social Psychology*, *83*, 340–354.

Campbell, W. K., and Foster, J. D. (2007). The narcissistic self: Background, an extended agency model, and ongoing controversies. In C. Sedikides and S. Spencer (Eds.), *Frontiers in social psychology: The self* (pp. 115–138). Philadelphia: Psychology Press.

Campbell, W. K., Goodie, A. S., and Foster, J. D. (2004). Narcissism, confidence, and risk attitude. *Journal of Behavioral Decision Making*, *17*, 297–311.

Campbell, W. K., Reeder, G. D., Sedikides, C., and Elliot, A. J. (2000). Narcissism and comparative self-enhancement strategies. *Journal of Research in Personality*, *34*, 329–347.

Campbell, W. K., Rudich, E., and Sedikides, C. (2002). Narcissism, self-esteem, and the positivity of self-views: Two portraits of self-love. *Personality and Social Psychology Bulletin*, *28*, 358–368.

Campbell, W. K., Sedikides, C., Reeder, G. D., and Elliot, A. J. (2000). Among friends? An examination of friendship and the self-serving bias. *British Journal of Social Psychology*, *39*, 229–239.

Carroll, L. (1987). A study of narcissism, affiliation, intimacy, and power motives among students in business administration. *Psychological Reports*, *61*, 355–358.

Cassin, S. E., and von Ranson, K. M. (2005). Personality and eating disorders: A decade in review. *Clinical Psychology Review*, *25*, 895–916.

Chatterjee, A., and Hambrick, D. C. (2007). It's all about me: Narcissistic chief executive officers and their effects on company strategy and performance. *Administrative Science Quarterly*, *52*, 351–386.

Cho, G. E., Sandel, T. L., Miller, P. J., and Wang, S. (2005). What do grandmothers think about self-esteem? American and Taiwanese folk theories revisited. *Social Development*, *14*, 701–721.

Crockett, R. J., Pruzinsky, T., and Persing, J. A. (2007). The influence of plastic surgery "reality TV" on cosmetic surgery patient expectations and decision making. *Plastic and Reconstructive Surgery, 120,* 316–324.

Donnellan, M. B., Trzesniewski, K. H., Robins, R. W., Moffitt, T. E., and Caspi, A. (2005). Low self-esteem is related to aggression, antisocial behavior, and delinquency. *Psychological Science, 16,* 328–335.

Dorsey, E. R., Jarjoura, D., and Rutecki, G. W. (2003). Influence of controllable lifestyle on recent trends in specialty choice by US medical students. *Journal of the American Medical Association, 290,* 1173–1178.

Downey, G., and Feldman, S. I. (1996). Implications of rejection sensitivity for intimate relationships. *Journal of Personality and Social Psychology, 70,* 1327–1343.

Emmons, R. A. (1984). Factor analysis and construct validity of the narcissistic personality inventory. *Journal of Personality Assessment, 48,* 291–300.

Emmons, R. A., and McCullough, M. E. (2003). Counting blessings versus burdens: An experimental investigation of gratitude and subjective well-being in daily life. *Journal of Personality and Social Psychology, 84,* 377–389.

Exline, J. J., Baumeister, R. F., Bushman, B. J., Campbell, W. K., and Finkel, E. J. (2004). Too proud to let go: Narcissistic entitlement as a barrier to forgiveness. *Journal of Personality and Social Psychology, 87,* 894–912.

Forsyth, D. R., Kerr, N. A., Burnette, J. L., and Baumeister, R. F. (2007). Attempting to improve the academic performance of struggling college students by bolstering their self-esteem: An intervention that backfired. *Journal of Social and Clinical Psychology, 26,* 447–459.

Foster, J. D., and Campbell, W. K. (2007). Are there such things as "narcissists" in social psychology? A taxometric analysis of the Narcissistic Personality Inventory. *Personality and Individual Differences, 43,* 1321–1332.

Foster, J. D., Campbell, W. K., and Twenge, J. M. (2003). Individual differences in narcissism: Inflated self-views across the lifespan and around the world. *Journal of Research in Personality, 37,* 469–486.

Foster, J. D., Shrira, I., and Campbell, W. K. (2006). Theoretical models of narcissism, sexuality, and relationship commitment. *Journal of Social and Personal Relationships*, *23*, 367–386.

Foster, J. D., and Trimm IV, R. F. (2008). On being eager and uninhibited: Narcissism and approach-avoidance motivation. *Personality and Social Psychology Bulletin*, *34*, 1004–1017.

Gabriel, M. T., Critelli, J. W., and Ee, J. S. (1994). Narcissistic illusions in self-evaluations of intelligence and attractiveness. *Journal of Personality*, *62*, 143–155.

Heatherton, T. F., and Vohs, K. D. (2000). Interpersonal evaluations following threats to self: Role of self-esteem. *Journal of Personality and Social Psychology*, *78*, 725–736.

Heine, S. J., Lehman, D. R., Markus, H. R., and Kitayama, S. (1999). Is there a universal need for positive self-regard? *Psychological Review*, *106*, 766–794.

Horton, R. S., Bleau, G., and Drwecki, B. (2006). Parenting narcissus: What are the links between parenting and narcissism? *Journal of Personality*, *74*, 345–376.

Johnson, J. G., Cohen, P., Brown, J., Smailes, E., and Bernstein, D. (1999). Childhood maltreatment increases risk for personality disorders during young adulthood: Findings of a community-based longitudinal study. *Archives of General Psychiatry*, *56*, 600–606.

Joiner, T. E., and Metalsky, G. I. (1995). A prospective test of an integrative interpersonal theory of depression: A naturalistic study of college roommates. *Journal of Personality and Social Psychology*, *69*, 778–788.

Judge, T. A., LePine, J. A., and Rich, B. L. (2006). Loving yourself abundantly: Relationship of the narcissistic personality to self—and other perceptions of workplace deviance, leadership, and task and contextual performance. *Journal of Applied Psychology*, *91*, 762–776.

Kaplan, L. S. (1995). Self-esteem is not our national wonder drug. *School Counselor*, *42*, 341–345.

Kasser, T., and Ryan, R. M. (1996). Further examining the American dream: Differential correlates of intrinsic and extrinsic goals. *Personality and Social Psychology Bulletin*, *22*, 280–287.

Kim, H., and Markus, H. R. (1999). Deviance or uniqueness, harmony or conformity? A cultural analysis. *Journal of Personality and Social Psychology, 77*, 785–800.

Kitayama, S., Markus, H. R., Matsumoto, H., and Norasakkunkit, V. (1997). Individual and collective processes in the construction of the self: Self-enhancement in the United States and self-criticism in Japan. *Journal of Personality and Social Psychology, 72*, 1245–1267.

Knee, C. R., and Zuckerman, M. (1996). Casuality orientations and the disappearance of the self-serving bias. *Journal of Research in Personality, 30*, 76–87.

Knee, C. R., and Zuckerman, M. (1998). A nondefensive personality: Autonomy and control as moderators of defensive coping and self-handicapping. *Journal of Research in Personality, 32*, 115–130.

Konrath, S., Bushman, B. J., and Campbell, W. K. (2006). Attenuating the link between threatened egotism and aggression. *Psychological Science, 17*, 995–1001.

Kwan, V. S. Y., Kuang, L. L., and Zhao, B. (2008). In search for optimal ego: When self-enhancement bias helps and hurts adjustment. In H. Wayment & J. Bauer (Eds.), *Transcending Self-Interest: Psychological explorations of the quiet ego.* Washington, D.C.: American Psychological Association.

Lakey, C. E., Rose, P., Campbell, W. K., and Goodie, A. S. (2008). Probing the link between narcissism and gambling: The mediating role of judgment and decision-making biases. *Journal of Behavioral Decision Making, 21*, 113–137.

Lucas, A. R., Beard, C. M., O'Fallon, W. M., and Kurland, L. T. (1991). 50-year trends in the incidence of anorexia nervosa in Rochester, Minn.: A population-based study. *American Journal of Psychiatry, 148*, 917–922.

Markus, H. R., and Kitayama, S. (1994). A collective fear for the collective: Implications for selves and theories of selves. *Personality and Social Psychology Bulletin, 20*, 568–579.

Mattia, J. I., and Zimmerman, M. (2001). Epidemiology. In W. J. Livesley (Ed.), *Handbook of personality disorders: Theory, research, and treatment* (pp. 107–123). New York: Guilford.

Menon, M., Tobin, D. D., Corby, B. C., Menon, M., Hodges, E. V. E., and Perry, D. G. (2007). The developmental costs of high self-esteem for antisocial children. *Child Development, 78*, 1627–1639.

Miller, J. D., and Campbell, W. K. (2008). Comparing clinical and social-personality conceptualizations of narcissism. *Journal of Personality, 76*, 449–476.

Miller, J. D., Campbell, W. K., and Pilkonis, P. A. (2007). Narcissistic Personality Disorder: Relations with distress and functional impairment. *Comprehensive Psychiatry*, 170–177.

Miller, J. D., Campbell, W. K., Young, D. L., Lakey, C. E., Reidy, D. E., Zeichner, A., and Goodie, A. S. (in press). Examining the relations among narcissism, impulsivity, and self-defeating behaviors. *Journal of Personality*.

Morf, C. C., and Rhodewalt, F. (2001). Unraveling the paradoxes of narcissism: A dynamic self-regulatory processing model. *Psychological Inquiry, 12*, 177–196.

Murray, S. L. (2005). Regulating the risks of closeness: A relationship-specific sense of felt security. *Current Directions in Psychological Science, 14*, 74–78.

Murray, S. L., Holmes, J. G., and Griffin, D. W. (1996). The benefit of positive illusions: Idealization and the construction of satisfaction in close relationships. *Journal of Personality and Social Psychology, 70*, 79–98.

Murray, S. L., Rose, P., Bellavia, G., Holmes, J. G., and Kusche, A. (2002). When rejection stings: How self-esteem constrains relationship-enhancement processes. *Journal of Personality and Social Psychology, 83*, 556–573.

Nasser, M. (1988). Eating disorders: The cultural dimension. *Social Psychiatry and Psychiatric Epidemiology, 23*, 184–187.

Nathanson, C., Paulhus, D. L., and Williams, K. M. (2006). Predictors of a behavioral measure of scholastic cheating: Personality and competence but not demographics. *Contemporary Educational Psychology, 31*, 97–122.

Neff, K. D., Hseih, Y., and Dejitthirat, K. (2005). Self-compassion, achievement goals, and coping with academic failure. *Self and Identity, 4*, 263–287.

Neff, K. D., Rude, S. S., and Kirkpatrick, K. (2007). An examination of self-compassion in relation to positive psychological functioning and personality traits. *Journal of Research in Personality, 41*, 908–916.

Newsom, C. R., Archer, R. P., Trumbetta, S., and Gottesman, I. I. (2003). Changes in adolescent response patterns on the MMPI/MMPI-A across four decades. *Journal of Personality Assessment, 81*, 74–84.

Ogden, C. L., Fryar, C. D., Carroll, M. D., and Flegal, K. M. (2004). Mean Body Weight, Height, and Body Mass Index, United States 1960–2002. *Advance Data from Vital and Health Statistics, 347*, October 27, 2004.

Otway, L. J., and Vignoles, V. L. (2006). Narcissism and childhood recollections: A quantitative test of psychoanalytic predictions. *Personality and Social Psychology Bulletin, 32*, 104–116.

Overbeck, J. R., Correll, J., and Park, B. (2005) Internal status sorting in groups: The problem of too many stars. *Research on Managing Groups and Teams, 7*, 171–202.

Paulhus, D. L. (1998). Interpersonal and intrapsychic adaptiveness of trait self-enhancement: A mixed blessing? *Journal of Personality and Social Psychology, 74*, 1197–1208.

Paulhus, D. L., and Harms, P. D. (2004). Measuring cognitive ability with the overclaiming technique. *Intelligence, 32*, 297–314.

Paulhus, D. L., Harms, P. D., Bruce, M. N., and Lysy, D. C. (2003). The over-claiming technique: Measuring self-enhancement independent of ability. *Journal of Personality and Social Psychology, 84*, 890–904.

Polak, E., and McCullough, M. E. (2006). Is gratitude an alternative to materialism? *Journal of Happiness Studies, 7*, 343–360.

Raskin, R. N. (1980). Narcissism and creativity: Are they related? *Psychological Reports, 46*, 55–60.

Raskin, R. N., and Hall, C. S. (1979). A narcissistic personality inventory. *Psychological Reports, 45*, 590.

Raskin, R. N., and Hall, C. S. (1981). The narcissistic personality inventory: Alternate form reliability and further evidence of construct validity. *Journal of Personality Assessment, 45*, 159–162.

Raskin, R. N., and Terry, H. (1988). A principal-components analysis of the Narcissistic Personality Inventory and further evidence of its construct validity. *Journal of Personality and Social Psychology, 54*, 890–902.

Reynolds, J., Stewart, M., MacDonald, R., and Sischo, L. (2006). Have adolescents become too ambitious? High school seniors' educational and occupational plans, 1976 to 2000. *Social Problems*, *53*, 186–206.

Rhodewalt, F., and Morf, C. C. (1996). On self-aggrandizement and anger: A temporal analysis of narcissism and affective reactions. *Journal of Personality and Social Psychology*, *74*, 672–685.

Roberts, B. W., and Helson, R. (1997). Changes in culture, changes in personality: The influence of individualism in a longitudinal study of women. *Journal of Personality and Social Psychology*, *72*, 641–651.

Robins, R. W., and Beer, J. S. (2001). Positive illusions about the self: Short-term benefits and long-term costs. *Journal of Personality and Social Psychology*, *80*, 340–352.

Robins, R. W., and John, O. P. (1997). Effects of visual perspective and narcissism on self-perception: Is seeing believing? *Psychological Science*, *8*, 37–42.

Rose, P. (2007). Mediators of the association between narcissism and compulsive buying: The roles of materialism and impulse control. *Psychology of Addictive Behaviors*, *21*, 576–581.

Rusbult, C. E., Verette, J., Whitney, G. A., Slovik, L. F., and Lipkus, I. (1991). Accommodation processes in close relationships: Theory and preliminary empirical evidence. *Journal of Personality and Social Psychology*, *60*, 53–78.

Russ, E., Shedler, J., Bradley, R., and Westen, D. (2008). Refining the construct of narcissistic personality disorder: Diagnostic criteria and subtypes. *American Journal of Psychiatry*, *165*, 1473–1482.

Sedikides, C., Campbell, W. K., Reeder, G. D., and Elliot, A. J. (1998). The self-serving bias in relational context. *Journal of Personality and Social Psychology*, *74*, 378–386.

Sprecher, S., and Regan, P. C. (1998). Passionate and companionate love in courting and young married couples. *Sociological Inquiry*, *68*, 163–185.

Steiger, H., Jabalpurwala, S., Champagne, J., and Stotland, S. (1998). A controlled study of trait narcissism in anorexia and bulimia nervosa. *International Journal of Eating Disorders*, *22*, 173–178.

Stinson, F. S., Dawson, D. A., Goldstein, R. B., Chou, S. P., Huang, B., Smith, S. M., Ruan, W. J., Pulay, A. J., Saha, T. D., Pickering, R. P., and Grant, B. F. (2008). Prevalence, correlates, disability, and comorbidity of DSM-IV Narcissistic Personality Disorder: Results from the Wave 2 National Epidemiologic Survey on Alcohol and Related Conditions. *Journal of Clinical Psychiatry*, 69, 1033–1045.

Trzesniewski, K. H., Donnellan, M. B., and Robins, R. W. (2008). Do today's young people really think they are so extraordinary? An examination of secular trends in narcissism and self-enhancement. *Psychological Science*, 19, 181–188.

Twenge, J. M. (1997). Changes in masculine and feminine traits over time: A meta-analysis. *Sex Roles*, 36, 305–325.

Twenge, J. M. (2001). Birth cohort changes in extraversion: A cross-temporal meta-analysis, 1966–1993. *Personality and Individual Differences*, 30, 735–748.

Twenge, J. M. (2001). Changes in women's assertiveness in response to status and roles: A cross-temporal meta-analysis, 1931–1993. *Journal of Personality and Social Psychology*, 81, 133–145.

Twenge, J. M. (in press). Birth cohort differences in the Monitoring the Future dataset: Further evidence for Generation Me. *Perspectives on Psychological Science*.

Twenge, J. M., and Campbell, W. K. (2001). Age and birth cohort differences in self-esteem: A cross-temporal meta-analysis. *Personality and Social Psychology Review*, 5, 321–344.

Twenge, J., and Campbell, W. K. (2003). "Isn't it fun to get the respect that we're going to deserve?" Narcissism, social rejection, and aggression. *Personality and Social Psychology Bulletin*, 29, 261–272.

Twenge, J. M., and Campbell, W. K. (2008). Increases in positive self-views among high school students: Birth cohort changes in anticipated performance, self-satisfaction, self-liking, and self-competence. *Psychological Science*, 19, 1082–1086.

Twenge, J. M., and Foster, J. D. (2008). Mapping the scale of the narcissism epidemic: Increases in narcissism 2002–2007 within ethnic groups. *Journal of Research in Personality*, 42, 1619–1622.

Twenge, J. M., Konrath, S., Foster, J. D., Campbell, W. K., and Bushman, B. J. (2008). Egos inflating over time: A cross-temporal meta-analysis of the Narcissistic Personality Inventory. *Journal of Personality*, 76, 875–901.

Vangelisti, A., Knapp, M. L., and Daly, J. A. (1990). Conversational narcissism. *Communication Monographs*, 57, 251–274.

Vazire, S., and Funder, D. C. (2006). Impulsivity and the self-defeating behavior of narcissists. *Personality and Social Psychology Review, 10*, 154–165.

Vazire, S., Naumann, L. P., Rentfrow, P. J., and Gosling, S. D. (in press). Portrait of a narcissist: Manifestations of narcissism in physical appearance. *Journal of Research in Personality*.

Vohs, K. D., and Heatherton, T. F. (2001). Self-esteem and threats to self: Implications for self-construals and interpersonal perceptions. *Journal of Personality and Social Psychology, 81*, 1103–1118.

Wallace, H. M., and Baumeister, R. F. (2002). The performance of narcissists rises and falls with perceived opportunity for glory. *Journal of Personality and Social Psychology, 82*, 819–834.

Watson, P. J., Hood, R. W., Jr., and Morris, R. J. (1984). Religious orientation, humanistic values, and narcissism. *Review of Religious Research, 25*, 257–264.

ACKNOWLEDGMENTS

J.M.T.

These acknowledgments will be very short, because I did all of the work on the book. No one else, not even my coauthor, agent, or editor, did very much, and when they did suggest changes they were always wrong. So if you didn't like the book, blame one of them. All the stuff you liked? That was me.

That's what I'd write if I were a narcissist who couldn't recognize narcissism after writing a book about it. But of course I am kidding—I could probably fill another book describing the work of the people who have improved this one, and I am immensely grateful.

It's unconventional to thank your coauthor, but I will nevertheless. Many people asked me, "What was it like to work with another author this time?" My answer was always the same: "It's been great. But that's because I have a great coauthor." I haven't taken a scientific poll, but I would bet that most writing collaborations are not this smooth. Not only did Keith do a great job writing about narcissism research, but he spent hours finding stats on everything from home sizes to articles in education journals. He was always gracious about my writing perfectionism and even tolerated numerous requests to change the location of tick marks on graphs by a tenth of an inch. He's the only person other than my husband to know just how big a pain in the ass I can be about details. My days are always better when I talk to Keith on the phone (especially the days when he answers the phone with "Welcome to hell, Keith speaking"), so I hope we will write another book together.

This book would not exist without the help and excellent advising of Roy Baumeister, who fortuitously hired both Keith and me as postdocs in 1998. Not only that, but Roy was among the first to realize that feeling good about yourself was not an unmitigated boon; his studies on self-esteem and narcissism were some of the first to show that positive self-views have a dark side. My postdoc years in Cleveland were the best in my career, and I am lucky to count my colleagues from that time as friends—I hope lifelong ones.

I have the extreme good fortune to work with the best three women in publishing. My agent, Jill Kneerim, is, in a word, amazing. As she did with *Generation Me*, she shaped this book from an unformed idea about narcissism and its negative effects into the wide-ranging cultural analysis you just read. I have Jill to thank for everything from the book's structure to its cover. Our editor, Leslie Meredith, did a fantastic job whipping the book into shape and stopping us from repeating ourselves. Special thanks for the mention of *South Park*'s "Stupid Spoiled Whore Video Playset" and the controversy around Usain Bolt's premature Olympic celebration. Nicole Kalian has seen me through two books now, and I could not possibly ask for a better publicist, or a more wonderful person to work with. Nicole's organizational skills are beyond compare and her enthusiasm is unmatched. I also thank Jessica Elkin, Cara Krenn, and Donna Loffredo for their tireless work (Cara, thanks especially for alerting me to the startling existence of the song "I Believe the World Should Revolve Around Me").

Several students and colleagues deserve thanks for their hard work on the studies described in the book. First among these is Josh Foster, my partner in battle and the fastest in the South with a fantastic Excel graph or a great graphic (my favorite: the kid wearing the shirt that says "I'm in charge," or maybe the purse for girls that says "All About Me"). My students Emodish Abebe, Leah Bonds, and Brittany Gentile worked tirelessly on projects mentioned in the book, as did coauthors Brad Bushman and Sara Konrath. Thanks to Elise Freeman for giving me a firsthand account of a sermon at Lakewood Church.

I'd also like to thank the several hundred people who gave generously of their time to fill out our online survey at www.jeantwenge.com. Thanks for overlooking the ultimate irony of filling out a survey on narcissism hosted on the domain name of one of the authors. Our survey respondents really opened their lives and hearts when they wrote in with their stories and opinions, and I'm very grateful to them. Their vivid stories illustrated the frustration so many Americans feel over our narcissistic culture. I also got lots of opinions, questions, and stories from my undergraduates at San Diego State University—thanks for your enthusiasm and honesty. I also learned quite a bit from the audiences at companies and universities across the country who heard my presentation on Generation Me. And thanks to the fantastic folks at Together We Grow, especially Gina Guzman and Heather McBeth, for entertaining my daughter and putting her shoes back on all day.

Many friends and colleagues were polite enough to listen as I yammered on about this book, or the other one, or the latest study I was working on. Thanks to David Armor, Ken Bloom, Gretchen Brosch, Jeff Bryson, Stacy M. Campbell, Lawrence Charap, Maureen Crawford, Jennifer Crowhurst, Jody Davis, Thierry Devos, Nathan DeWall, Patti Dickson, Tracy Dunagan, Julie Exline, Eli Finkel, Craig Foster, Linda Gallo, Richard Graf, Jeff Green, Christine Harris, Kendrea Hilend, Brian Hoffman, Benita Jackson, Jason Jameson, Deborah Johnson, Mike, Kelly, Katie, and Faith Johnson, Sarah Kelen, Darlene and Rich Kobylar, Vanessa Malcarne, David Marx, David G. Myers, Georg Matt, Claire Murphy, Nell Newman, Sonia Orfield, Judy Price, Radmila Prislin, Cara Schoenley, Adam Shah, Amy and Paul Tobia, Kathleen Vohs, Robin Weersing, Sara Unsworth, May Yeh, and Steve and Eva Yeung. (If you're not here, it just means I liked you too much to bore you with my yammering.)

My family heard even more, and in more detail. Thanks to my parents, Steve and JoAnn Twenge, for all of your support over the years (and thanks in advance for all of the babysitting, now that I've talked you into retiring to paradise). Thanks to Susie and Jud Wilson and to Dave, Amanda, Joe, and Charlie Louden for being fantastic in-laws (and for listening to the yammering, too). Because Keith's family lives in Southern California, I get to thank them as well—especially Erik and Kathleen DiPaolo for opening up their home to me so many times and always making me feel welcome. Jane Moening and George, Hanley, and Olivia Ekeren-Moening, you are in my thoughts often. Mark, Kathy, and Katie Moening, thanks for the copy of Grandma's journal. Thanks to Dan Tvenge and Alexandra Berman for entertaining me so thoroughly and well during my visits to New York, and to Kim, Brian, and Abby Chapeau, Sarah and Dan Kilibarda, Bill and Joan Moening, Bud and Pat Moening, Anna and Dusty Wetzel, and Marilyn and Ray Swenson for doing the same during our visits to Minnesota. I'd say "Go Twins," but Craig would disown me.

So I will say "Go Angels" instead, because I owe the biggest thanks to my husband, Craig. During all of my trips to give talks, I never had to worry about our daughter being safe and well—that peace of mind is the best gift I could ever receive. Thanks for being the equal partner I have always dreamed of, and especially for not running away when I gave you the Narcissistic Personality Inventory on our fourth date. That, combined with your low score, is the secret to marital happiness.

And, last but not least, I would like to thank my daughter, Kate, for being the greatest and most special child in the world. Kidding. I would like to thank Kate for still speaking to me after she is old enough to read this book and realize I wrote about her. OK, one more time. I would like to thank Kate for her curiosity, her smile, and her enthusiasm, all of which, even in small doses, have the power to make my day.

W.K.C.

Writing this book has been an experience. Sometimes it felt like wrestling a bear; sometimes there was the joy of new insights; sometimes there was the pain of discovering that these new insights were actually correct; and sometimes I saw so many big connections that I thought the black helicopters would come and take me away. There is absolutely no way I could have done this without Jean. When I sank into despair she would get angry—and the ensuing rants would lead to some of the best ideas in the book. I would write a section that had the same structure and level of clarity as an episode of *Lost;* Jean would cut out the polar bear, get rid of the flashbacks, and the result would be something pretty good. Mostly, though, I just had a lot of fun working on this project with Jean. I hope that we can do it again.

Jean and I have worked together since our postdoc days at Case Western under the supervision of the eminent social psychologist Roy Baumeister. For this reason and others, I want to also express an enormous debt of gratitude to Roy. During my postdoc at Case Western I had the great good fortune to spend many a late evening in Roy's mask-covered office listening to Brazilian jazz and talking about "big ideas." This book is in many ways an outcome of that training. Also, I want to thank Constantine Sedikides—no one could ask for a better academic mentor and role model.

About twenty years ago I defined my goal in life as "snowboarding and hanging out with smart people." The snowboarding didn't work out, but I sure got to hang out with a lot of smart people. How cool is it to have a cultural psychologist in the office next to mine on one side, and a neuroscientist on the other? Plus, the neuroscientist keeps a basket of candy. I have too many great colleagues to list, but some whom I have discussed ideas in this book with are Steve Beach, Jennifer Bosson, Brad Bushman, Brett Clementz, Andy Elliot, Julie Exline, Eli Finkel, Craig Foster, Adam Goodie, Jeff Green, Randy Hammond, Brian Hoffman, Bobby Horton, Mike Kernis, Karl Kuhnert, Lenny Martin, Jennifer McDowell, and Kathleen Vohs. In particular, I want to thank clinical psychologist Josh Miller, who has played a huge role in shaping my views on narcissism. We have had a great time trying to develop models of narcissism that span the normal and clinical worlds. Also, I owe a debt to Vicky Plaut for turning me into a cultural psychologist—at least I think of myself that way now, although I am not officially in the club.

There's a saying in academics: "There's nothing better than a good graduate student and nothing worse than a bad graduate student." I have been fortunate enough to have had and have only good ones: Josh Foster (now on the faculty at the University of South Alabama), Amy Brunell (Ohio State University at Newark), Chad Lakey (East Tennessee State University), Laura Buffardi, Elizabeth Krusemark, and Brittany Gentile. Without these folks I would be lost. Literally. It has been a pleasure to collaborate with all of them. I also want to thank many undergraduate research assistants who have worked in the lab; the research participants; and everyone who has spoken with me about narcissism and shared their stories.

This book would not have happened without the guidance and wisdom of my agent, Jill Kneerim. She played a huge role in taking the vague idea at the core of this book and turning it into something interesting. She is also just a pleasure to work with. Similar thanks go to our editor, Leslie Meredith. She managed to shape a long and winding manuscript into something that is much more of a straight path. She also had some terrific input into the structure and content of the book. I also want to thank Jessica Elkin, Cara Krenn, and Donna Loffredo. They really deserve the credit for keeping the train on the track. Last but not least, I want to thank our publicist, Nicole Kalian, for her enthusiasm and hard work at getting this book actually read by someone other than my mother and my grad students.

Outside of the publishing world, my thanks go out to my parents, Linda and Denny Campbell, for their 100% support and friendship; Kathleen and Erik DiPaolo for always going out of their way to bring the family together; Lisa and Erich Reichenbach for making me laugh when things are bouncing off rock bottom; Scott and Jennifer Campbell for keeping me paddling out; Bill McMahan for being the best guy in the world to accompany on a long road trip; all our friends in Athens who have made living here such a pleasure: Carol, Kevin, Lisa, Doug, Jessica, Eric and many others; and the staff at McPhaul for being such a wonderful support to my daughters.

During the time I worked on this book, my wife, Stacy, managed to finish her Ph.D., get an academic position in the same state (thus solving the classic academic "two body problem"), raise one daughter, and bring another into the world. Through all this she has unfailingly supported my writing and my career. Her strength has been an inspiration, and her tolerance of my crazy schemes and loose associations has been a dream. I am a lucky guy.

Finally, I have dedicated this book to my daughters, McKinley and Charlotte. Having a father with a sarcastic sense of humor is tough. And getting twenty-minute answers to questions that you didn't even mean to ask probably turned you off science as a career forever. Add to that a year or so of a father working on a book and I imagine it hasn't been ideal. But, when you read this in 10 or 15 years, know that you have my thanks and that I love you both more than words can tell.

INDEX

ABOUT THE AUTHORS

Jean M. Twenge, Associate Professor of Psychology at San Diego State University, is the author of more than 60 scientific publications and the book *Generation Me: Why Today's Young Americans Are More Confident, Assertive, Entitled—and More Miserable Than Ever Before* (Free Press, 2006). Accounts of her research have appeared in *Time*, *Newsweek*, *USA Today*, *The New York Times*, *The Wall Street Journal*, *U.S. News & World Report*, and *The Washington Post*, and she has been featured on *Today*, *NBC Nightly News*, *Fox & Friends*, *Dateline NBC*, and National Public Radio's *Morning Edition*, *All Things Considered*, and *Day to Day*, in addition to numerous talk radio and local TV appearances. She received a B.A. and M.A. from the University of Chicago in 1993 and a Ph.D. from the University of Michigan in 1998. She lives in San Diego, California, with her husband and daughter.

W. Keith Campbell, Associate Professor of Psychology at the University of Georgia, is the author of more than 70 scientific publications and the book *When You Love a Man Who Loves Himself: How to Deal with a One-Way Relationship* (Sourcebooks, 2005). He has published over 30 journal articles and chapters on narcissism. Accounts of his research have appeared in many news outlets including *USA Today*, *Newsweek*, and *The Washington Post*. He has been featured on Fox News's *The Big Story* and made numerous radio appearances. He holds a B.A. from the University of California at Berkeley, an M.A. from San Diego State University, and a Ph.D. from the University of North Carolina at Chapel Hill. He lives in Athens, Georgia, with his wife and daughters.